Slavery and British Society
1776-1846

Each volume in the 'Problems in Focus' series is designed to make available to students important new work on key historical problems and periods that they encounter in their courses. Each volume is devoted to a central topic or theme, and the most important aspects of this are dealt with by specially commissioned studies from scholars in the relevant field. The editorial Introduction reviews the problem or period as a whole, and each chapter provides an assessment of the particular aspect, pointing out the areas of development and controversy, and indicating where conclusions can be drawn or where further work is necessary. An annotated bibliography serves as a guide to further reading.

PROBLEMS IN FOCUS SERIES

FURTHER TITLES ARE IN PREPARATION

Slavery and British Society 1776-1846

EDITED BY
JAMES WALVIN

First published 1982 by
THE MACMILLAN PRESS LTD
London and Basingstoke
Companies and representatives throughout the world

ISBN 0 333 28073 3 (hc)
ISBN 0 333 28074 1 (pbk)

Typeset by
STYLESET LIMITED
Salisbury · Wiltshire
and Printed in Hong Kong

emancipation setting free from Slavery

Contents

Introduction

JAMES WALVIN

The direct British involvement with black chattel slavery, the institution which had proved instrumental in the development of the Caribbean islands and other parts of the Americas, was brought to a relatively swift end in the years 1776–1838. The main produce of the region – sugar – lost its former primacy when the system of economic protection was terminated in the years 1846–52 under pressure from a changing economic philosophy. Thus ended not only the labour system which had come to characterise plantation life in the Caribbean but also the economic rationale for the plantation system itself. The essays which follow address themselves to some of the major themes in the history of the tortuous and sometimes tortured relations between the British imperial metropolis and the Caribbean slave islands in these years of major change.

Some comments need to be made about chronology. The years under review here are not merely a haphazard choice but form a clear and coherent episode in the history of British slavery and its immediate aftermath. The separation of the American colonies in 1776 saw the articulation of political ideals and ambitions which, despite their undeniably older intellectual and political roots, brought immediate attention to the wider issues of representation and social rights. The 'self-evident truth' enshrined in American Independence that all men are created equal and are endowed with 'certain unalienable Rights' notably 'Life, Liberty and the Pursuit of Happiness' served, among other things, to highlight the base and dispossessed status of black slaves in the northern mainland colonies and throughout the British possessions. This paradox – of slavery persisting and thriving in a society formally dedicated to the ideals of liberty – has long attracted the attention and efforts of notable historians of the USA.[1] But it is important to stress that the debate about political and social rights which was sponsored by the upheavals in America went far beyond the confines of the thirteen colonies. It formed the effective political origin of a much wider and more comprehensive 'age of democratic revolution' which in its turn was to transform the political shape of the Western world.[2] In this, slavery — and the struggle to overturn it — were important ingredients. While this was the case for those societies which possessed their own slave communities it may appear to have been less important when viewed from Europe. It would, however, be a mistake to imagine that Europe remained isolated from the problems posed by black slavery.

Although physically distant from the centres of black slave populations in the Americas (and from the source of slaves in Africa), Europe was inextricably involved in the evolution, development and ultimately the ending of black slavery. Britain had long been closely involved with black slavery and the slave trade, both of which were to remain major issues of British politics and diplomacy well into the nineteenth century. As early as the sixteenth century British merchant adventurers had begun trading in Africans and, even before the successful establishment of British settlements in the Caribbean and North America, British sailors and merchants had conducted a growing and thriving trade in supplying Iberian settlements in the New World with imported Africans.[3] If the British were not the initiators of the slave trade and chattel slavery in the Americas, they were none the less instrumental in elevating both, related, institutions to new levels of economic and social importance in the Atlantic world of the eighteenth century.

It could be claimed that the British played a major and innovatory role in bringing to an end both the slave trade and slavery, although their motives for doing so continue to be hotly debated by historians.[4] There are two major and obvious landmarks which dominate the history of British slavery in these years: the abolition of the slave trade in 1807 and the emancipation of the slaves between 1833 and 1838. Both measures were legislative acts of the British Parliament but both were also functions of a complexity of social and political forces. The parliamentary and public struggle to effect both these measures gave the slave trade and slavery an unprecedented position in British political affairs. While slavery's social and economic importance pre-dates these struggles, as a political and contentious issue, the fate and future of enslaved humanity was elevated to levels of unusual public significance.

Throughout the period covered by this book slaves continued to pour into the Americas. In a little over a century up to 1810 some one and three quarter million slaves had been imported into British possessions. When slavery ended in 1838, more than three quarters of a million slaves were freed in British colonies (excluding the expanding slave populations of the newly emergent USA or the slaves in southern Africa).[5] Long after the abolition of the slave trade in 1807, the flow of Africans across the Atlantic continued, more especially because of the new economic booms in Brazil and Cuba and their consequent demand for cheap black labour. Having abolished their own slave trade, the British embarked on the major task of suppressing the trade to those nations who continued to feel the need for fresh slaves. Consequently and throughout much of the nineteenth century a substantial part of the activity of the Royal Navy was involved in suppression on the West and East African coasts.[6]

The slave plantations, producing a variety of tropical crops for European and, later, local consumption, were proto-industrial organisations in a rural setting. Long before the coming of modern Western industries the plantations consumed cheap and easily recruited labour in a fashion which was to become so commonplace in nineteenth century Europe and North America. Both in the industrialising West and in the frontier settlements of the Americas the prime need was for cheap labour. In the case of the plantations it took the form of imported slaves.[7] The consequent institution of black slavery — which varied remarkably throughout the Americas — did not develop solely because of unbridled and unlicensed economics. While it is true that private capital and enterprise were prerequisites in the organisation of the slave trade and the establishment of the plantation economies, the imperial

Governments took a close and growing interest in the nature and conduct both of the trade in African slaves and of the British tropical settlements.

From the earliest days of speculative ventures by merchant adventurers to Africa, the Royal Government often took an economic or diplomatic interest in the outcome. It was with the British settlements in the Caribbean and North America that British Government became ever more deeply committed to the encouragement and regulation of black slavery. Companies with Royal Charters organised the early trade to and on the African coast. The trade to Africa and beyond was regulated by a series of Navigation Acts.[8] As a result the Royal Navy, throughout much of the eighteenth century was used as an instrument in the Caribbean and mainland America for the supervision and regulation of those Acts (much to the growing annoyance of the economically restricted northern colonies). It was in the Caribbean islands that black slavery became more especially important as waves of slaves poured in to undertake the demanding tasks in the tropical field crops.

It was not so much a question that Europeans could not do this work (they had in fact worked side by side with Africans in the early pioneering days) but that African labour was abundant, more easily recruited and, apparently, cheap. As the tropical colonies thrived, so did their populations become ever more Afro-American. Soon the white master and slaveowning class found itself greatly outnumbered by Africans and their Creole descendants whose sole rationale in life was to labour for their white owners.[9] It was soon apparent that this was a labour force which required a careful and minute regulation and there hence evolved complex social and legal institutions – supported by fearful punishments – to subdue and marshal the alien and alienated black populations. Such slave laws and codes though initiated by local island assemblies were approved or amended by the King in Parliament in London. The degree of British involvement at this level of supervision of the slaves was more remote and more indirect than, for instance, in the drafting and implementation of the Navigation Acts. It needs to be stressed that British Governments and legislative agencies and representatives of the Crown were closely involved in the legal and economic evolution of black slavery — in West Africa, on the high seas and in the Americas. And all this was in addition to the more specific problems posed by the importation of black slaves into Britain itself.

Slavery had posed a problem — or rather a series of problems — ever since its introduction into British possessions. After 1776 it was an issue which became ever more pressing and more widely appreciated and discussed. In large measure this was because of the growing abolitionist pressures mounted in Britain and North America which sought to end the slave trade through a carefully orchestrated campaign directed towards both the public and Parliament. In Britain the initial abolitionist efforts had been through courts where, since the 1760s, Granville Sharp had sought to secure a legal judgement outlawing slavery in England. His efforts, aimed primarily at improving the lot of blacks living in England, had mixed fortunes but helped create growing public awareness of the existence of slavery in Britain and of the wider problems of slavery at large. Sharp's indefatigable legal efforts, his persistent correspondence with influential men, his tracts and well-timed publicity — in addition to the documented horrors of slavery which he laid before the public — all generated a remarkable interest in slavery.[10]

The end of the American War reinforced awareness of the problems of slavery. Many of the former slaves who had fought on the losing British side found themselves in Britain where they joined the ranks of many other dispossessed poor blacks. The charitable efforts on their behalf and the unsuccessful Sierra Leone scheme to 'repatriate' them to Africa brought further political attention to this.[11]

The Sierra Leone scheme immediately preceded the formation in 1787 of the Abolition Society, although the intellectual roots of that organisation are to be found in the well-established Quaker antipathy to black slavery.[12] It was an antipathy which existed on both sides of the Atlantic and formed, in embryo, what became a major international drive against slavery and the slave trade. Early abolitionists and Quakers made deliberate efforts to forge international links with people of similar feelings in other countries. The spread of anti-slavery as an international phenomenon was substantially assisted by the political upheavals which shook Europe and North America in the last quarter of the eighteenth century. This 'age of revolution' saw the emergence of the USA, the end of the *ancien régime* in France, the establishment of revolutionary Government, and the Napoleonic imposition on vast tracts of Europe of French ideals and institutions. It also witnessed as a by-product of the French Revolution, and slave resistance, the destruction of the slave society in the French Caribbean island of St Domingue (Haiti). Throughout these turbulent years, Britain remained physically isolated and relatively immune, notwithstanding the naval mutinies of 1797 and the fearful Irish rebellion in 1798.[13] It was, however, quite impossible to avoid the influence of the new political ideology which, although apparently French, was first enunciated and propagated on a major scale in the 1770s and 1780s in the highly literate and politically sensitive British possessions in North America.

The radical ideology which emerged in both America and Europe in these years transcends the work and writings of any one group or individual. Yet, in the English-speaking world Tom Paine offers a personification of the major issues involved. Paine was at the heart of the American independence movement in the 1770s, a friend of the resurgent plebeian radical societies in Britain in the 1790s, a member of the French revolutionary Convention and, above all, the prophet and scribe of a new political ideology which demanded rights for all men — irrespective of rank or colour. In America Paine had sought to persuade Jefferson of the justice of black freedom. In Britain his message had a major impact on popular radicalism. The rights of man, said Thomas Hardy, Paineite founder of the London Corresponding Society, 'are not confined to this small island but are extended to the whole human race, black and white, high or low, rich or poor'.[14] It was appropriate that when Paine died, a lonely and rejected figure in New York, he was followed to the grave by two blacks.[15]

After 1787 it was a prime ambition of the abolitionists to establish slavery as a major British political issue. But slavery sprang to prominence not merely because of their efforts. A peculiar conjunction of factors – abolitionist efforts, the impact of the new radical ideology and the rapid spread and penetration of nonconformist churches – all served to bring attention to an institution which had long gone unchallenged. Once raised in public slavery soon entered the mainstream of British political affairs, defended by those with an interest in its survival and attacked by a growing body of opponents who found it offensive for a great variety of reasons. It was natural that the West India lobby – the planters, merchants, bankers, brokers, traders and others whose livelihoods depended upon or were associated with slavery and the slave trade – would rush to its defence.[16] Less obvious is why so many of their opponents found anti-slavery so attractive. While it was formerly traditional to view anti-slavery primarily as the work and preserve of men of evangelical persuasion and of property, recent work has shown the much wider support attracted to the cause. Slavery as a political issue was not merely restricted to the propertied and privileged world of traditional politics (inside and outside Parliament) but, like the parallel demands for parliamentary reform, became an issue in the world of popular and radical politics.[17]

For many people in late eighteenth-century Britain, slavery was no political abstraction. The human flotsam and jetsam of the slave trade, the thousands of blacks imported or deposited, could be seen, normally in abject conditions, throughout Britain but more especially on the streets of London. The existence of slavery in Britain – the advertisements for slave sales in British newspapers and the regular slave cases in the courts, also brought attention to the matter.[18]

There was, however, an even more striking knowledge and immediate experience of slavery to be found in British ports. There, as Thomas Clarkson discovered, were to be found thousands of men who, via the slave trade, had personal experience of trading in humanity on the Middle Passage.[19] It is impossible to assess how influential these men were in conveying the realities of slavery to a wider public but it seems likely that in the major slaving ports of London, Bristol and Liverpool an awareness of the nature of slavery was widespread throughout local society. This would have been true throughout the history of the local involvement in slave trading and we must not assume that such knowledge would produce revulsion against slavery.

Whatever knowledge about slavery existed before 1787 the formation of the Abolition Society in that year ensured a massive upsurge in anti-slavery propaganda with an attendant interest in slavery itself. Through lectures, publications, tracts, evidence to Parliament and personal persuasion, the initial band of abolitionists, led by their extraordinary lecturer and researcher Thomas Clarkson, overwhelmed the public with a quite remarkable output of evidence about slavery and the slave trade.[20] Their efforts were not merely to inform but to recruit support and the focal point of their efforts became the petition — a garnering of public sentiment about the slave trade — to be presented to Parliament. Not only were these petitions numerous and numerously signed but they became a key instrument of abolitionist politics from 1787 to 1838. Throughout the period the petition, unless outlawed by the vagaries of governmental suppression of popular politics, was perhaps *the* most striking feature of abolitionist tactics, attracting relatively more names than any other comparable reforming movement — including Chartism.[21]

The British appreciation of slavery in these years did not stem solely from the efforts of the abolitionists. In all this the blacks themselves made a major contribution. There were, in the late eighteenth century, a number of prominent blacks in Britain who played a considerable role is disseminating information about slavery. Most notable were Ottobah Cugoano and, particularly, Olaudah Equiano, both of whom wrote widely publicised denunciations of slavery. Equiano was moreover an active political campaigner in the black cause.[22] There was another area of black activity which, though geographically distant, proved important. Black resistance to slavery — on the Middle Passage and more particularly in the Caribbean colonies — had, from the first, characterised the history of black slavery. Indeed, slave revolts of varying nature and intensity had been endemic in slave society. Some, like the 1760 Jamaican revolt, had been on a horrifying scale of violence and reprisal.[23] But there was nothing in the British slaving experience to compare with the slave revolt in Haiti in the 1790s. In many respects that French colony seemed ripe for revolt. It had been developed only in the recent past and its luxuriant geography encouraged swift and massive economic development, with rapid and regular infusions of large numbers of African slaves. On the eve of the revolt Haiti was a predominantly African society, unlike the other settled islands where a growing proportion of the labour force was becoming Creole (or local-born). Thus when the revolt erupted it was an African revolt, and the bitterness of local racial and class feelings produced a devastating revolution.[24] The ensuing violence and destruction simply destroyed slave society and provided a moral for the main British groups committed to the argument about slavery, though they drew conflicting conclusions. The West India lobby, who feared the spread of black revolt to the British islands, saw in Haiti an awful illustration of the results of tampering with slavery, while abolitionists tended to view it as an unfortunate but inevitable consequence of the evils of slavery itself.

The revolt did more than destroy the local slave society. It also swallowed a British army. Pitt's Government was drawn into the Haitian disaster for a confusion of reasons, some military, some economic and some purely opportunistic. But instead of curbing the revolt and capitalising on French misfortunes, the ill-prepared invasion produced the worst military disaster of those years. The British faced the unexpectedly brilliant tactics and leadership of Toussaint and his well-trained black army (itself a shock and a revelation to whites accustomed to dismissing blacks to mere slavish tasks). But even more devastating than the attacks of the black insurgents were the fearful ravages of tropical disease. Once again the British were forced to count the cost of slavery in terms of human suffering, only this time they were the most obvious sufferers.[25]

Ironically perhaps, in the years of the French Wars (1793—1815) the slaves in the British West Indies were relatively quiet, despite the constant fear of contagion from Haiti. There were a number of small revolts and Maroon troubles but nothing on the scale of the earlier — or later — risings. There was a massive military presence in the Caribbean throughout the wars but it is significant that the British had been forced

...se several regiments of slaves to keep their colonial house in peace and order. Despite the appearance of calm, however, slave unrest simmered below the surface.

The greatest upheaval in those years, the abolition of the slave trade in 1807, was peaceful. The history of the movement to abolish the slave trade has been well charted by Roger Anstey. It seems clear that it was accidental that abolition had not succeeded earlier in the 1790s and had only been held up by fears created by the Haitian revolt and the shadow of the French Revolution (which transmuted all aspects of reform into a sinister all-pervasive 'Jacobinism'). By 1792 abolition had been firmly planted in Parliament and henceforth its fate depended on manoeuverings within Parliament and the Government. The exact timing of abolition was to a large degree fortuitous and was dependent on the incalculable vagaries of parliamentary and governmental politics. Moreover throughout these years the slave trade continued to thrive. Few thought at the time (and subsequent research bears them out) that the slave trade was economically outdated or unprofitable.[26]

Planters had needed regular infusions of African slaves to 'top up' their slave communities which, in the tropical colonies, rarely reached levels of demographic self-sufficiency. In large part this was a result of sexually imbalanced slave communities and the excess of mortality over birth rates. Faced with an end to slave imports after 1808 planters were forced to rethink and rationalise their labour force on the plantations. The most obvious consequence was that planters now 'squeezed' their black labour force as never before, a process which altered and destroyed many expectations of certain groups of slaves who henceforth found themselves forced into humbler, less rewarding tasks.[27] In fact even the proponents of abolition had been uncertain about their expectations of the ending of the slave trade. In general it was hoped that it would lead to amelioration in slave conditions. The argument ran that planters, unable to buy new slaves, would be obliged to treat their existing slaves better and hence make good the demographic shortfall. It is then not surprising to learn that, initially, abolition disappointed more than it encouraged.

Planters regarded abolition as a serious blow to their efforts to maintain economic viability. Abolitionists for their part could see no obvious or immediate improvement in slave conditions, while the slaves themselves felt no appreciable benefits at a time when the campaign for abolition had raised their expectations (via those garbled communications which transmitted plantocratic tabletalk and metropolitan news back to the slave quarters). The consequent slave frustrations were in part responsible for the outbreak of slave revolts, in Barbados in 1816, in Demerara in 1823 and, most violent of all, in Jamaica in 1831.[28] Although each revolt had its own specific roots, the revolts — news of which seemed to arrive regularly from the Caribbean — convinced ever more people (more of whom scrutinised the news from the West Indies) that slavery was a barbaric and doomed institution. Viewed from Britain, planters seemed to refuse to improve the lot of their slaves while the slaves themselves appeared unable to find an outlet for their legitimate grievances and expectations save for open and violent revolt, followed by the inevitable white reprisals. It was a dreadful spiral of violence and counter-violence which increasingly appalled and ashamed observers in Britain.

Planters could do little right in the eyes of their opponents who after 1807 anxiously awaited the results of abolition. One problem was which source of evidence they could rely on to judge accurately the consequences of abolition. Firm data was needed, for instance, to assess whether or not abolition of the slave trade had led to amelioration of slave conditions. After 1801 the British had their own census data; after 1810 the abolitionists began to demand a similar slave registration (census) in order to discover the effectiveness of abolition in preventing illegal slave imports and to assess the expected social improvements in slave life. The parliamentary struggle for complete slave registration (already established in Trinidad and Guiana in 1813) did not succeed until 1816 but thereafter an invaluable wealth of data became available which immediately transformed the contemporary debate about slavery. The nature of slave demography had for some time played an important role in abolitionist arguments but this evidence became particularly important in the 1820s and 1830s, just as the statistics gleaned from Clarkson's research

on the slave trade had been influential in the 1780s and
1790s. In both campaigns statistics and hard empirical data
became major themes in political argument — a remarkably
early example of a phenomenon which was to dominate
British social investigation throughout the nineteenth century
and which was to influence the distinctively empirical nature
of early British sociology.

The details about slave populations which emerged from
the registration returns did not encourage the abolitionists.
Their unhappiness with the results of 1807 was compounded
by news of the slave revolts and by evidence about slave
conditions sent back by a new generation of missionaries
working in the West Indies. This latter source of information
was extremely important. The absence of Christianity among
the slaves had long been a complaint and planters had been
reluctant for a number of reasons to permit their slaves to be
converted by missionaries, distrusting in particular the establishment of an alien institution which would provide their
slaves with a life beyond plantocratic reach and control. Such
fears were in fact more than amply confirmed once the nonconformist churches, notably the Baptists and Methodists,
began to penetrate slave societies from the late eighteenth
century onwards. Churches and chapels could, and did, sow
the seeds of discord among slaves while those churches cater-
ing overwhelmingly for black congregations provided a framework for black organisation and self-expression and could
become a training ground for black leaders and spokesmen.[29]
Much the same pattern was discernible in British working-class
communities in the same period, when the chapel became an
important agent for social and political change.[30] There were
direct connections between chapels among the slaves and
those in the British working-class communities. Those organisations with missionaries in the Caribbean kept their British
congregations and friends informed about the progress — or
otherwise — of their efforts to convert the slaves and of
encouraging them to adopt European institutions of marriage
and family life, though this is not to deny the earlier, indigenous existence of both these institutions among the slaves.
Normally they passed unnoticed by white observers. Missionaries to the slaves also told of obstacles and dangers placed in

their collective path by a resistant and at times aggressive plantocracy. Returning missionaries, who from the 1820s onwards became a major attraction and source of information on the abolitionist lecture circuits, told a uniformly bleak picture of black Christianity obstructed and even violated by whites throughout the Caribbean. The death of missionary John Smith in a Demerara jail in 1824 seemed tragic proof of the corruption of the slave system and of the men who were wedded to it.

There were a number of obvious and well-tried lines of defence for the West India lobby. From the first their arguments had depended upon economic evidence; their case was both determined by their own self-interest and advanced by the alleged benefits accruing to Britain from the slave system. Much more complex was the formulation of an economic critique of the slave system. In terms of the recent historiography of this topic, the parameters of the debate continue to be those established by Eric Williams in his seminal book *Capitalism and Slavery* (1944). Williams's argument transformed our understanding of the whole problem but a number of his main lines of argument now seem less than convincing. His assessment, for instance, of the role and importance of the slave trade and slavery within the wider British economy and hence its contribution to the emergence of the Industrial Revolution now seems greatly simplified and overdrawn. Similarly, Williams's identification of the particular interest groups at work behind abolition now appears to be exaggerated. None the less Williams established historical problems which continue to puzzle and, to a degree, to defy historians. It continues to be an important and legitimate exercise to trace and weigh in the balance the shifting contemporary economic values which enabled or persuaded British society to shed its former unquestioned commitment to the slave system and to resort, in the West Indies as in Britain, to a free labour economy.[31]

The argument that slavery was an inefficient labour system, first effectively advanced by Adam Smith in *Wealth of Nations* (1776), might seem to point to an obvious economic school critical of the slave system. Yet by seeking an explanation for abolition in terms of rather stark alternatives (humanitarian

versus economic factors) many historians since Williams have
led themselves into an impasse. Much more plausible is to set
the attack on slavery in the context of a much wider ideology
espoused by newly emergent classes who were themselves
playing an increasingly important role in early nineteenth
century Britain. And it is perfectly feasible to argue that
this ideology, in relation to slavery, was shared by bourgeois
industrialists as much as plebeian groups. It is striking that
substantial sections of the new bourgeois industrial class were
at one with representatives of new plebeian political and
religious organisations in demanding an end to slavery. Largely
because anti-slavery was sometimes couched in terms of the
benefits — to master and man — of free labour it is tempting
to view the abolitionist urge as one facet of a new capitalist
ethos. But as David Eltis shows this view is also oversimplified.
None the less the current historiographical debate has shifted
away from a narrow interpretation which sought to explain
the ending of slavery as a result of either humanitarian or
economic factors. Now the main thrust of the historical
effort in this field is to locate and explain abolition in terms
of shift in a much more all-embracing ideology or world-view
which could encompass both of these once competing factors.

It is no accident that the newly emergent economic order
in early nineteenth century Britain was committed to free
trade rather than to protection, and began to demand an end
to a slave system which had been highly protected. There
were growing numbers of people by the mid-1820s who
regarded slavery not merely as an affront to the nation's
religious sensibilities but as an economic irrelevance. Equally,
it is striking that arguments about the economics of slavery
obtruded more and more into the propaganda disseminated
by the abolitionists from the 1820s onwards. And while the
West India lobby persisted in asserting the continuing economic need for slavery, both by Britain and the Caribbean,
these were assertions which proved ever less convincing.
Newer arguments enunciating the concepts of freedom — of
labour, conscience and religious worship — and social rights
proved more persuasive to ever more people — of all ranks.

We ought not to imagine that the outcome of the anti-
slavery effort hinged entirely or even largely on economic

arguments. If we are to regard the abolitionists' own words as an indication of their feelings then the economics of slavery played a relatively minor role in their considerations and the overwhelming thrust of their case against slavery was couched in moralistic and religious terms.[32] This may have been less true of ministers who played a crucial role in parliamentary discussions. Yet even here the bulk of the evidence does not suggest that an economic appreciation of slavery was a central determinant in the downfall of that institution. In fact the debate about British slavery has defied the application of rational economic analysis. It would be simplistic to assume that people behaved politically in what appears, in retrospect, to have been the most economically rational fashion.

It was not always clear, even to the most active participants in the slave system, what constituted the best and most rational economic policy to follow. The affairs of the planters provide a useful case in point. Throughout their history there had hovered the prospect of economic incalculability: of not knowing, for example, the price and availability of slaves and not being able to predict the market value of their produce on the European market — or even the time it would take to arrive there. For supplies, labour and sales the planters were at the end of long, dangerous and unpredictable lines of communication. The abolition of the slave trade in 1807 undoubtedly dealt the planters a severe economic blow. Yet in their subsequent efforts to readjust their slave labour force to accommodate the consequent demographic change, the planters merely compounded their own problems while simultaneously fuelling the slaves' frustrations. If any single factor loosened the structure of slavery it was the abolition of the slave trade itself. The ending of that trade to the British Caribbean was the cause and not the result of the economic dislocation of the British slave system. Equally we need to remind ourselves that the abolition of the slave trade was the result not of economic change but of distinctive and unique political and social circumstances in Britain in the 1780s and 1790s. Even in the last phase of the struggle to end slavery (from the mid-1820s) it is worth noting that the most bitterly debated economic aspect of slavery was not so much slavery's place within a changing imperial economy but the level of compensation (eventually agreed at £20 million) offered to the planters. To many, such compensation smacked unpleasantly of slave trading itself, of conceding the fundamental point that the slaves were chattel with an agreed market value.

The abolitionists had become hugely successful politically speaking by the mid-1820s. The West India lobby, despite great efforts and substantial funds, proved incapable of generating effective or widespread public sympathy for slavery. To a marked degree their failure was merely the reverse of the abolitionists' remarkable success. Anti-slavery now occupied the middle ground of British politics. Fewer and fewer newspapers and periodicals supported the planters. Pro-slavery publications were swamped by a remarkable outpouring of anti-slavery literature – in newspapers, magazines, tracts, sermons, handbills and even children's literature. Abolitionists' meetings and lectures proliferated; meetings through the country were crowded with people of all classes and both sexes. It became *de rigueur* for parliamentary candidates to denounce slavery as part of their electoral address. And the established abolitionist tactic of recruiting support via petitions continued to attract vast numbers of names. Government ministers, having given a firm commitment to eventual black freedom, found themselves squeezed between skilfully orchestrated public pressure and astute parliamentary lobbying. Slavery was far from being the sole reform issue at the forefront of politics. The campaigns for factory reform, Catholic emancipation and particularly the push for the reform of Parliament itself in conjunction with anti-slavery, all produced a remarkably volatile political climate worsened by domestic social tensions and news of the political upheavals in Europe. By 1830 – and even earlier – it was clear to many that black freedom was but a matter of time, a conviction reinforced by news of the devastating Jamaican slave revolt of 1831 and the appallingly violent reprisals. By then of course emancipation was dependent upon the vagaries of political manoeuverings – the movement of parliamentary and ministerial backing one way or the other. The passing of the 1832 Reform Act, however, made emancipation imminent.[33] William Knibb, a missionary returning from Jamaica, was told of the Reform Act by the pilot guiding his ship into Bristol.

'The Reform Bill has passed.'

'Thank God,' he rejoined. 'Now I'll have slavery down.'[34]

A reformed Parliament, with a sympathetic abolitionist Government and a weakened West India lobby, paved the way for freedom. All that remained were the details.

Unfortunately these details proved more troublesome than many had hoped. Compensation for the planters (why not, some asked, for the slaves?), a protracted 'apprenticeship' period (a transition between slavery and freedom which varied between the islands), a complex and perhaps unmanageable machinery for supervision, these and more provided a further four years of campaigning. Finally on 1 August 1838 some three quarters of a million black slaves in the British Caribbean were freed. Despite white fears to the contrary it was a peaceful transition. Slavery, which had been born in and characterised by persistent violence, ended quietly.

It had taken a period of about fifty years to transform slavery into freedom (though this was far from the original ambition of all those men who first raised their voice against the slave trade in 1787). Although economically the freeing of the slaves was very much a leap in the dark, the economic uncertainties about freedom for the slaves could never prove a political counterweight to the overriding public insistance on freedom *tout court*. The undermining of the Caribbean economy had begun even before emancipation. But within a few years of full freedom, the economic distress which was to characterise the region thereafter descended on the Caribbean. In 1842 a committee of the Commons reported that there had already been 'a great diminution of the staple productions of the West Indies, to such an extent as to have caused serious, and in some cases, ruinous injury to the proprietors of estates'.[35] This was the beginning of a new West-Indian demand for fresh sources of imported labour, demands which were satisfied by the schemes to settle Indian and Chinese indentured labour. Those waves of new immigrants were to descend on the Caribbean until the years of World War I and were, once again, to transform the demographic and social face of the region. Of course it had been a common plantocratic claim before 1833 that black freedom would leave a labour vacuum on the plantations, since former slaves would simply quit the place of their former bondage for the life of independent peasants. This clearly happened, although the process varied greatly between the islands. On the smaller more crowded islands there was relatively little spare land on which free blacks could settle. None the less the subsequent fate of the Caribbean, more especially of its plantations and labour force, was to plague the relevant British departments throughout the nineteenth century and beyond.

The British involvement with black slavery did not cease with the ending of Caribbean slavery. The transatlantic slave trade continued to thrive on the economic resurgence particularly in Brazil and Cuba. The USA on the other hand, with its expansive slave population, had no need of a transatlantic trade to supply its own buoyant slave-based southern and frontier economies. While it is true that a great deal of British abolitionist effort was directed towards the USA, with American abolitionists regularly travelling the British circuits, the great bulk of British anti-slavery effort was directed towards Africa. The Royal Navy patrolled the West and East African coasts, the Foreign Office concluded a great number of anti-slavery treaties and missionaries sought to dispel the scourge of slavery from among their African hosts. Yet it does not take a cynical mind to appreciate the paradox here. For two centuries the British had enslaved countless Africans but now resolved, for a complexity of reasons, to have done with it and henceforth sought to force, cajole, persuade and prevent other people from slaving. Having imposed their slaving systems on vast tracts of Africa and the New World, the British with an almost evangelical zeal henceforth hawked their abolitionist conscience around the world and, in a no less imperious manner, obliged others to accept their revulsion and reject slavery.

It is commonly and justifiably claimed that many historians writing in this field before 1944 — Coupland, Ragatz, Mellor, for instance — have displayed ethnocentricity and a pre-occupation with élitist politics which seem unacceptable today. The work of Michael Craton directs similar accusations against more modern historians. Too often the slaves in the Caribbean have been portrayed as the passive victims in their own history, people whose lives and fates were shaped and decided by outsiders, be they planters, slave traders or abolitionists. In the light of Craton's work on the slave revolts such a view is no longer tenable and there is now a need to view the role of the slaves as integral to the progress of abolition.

Among earlier pioneering historians who sought to bring attention to the role of the slaves the two Trinidadians, C. L. R. James and Eric Williams, are pre-eminent. Both pointed to the dramatic impact which the Haitian Revolution had on the course of black slavery and freedom. Understandably enough, as modern scholars follow the leads of James and Williams, many of their early historical formulations will be overturned. The essay by David Geggus, for instance, raises a number of questions about the British involvement in Haiti, showing in particular how much more complex than is generally recognised was the British decision to invade Haiti. The British invasion and occupation were characterised by muddle, logistical confusion, military disaster and the ravages of disease. In all this it is difficult to spot any coherent or systematic British policy which might shed light on the wider attachment to slavery (or freedom) allegedly revealed by Pitt's policy towards Haiti.

Just as many historians have tended to ignore or dismiss the role of the slaves, so too have historians of abolition tended to conceive of anti-slavery in terms of established formal politics, of men of property and sensibility battling in public and private for the minds, support and votes of their peers. Three essays here (by Seymour Drescher, Betty Fladeland and James Walvin) add substance to other recent work which suggests that abolition had an unusually wide constituency — of all classes and both sexes. Abolition became a species of contemporary popular politics attracting support which surpassed many other popular movements. There is a need to relocate the campaign against slavery more firmly in the wider world of contemporary radical and popular politics.

One group which played a particularly important role in expanding the public's knowledge of slavery was the missionaries. Duncan Rice shows that missionary activity among the slaves was but one facet of a more broadly based proselytising impulse which directed itself at large areas of the world's 'heathen' population. In part the growth of missionary activity was a result of the professionalisation of missionary training (itself part of a more general professionalisation within British society). The men who emerged as missionaries were instrumental in imposing, in Africa, the Caribbean and elsewhere, structures of informal empire which were to outlast both the edifice of slavery and, later, the formal trappings of imperial control.

By the mid-nineteenth century many British observers were sorely disappointed with the outcome of black freedom. Indeed the 'failure' of the new West Indian peasantry to conform to the inflated and unrealistic hopes of their abolitionist sponsors became an ingredient in the complex evolution of mid-Victorian racism. Yet it is unclear what supporters of black freedom really expected abolition to achieve. Black freedom itself was only a partial goal and, as David Eltis suggests, there was disappointment among those abolitionists who expected to see a black peasantry grateful for its freedom and anxious to work industriously to justify the benefits of free labour. Freed slaves proved much less amenable to the dictates of early Victorian bourgeois philosophy than had been expected.

Anyone familiar with abolitionist literature will be aware of the significance attached to demographic data. Abolitionists were especially partial to theorising about the origins, nature and future trends of slave populations. Barry Higman's work is an important reminder of the broader context in which such theories of population emerged and were discussed. Although Malthusian principles provided a basic methodological tool for the analysis of slave populations, the demographic pattern of slave populations seemed to veer sharply away from Malthusian theory. None the less it is true that the abundance of demographic slave data lent itself ideally to such analysis. Indeed it is striking that a great deal of modern historical analysis of slavery concerns itself precisely with the demographic minutiae which in the early nineteenth century were the subjects both of contemporary political argument and of population theory.

The purpose of each of the following essays is more specific than the overall ambition of the collection which, as much as providing the reader with an analysis of current research, is intended to suggest possible future directions of work in the field. Viewed collectively they suggest the complexity of ways in which the issue of slavery became a major preoccupation of British society in these years. They tell how, through a tortuous political process, the British came to divest themselves of an institution which had, until recently, been an unquestioned and highly valued feature of Britain's Atlantic pre-eminence.

1. Public Opinion and the Destruction of British Colonial Slavery

SEYMOUR DRESCHER

Embedded in most histories of the abolition of British imperial slavery is what one might call a downward flowing model. From Thomas Clarkson's graphic figure of abolitionism as a converging system of leading moralists, in 1808, to David Brion Davis's hypothesis of anti-slavery as an expression of the hegemony of the British ruling class, in 1975, the emphasis has been on how leading members of cultural, political or economic sectors of society generated and directed the force which ultimately destroyed the British slave trade and slavery.[1] In individual accounts saints are pitted against slave-driving planters and merchants, or statesmen and political economists join forces against imperial slave interests, but attention centres on leading economic interests, on clusters of intellectuals or philosophers, on lines of division in Cabinets and Parliament. When historians have introduced the larger public into the story, it is generally and briefly treated as a 'mass sentiment', consciously or unconsciously worked on by élites for good or ill.[2]

This model of the movement of public opinion is by no means purely a retrospective imposition by later historians. Indeed most contemporary chroniclers of British anti-slavery adopted a similar perspective. Historians continue to be concerned with economic profitability and interests, with the ideology of the anti-slavery leadership and with the proceedings of the British Parliament. Most recently, both Roger Anstey's major finished study on the abolition of the slave trade and his unfortunately fragmentary chapters on subsequent emancipation are organised in terms of the stages of parliamentary action.[3] There have been brief forays which look more closely at 'popular' aspects of abolition,[4] but there has as yet been no attempt to define the kinds of questions that must be systematically raised or the data that should be looked at in order to comprehend the role of public mobilisation in the destruction of the British imperial slave system.

This essay will ask a number of questions about mass abolitionism in Britain. A first set of questions is directed towards the relationship of the movement to the broader social and political setting:

(1)   How extensive was mass mobilisation against slavery in an international context?

(2)   How extensive was abolitionism in relation to other contemporary issues in Britain for which there were similar attempts at pressure from without?

(3)   To what extent should this movement be looked upon as an extension of a parallel religious mobilisation — the rise of evangelical nonconformity in Britain?

(4)   To what extent should 'mass' public abolitionism be considered a class rather than a mass movement?

A second set is directed towards results:

(1)   How important was the role of public opinion in determining the timing or outcome of emancipation?

(2)   How does public opinion relate to other considerations, notably the economy or social conditions in the West Indies?

(3)   What impact might it have had on the fiscal constraints of the British Government?

A brief essay cannot definitively address all these questions but it can indicate those answers which seem most plausible, or challenge assumptions which have hitherto seemed acceptable beyond question.

It is important first to clarify the relative significance of British mass anti-slavery in spatial and temporal perspective. The British movement formed part of an international movement which emerged in the 1780s.[5] Anti-slavery took institutionalised form in countries on both sides of the Atlantic,

from Germany to Brazil. On the north-eastern side of the
Atlantic, however, the period of institutional mobilisation
was much briefer in time and much narrower in appeal.
Abolitionism became an identifiable massive movement only
in the United Kingdom, with minor reverberations in France,
first at the very end of the *ancien régime* and again at the end
of the July Monarchy.[6]

In Britain mass anti-slavery definitively emerged at the end
of the 1780s and reached peaks in the campaigns for abolition
of the slave trade (1788, 1792 and 1814), for emancipation
(1823, 1830 and 1833), and for the end of Negro apprenticeship (1838). It then ebbed and fragmented, with a final
lower-level revival during and immediately after the American
Civil War.[7] It survived as a minor lobby into the twentieth
century. Outside Parliament the movement took the form of
massive propaganda, petition and subscription campaigns
intended to make the issue a priority item on both the public
and parliamentary agendas. During the principal peaks of
agitation, local accounts of petitioning rallies would often
casually note that the gatherings or numbers of signatories
were the largest in a generation or in recorded memory.
Although brawls and broken heads were exceptional,[8]
enough emotion was aroused to generate angry heckling at
public meetings and disruption of related functions such as
the auctions in Britain of West Indian estates.

British anti-slavery was organised on the basis of a national
network which became increasingly formal and durable with
each successive campaign. Beginning as a single committee
of individuals in 1787, and relying heavily on the Quaker
connection, it gradually evolved into a movement of well-
defined local associations. Over 200 existed in 1814, 800 in
the mid-twenties, and 1300 at the climax of emancipation.[9]
Moreover, after 1806 the abolitionist network lay in reserve,
ready to apply either discreet or highly visible pressure on the
legislature. This reservoir of abolitionist power as well as the
periodic upsurges were used to prod ministers and ordinary
MPs on specific issues. Correspondingly, when, after about
1840, anti-slavery was no longer able to invoke such a united
national constituency, the power of the abolitionist leadership was severely reduced.[10]

As a comparative indicator of public opinion, we will focus on the petitions which were the rallying point of all the major campaigns between 1787 and 1838, except 1806–7. They signified more than the mere deposition of a number of signatures before Parliament. Almost all petitions were the end product of extensive expenditures of energy, ingenuity, material resources, organisation, propaganda and public discussion. Almost all petitions resulted from public meetings called for that specific purpose. The number of petitions, as well as of signatures, was important because each particular one enabled the MPs presenting them to Parliament repeatedly to draw attention to the issue before an abolition bill was discussed and put to a vote.

In cases of exceptionally numerous petitioners, an MP could also place their number in the parliamentary record. He might also dramatically impress the legislature with the size or weight of the sheets, sewn together like great scrolls. When a number of strong men were required to haul a single petition into Parliament the visual impact of volume and weight was added to number. When soaring numbers of petitions finally caused the Commons to tabulate officially the weekly flood of signatures in 1833 (precisely at the peak of the emancipation campaign), newspapers gave a running account of the number of signatures piling up for each subject.[11] By the 1830s, then, petitions were regarded as an imprecise but none the less tangible indicator of public feeling about social problems. The canvassing, gathering and presentation of these requests for parliamentary action had developed into an elaborate ceremony for the creation and expression of public opinion and became a symbol of the people mobilised. The abolitionist petitions were, in fact, the single most important embodiment of that phenomenon in the fifty years between 1788 and 1838.

The process of gathering petitions therefore implied far more than the mere exercise of the right to have individual names placed on the tables of the two Houses. It required the existence of a complex political and social network which could foster the easy circulation of political literature and agitators throughout society, and of associations capable of well-timed agitation on a broad scale. The vastly different levels on which such mobilisation might occur is shown by comparing Britain and France. In figure 1, column 2 represents the total number of petitions submitted to the French legislature in the ten years before the emancipation of French colonial slaves in 1848. Petitioning the legislature in France was quite legal, but there were severe restrictions on the press and on political organisation. Column 3 represents the number of petitions presented when political association became easier after the revolution of 1848.[12] A comparison with England (column 1) is equally revealing. The number of petitions submitted to the House of Commons for just two major public issues during the single session 1830–1 easily exceeded the total number of petitions presented to the French Chamber of Deputies in the last ten years of the July Monarchy.

The emergence of public abolitionist petitions was a major example of the wider use of public petitions to Parliament in the 1780s.[13] British anti-slavery reached an early peak in 1792, just before the Government's disillusionment with popular politics. After the imposition of legal restrictions, mass petitioning practically disappeared for more than a decade.[14] In this respect the rhythm of the anti-slavery movement developed in tandem with egalitarian and liberalising trends in general. But the anti-slavery petitions also seem to have held a special place in comparative national mobilisations which deserves emphasis. Figure 2 shows that in pre-1848 France, modification of the electoral franchise attracted far greater numbers of signers than even the peak level for slave emancipation before 1848. Across the Channel, however, anti-slavery in Britain (1833) probably attracted more signatures than either parliamentary reform (1830–1) or Catholic emancipation (1829), despite the fact that the latter was treated as a quasi-public opinion poll in many areas of Britain.[15] British colonial emancipation successfully competed with the most popular of domestic issues of a peculiarly volatile political period.

Even more clearly, anti-slavery was strikingly more popular in Britain than in France in the period just prior to their respective emancipations. More than one British male in five over the age of fifteen probably signed the anti-slavery petitions

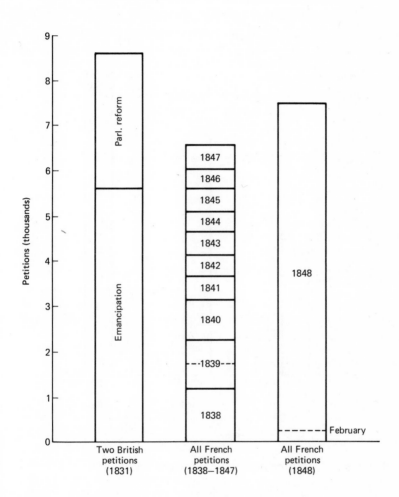

FIGURE 1   Petitions to legislatures of Britain and France

SOURCES: First column, *House of Commons Journals*, 1830–1; second and third columns, Archives Nationales, series C Register of Petitions, 1838–48.

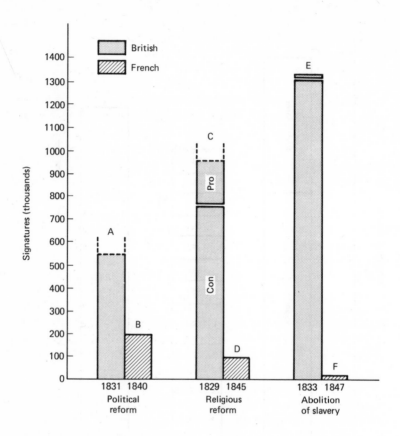

FIGURE 2   Three petition campaigns 1829–47

SOURCES: Columns A and C represent approximate figures tallied from statements in *Hansards Parliamentary Debates*, concerning the numbers signing individual petitions. The figures for some smaller petitioning areas were not announced. Figure E comes from the official tally of the Select Petition Committee of Parliament. Figures B and D are derived from Tudesq, *Les Grands Notables* I, p. 517 and II, p. 701. Figure F comes from *L'Abolitioniste Française*, and Archives Nationales, Section Outre-Mer, SA 197 (1489), petition of 1847 in 48 cahiers.

of 1814 and of 1833. In France less than one man in a thousand did so in 1847.[16] Even at its relatively modest beginning, in 1787, British abolitionism outpolled French popular abolitionism at its height, in 1847. The first British mass petition against the slave trade was launched in Manchester at the end of 1787. This city, with fewer than 50,000 souls (including women and children), mustered about 10,700 signatures against the trade. Just sixty years later, the entire French petition campaign of 1846–7 accumulated just over 10,700 signatures, out of a population of thirty-five million.[17]

If one looks at petition mobilisation over the long run the performance of British abolition is equally striking. During the entire half-century between the first and last campaigns against the British imperial slave system, abolitionist petitions consistently surpassed those from other campaigns. In the seed time of parliamentary public petitioning in the 1780s,[18] the first slave trade campaign attracted more petitions than any other. In the 1790s the slave trade campaign of 1792 was again at the top, as was the one in 1814 against the revival of the international trade. In the twenties, anti-slavery again demonstrated its attractive powers, although it was not as spectacularly ahead of a host of competitive issues, and was momentarily outpaced by the Catholic emancipation campaigns at the very end of the decade. In the 1830s anti-slavery regained its pre-eminence as a petition issue.

Another distinguishing characteristic of anti-slavery was the imbalance in opinion mobilised for and against change. On most other issues involving civil, political, religious or economic reforms between 1780 and 1838 it was possible for the opponents of change to mobilise respectable, and sometimes superior, numbers of counter-petitions or signatures. The differential on anti-slavery was greater than on most major issues at the climax of their respective campaigns. On Catholic emancipation in 1829, for example, the proportion of signatures against reform in Britain (excluding Ireland) was something in the order of five to one.[19] In 1833 the proportion in favour of immediate emancipation against all alternatives was over seventy-five to one. In such terms it seems safe to say that slave emancipation, in 1833, had as

much claim to being a national opinion as any other identifiable political issue.

Anti-slavery reached its climax in the 1830s, sending over
4000 petitions to Parliament during three separate sessions, a
feat unequalled by any other national movement. In terms of
signatures, only the first Chartist petition at the very end of
the 1830s came close to matching anti-slavery in total numbers. In signatures *per capita*, the abolitionist campaigns of
both 1814 and 1833 probably represented peaks or near
peaks of mobilisation in the period before 1840, and were
possibly not surpassed even by the spectacular campaigns of
Chartism or the Anti-Corn Law League in the following
decade.

Traditional accounts are correct in their outlines of the
climactic campaigns of 1830–3. The abolitionist intention
to place immediate emancipation high on the political agenda
of the first reformed Parliament in 1833 was also a resounding
success. During the election of 1832 anti-slavery managed to
impose itself on political discourse. An extensive survey of
campaign rallies and acceptance speeches shows an almost
universal acknowledgment that emancipation was one of the
items requiring the attention of the reformed Parliament,
even where explicit reservations were made regarding the
need for social order or the claims of vested property rights.[20]
An apparent betrayal of anti-slavery commitments, like that
of the Methodist 'Pope' Jabez Bunting in voting for a 'West
Indian' at Liverpool, was an occasion for scathing comment.[21]
By 1832 the abolitionist movement felt powerful enough to
weigh prior legislative reliability as well as verbal promises.
They demanded pledges by candidates to support immediate
emancipation. 'Schedules' of reliables and unreliables (denounced as proscription lists by the opposition) were published
in order to focus attention and force clarification of individual
positions. Local anti-slavery associations backed candidates
who supported emancipation across the political spectrum.
They thereby strengthened the role of advanced pledging and
of legislative responsiveness to direct constituent pressure
over a traditional emphasis on the independent function of
the elected MP.[22]

Symptomatic of the way anti-slavery intruded on political

behaviour in the electoral process of 1832 was the election at Salford. The candidate who took the 'immediacy' pledge won the election. Even more interesting was the concession speech of the defeated condidate, Garnett. He insisted that he would have voted for emancipation, but having been approached late in the campaign, he did not want to look as though he was pledging only to gain votes.[23] If candidates associated with anti-slavery by birthright, like the Whig Thomas B. Macaulay, rested on their ancestral oars, they might find themselves excoriated from both the right and left as really being soft in their commitment to emancipation. Anti-slavery banners and hecklers were often noted in newspaper accounts of the verbal battles at the hustings. The list of 163 pledged candidates published by the central agitational anti-slavery organ (*The Tourist*) therefore considerably under-states the numbers of candidates who were belatedly forced to add at least a precise reference to the need for immediate emancipation in the 1832 campaign,[24] and could no longer evade the issue through silence.[25] In a sample of dozens of campaign accounts I have found few contenders who simply avoided slavery, or who even claimed that it was not a para-mount issue before the new Parliament.

The speeches to the electorate in 1832 reflected the in-fluence of an earlier mobilisation. The ground work had been prepared by a host of speakers touring the country from 1830 onwards to focus interest on the problem of colonial slavery. One part of this effort was the centrally co-ordinated cam-paign of paid agents who systematically visited the major population centres throughout the Kingdom. Anti-slavery agents required a local network to work most effectively at local and regional meetings. Lecturers with personal experi-ence of slavery, especially colonial missionaries, systematically transformed colonial persecution into metropolitan sympathy. As a result, politicians took the resulting anti-slavery public with particular seriousness by 1832. When abolitionist agent George Thompson came to give his immediate emancipation lecture in Sheffield, all the local parliamentary candidates either attended or sent regrets which were read to the meet-ing. At Bradford, all three contenders appeared at the main anti-slavery rally.[26]

Because of the disproportion between pro- and anti-emancipation audiences in Britain itself, even the West Indian efforts at counter-lecturing could be converted into occasions for pro-abolitionist mass demonstrations. George Thompson claimed to have spoken to 750,000 listeners when he passed through Manchester in 1832. In the same city the West Indian agent found himself confronted by a heckling phalanx who reduced his lecture to a splintered liturgy of statements and responsive hoots and hisses. Newpapers hostile either to anti-slavery or to its rough open-air tactics reacted with a mixture of wonder and disgust at the behaviour of people who were so obviously 'respectably attired'. Even in Liverpool, where West Indian capital was heavily over-represented, thousands attended lectures on slavery and many were turned away.[27] The lecture campaigns of 1830–3 were intended to generate a clear message of common anti-slavery sentiment to audiences throughout the country, and to forge a temporal national solidarity around the principle of emancipation.

Accounts of the abolitionist campaigns almost always conveyed the impression that, in gathering and signing, the public was playing a unique role in precipitating changes in parliamentary opinion and in the legislative process. On the part of the opposition the reproof that popular passions were inflamed was implicit acknowledgement that the movement was both popular and passionate. On the other side, abolitionists invoked symbolism linking divine and popular inspiration: 'For the *vox populi erit vox Dei*, the voice of a united people shall be as the voice of God', declared the *Sheffield Iris*. 'What arguments could be urged for staying execution upon the sentence . . . by the *vox populi vox Dei* . . . that slavery shall be no more', asked the *Manchester and Salford Advertiser*.[28] Hostile conservative opinion might consider the demand for anti-slavery pledges as a test for public office to be 'unparalleled affrontery', but radicals, even when later embittered by the 'perversion' of compensation for planters and apprenticeship rather than unconditional emancipation for ex-slaves, saw petitions as an eminently useful tactic for forcing Governments at least to confront grievances.[29]

The perception of 'forcing attention' was accurate. None

of the Governments between 1792 and 1837 could claim full credit for taking the initiative in dismantling the overseas slave system, although the ministers of 1806—7 came closer than others in that respect. Concerning the breadth of pressure from without, anti-slavery continually broke new ground. As early as the 1780s it appears that a good deal of care was taken by organisers to ensure authenticity in order to avoid parliamentary devaluation through fraudulent adhesions. Women began to petition *en masse* at the beginning of the 1830s and anti-slavery was in the vanguard. In 1833 a single petition of 187,000 'ladies of England — a huge featherbed of a petition' — was hauled into Parliament by four sturdy Members.[30] The impact of the movement created new precedents in governmental public relations. When anti-slavery delegates meeting in London were given a mass audience with the Colonial Secretary in order to lobby collectively for changes in the emancipation bill, the *Manchester Guardian* could not recall any previous case in which 'such a body of delegates have been admitted to the presence of ministers'.[31]

Anti-slavery also assimilated agitational styles from radical and working-class rallies. The hostile reporter of the *Manchester Courier* wrote of one such major meeting: 'I was *astonished* to see so many well-dressed professing Christians keep such a continual noise of applause, while the cause of the suffering negroes was trifled with and the sacred language of revelation was prostituted'.[32] At the height of the agitation over emancipation so impressive was the breadth of public opinion that contemporaries projected popular abolitionist opinion back into the early eighteenth century.[33] None the less, if one considers numbers of signatures, petitions or public meetings as measures of 'popularity' it is impossible to identify anti-slavery as less than one of the most extensive movements of national opinion in the first half of the nineteenth century.

So much for the voice of the people. But what of the voice of God? We have dealt with popular abolitionism only in terms of other single issues at the national and international level, but historians have seen abolitionism as intimately linked to the religious development of Britain, from the initial eighteenth-century Quaker impetus and the leadership of the Clapham 'Saints', to its nonconformist climax in the

1830s. A number of recent works reflecting on this aspect of the British anti-slavery crusade see it as an indication of the triumph of the spiritual over the material, and more specifically as the result of the mobilisation of one variety of British Protestantism. For Edith Hurwitz this mobilisation occurred both in theological and in liturgical terms: 'Antislavery thought cannot be divorced from the general body of Protestant theology. Antislavery societies and Antislavery meetings followed the Protestant congregationalist community—organisational pattern.'[34] Hurwitz rightly focuses on the theological transference of evangelical symbols to the issue of black slavery, as well as on the mobilisation of religious fervour into the goals, techniques and indeed the cadences of anti-slavery reform. In her view, the formation of anti-slavery societies and petition meetings derived from Protestant organisation and evangelical dissent.

There is a general chronological correlation between the burgeoning of British anti-slavery and the rise of evangelical nonconformity.[35] Although Thomas Clarkson emphasised the significance of the Quakers rather than the new nonconformity in the early organisation of the movement, the more one moves toward the climax of anti-slavery in the early 1830s, the more clearly the evangelical ties appear. From contemporary evaluation we also have the testimony of the agitator-general, George Stephen that his campaign was aimed at the 'religious' public. Indeed, to Stephen, it was self-evident 'that if the religious world could be induced to enter upon the subject . . . viewing it simply as a question between God and man, the battle was won'.[36] Stephen's strategy was to insist on the link with the Christian imperative as a response to all nuances of opposition argument. From the opposition, a resentful linking of anti-slavery and nonconformity was equally emphatic. The tendency of those commentators relying on these sources is therefore to see anti-slavery as an extension of the British nonconformist revival.

Viewed in broad international perspective this seems to be a fair general statement of the historical nexus. This has already been the subject of extensive analysis. It must be remembered that the same Protestant—evangelical revival in the American South took religious organisations and theology in quite a different direction in relation to slavery.[37] More-over, although anti-slavery was usually heavily dependent on denominational support for funding and organisation in Britain, this does not demonstrate that anti-slavery was merely an offshoot of the nonconformist religious revival. In the initial phase of the movement the focus of abolitionist organ-isation was communal not denominational. The local civic centre and the tavern were far more frequently the venue of meetings and petitions than either church or chapel. One cannot ignore the vigorous support for early anti-slavery by a popular secular radicalism which was driven to the periph-ery, but not out of the picture, by the conservative reaction of the 1790s. The democratic tradition of Yorkshire proudly dated its contribution back *beyond* Wilberforce to David Hartley, who made the first parliamentary motion denounc-ing colonial slavery in the 1770s. It was, in fact, only toward the end of the 1820s that nonconformity began to play its overshadowing role in the anti-slavery movement.[38] In the famous Yorkshire 'slave trade' election of 1807, only one of twenty-four dissenting clergy voted for Wilberforce, although the Methodists already gave him disproportionate support. As for the latter, as late as 1819, when Wilberforce canvassed the Methodists (who had objected to the Jamaica slave laws in 1809) on further anti-slavery initiatives, he found that they were 'for leaving to their masters all improvements in the condition of the slaves', and postponed immediate action.[39] The pressure of countervailing forces on Methodist conserva-tives was manifest as late as the controversial vote of Jabez Bunting in 1832, mentioned above.

Even at the height of the nonconformist presence in 1830–3, however, the pattern of religious support reached well beyond organised nonconformity. If the Wesleyan Methodists began moving away from earlier political quietism over the issue of slavery, and if the Baptists rigorously or-ganised petitions and revived the early abolitionist tactic of boycotting slave-grown sugar, even the anti-Claphamite Anglican *Record* published model petitions and faithfully recorded those Anglican gentry or clergy who attended peti-tion rallies.[40] Anti-slavery therefore demonstrated an appeal well beyond the boundaries of nonconformity. Contrary to

Hurwitz's assessment, the pattern of petitioning in Parliament was not 'by denomination in a given local community' even in the 1830s.[41] The denominational effect was indeed strong enough to receive special note by the parliamentary report on public petitions. However, the same report showed that communal petitioning continued to be the predominant source of affiliated signatures. Denominations collectively accounted for 56 per cent of the 5000-plus anti-slavery petitions in 1833, but they accounted for less than 27 per cent of the signatures.[42] Only after 1840 did it become more exclusively identified with nonconformity. In the British public debate on policy in the American Civil War, what denominational petitioning occurred in favour of the North after Lincoln's Emancipation Proclamation was exclusively nonconformist. A less explicit religious identification with a pro-southern interventionist position, on the other hand, was Anglican. By then, however, the mass base of anti-slavery was rapidly vanishing.[43]

To consider anti-slavery in general as merely an extension of nonconformity is therefore to designate a part as the whole. In this context we can appropriately compare the petitions and signatures mobilised for anti-slavery with those accumulated on behalf of contemporary religious issues. In the late 1780s and early 1790s those who sought a repeal of the Text and Corporation Act clearly could not match abolitionism in mass support.[44] Two decades later, neither the petitions against Sidmouth's attempt to restrict nonconformity, nor those submitted in favour of Wilberforce's evangelical project for India, could approach the scope of the 1814 petition campaign against the slave trade clause in the treaty with France. Finally, if anti-slavery attracted more signatures in 1833 than the Catholic emancipation petition on both sides combined, it even more easily surpassed all religious issues dear to evangelical nonconformity.[45] Allowing for a large evangelical role in the organisation and rhetoric of the movement at its climax, anti-slavery's attraction of more than twice as many signatures as any nonconformist petition campaign in the 1830s impels us to think of abolitionism as far more than a spin-off of the evangelical revival.

Beyond the evidence from petitions, the more strictly

religious issues usually met with far more indifference and hostility than anti-slavery mobilisations. A meeting for stricter observance of the sabbath in Manchester in the wake of an anti-slavery rally was swamped by its opponents. This pleased the *Manchester Guardian* which hoped that such a result would reduce the growing number of 'promiscuous' public meetings. Now that the poor had felt the itch for public meetings 'the more intelligent and respectable classes' might be less disposed to attend.[46] At its most popular phase in 1833, anti-slavery was clearly attracting radical as well as evangelical support. The organ of the Anglican evangelicals began to denounce the popular movement as an ungodly alliance between Dissenters and contaminated radicals.[47]

This also raises the problem of class affiliation and anti-slavery. When socially characterised, anti-slavery is usually assumed to be a political movement directed by the ruling class, or a portion thereof, in Parliament, and expressive of the sentiment of the rising middle class in the country at large.[48] As in the case of the religious connection, the writings of the abolitionists themselves tend to encourage this conclusion. George Stephen, whose *Antislavery Recollections* have given historians the most detailed retrospective insight into the motivations of the organisation of popular agitation in 1832–3, explicitly designated the 'provincial respectability', not the saints of religious communities, as the prime target for the great final push.[49] The propaganda organ of his agency, *The Tourist*, for all its clear defence of the 'Rights of Man',[50] was directed more at the buyers than the sellers of manual labour, at farmers and landowners rather than agricultural workers.

Closer analysis of anti-slavery support gives us a somewhat different view. Even those historians who emphasise the middle-class evangelical nature of the anti-slavery constituency by 1830, concede that in its earlier period there was a vociferous source of support for anti-slavery which few would regard as middle class. The widely recognised abolitionist participation of English popular radicalism in the 1790s, outlined by James Walvin among others, casts doubt on any equation of middle class and abolitionism for the early period of political mobilisation. Popular radicalism gave unequivocal support for one of the earliest of the protest movements of the early 1790s to come to fruition – the abolition of the slave trade.[51]

On the other hand, during the early 1830s, there is also a good deal of evidence of radical working-class hostility to abolitionism.[52] Yet it does not appear that anti-slavery had lost its working-class constituency. The quantitative evidence is indirect and partial but worthy of attention. We have clear evidence from at least one large denomination, Wesleyan Methodism, which accounted for about one-sixth of the signatures on the 1833 petition. The great majority of that denomination's signatories must have been artisans and labourers.[53]

But we also have other direct evidence of working-class loyalty to anti-slavery which was sufficient to convert its most inveterate populist enemy. In 1832, just after the passage of the Reform Act, William Cobbett announced his conversion to emancipation at a Manchester campaign rally.[54] Cobbett had been one of England's most virulent Negrophobes. He also detested both Wilberforce and evangelicalism. His motivation in changing sides during his campaign is therefore of some interest. Cobbett was not speaking in Yorkshire, whose citizens he had more than once written off as religious fanatics. Nor was Cobbett's Manchester audience George Stephen's target, the newly enfranchised 'respectable' middle-class voter. It was a rally of the working-class population of the city. Perhaps Cobbett recalled his unsuccessful election campaign at Preston, in 1826, when he was singled out for his hostility towards emancipation, and for his description of blacks as 'degraded brutes'.[55] This time Cobbett pledged himself to support emancipation precisely because his working-class audience favoured such a position. At the Oldham hustings in another part of industrial Lancashire a few months later, he received support from the anti-slavery movement.[56]

It is equally significant that Cobbett had not relinquished his view that black slaves in the islands lived more comfortably and worked less arduously than many whites in England. While all of the radicals who claimed to represent the working class did not support emancipation, and some actually interrupted anti-slavery meetings with interjections about the proper relationship between charity at home and abroad, they were apparently not able to carry the rank and file of the industrial North along with them.

There was, however, at least a fraction of working-class sentiment which deeply resented the priority given by some abolitionist leaders to relief of suffering abroad. There seem to have been few cases in which a militant working-class contingent, or at least militant radical spokesmen, actually attempted to deflect or disrupt anti-slavery petition meetings in 1832–3, but there may also have been enough resentment in other cases to prevent petitions from being launched by public meeting. The Tory and anti-abolitionist *Leicester Herald* hinted that its local abolitionists avoided such a meeting for fear that radicals would move an amendment 'upon the present state of the white slaves in this country'.

The fears were not groundless. In the wake of the dismay over parliamentary action on compensation and apprenticeship the Blackburn working-men's Political Union condemned the activity of abolitionists as misleading the people. In two other recorded instances, however, this approach was overruled. After a disrupted anti-slavery meeting in Birmingham, its Political Union voted by three to one to send a petition to Parliament in favour of emancipation. And in Bolton, where an anti-slavery meeting had been disrupted in the name of the working class, the local operatives denied both that the speaker was an operative or that he spoke for their community.[57]

The older antagonistic tradition of Cobbett remained a staple but equivocal attitude of some of the radical working-class spokesmen into the mid-thirties. At a rally in Preston, a radical could casually invoke the pro-slavery symbolism of the sleek, well-clothed and lazy black, whose problems could be tabled pending the emancipation of white workers without bread or votes. In the next breath, however, the same speaker denounced slavery both at 'home and abroad', to the cheers of his audience.[58] Even the most radical anti-abolitionist MPs found colonial anti-slavery to be a popular political symbol. Orator Henry Hunt, hostile to anti-slavery to the bitter end of his electoral defeat in 1832, had cheerfully adopted its symbolism to attack opponents on the hustings who could be linked with the 'groans and anguish of poor creatures whose colour was their only crime'.[59]

Other segments of the working class were apparently less ambivalent. Although George Stephen's agency committee may have decided that influential 'respectability' was their principal target, the Methodist and Baptist petition campaigns obviously had far broader aims. The agitation, even among the unenfranchised, did not stop with the acquisition of their signatures. When the compensation clauses of the Government brought an angry backlash among both radical middle- and working-class spokesmen, a special campaign to maintain support for emancipation was conducted among the Methodist poor.[60] Working-class anti-slavery was neither ignored nor taken for granted.

Given the support for anti-slavery among other politically mobilised working-class groups in America and France, it would be odd if English urban artisans had completely abandoned a component of the democratic ideology they forged at the end of the eighteenth century. And there is evidence that they not only did not break with their anti-slavery tradition but, even after emigration, were most likely to be among the working-class supporters of American abolitionism as well. This evidence further reinforces the conviction that abolitionism had deep and continuing roots in British artisanry.[61]

Having indicated the range of anti-slavery support in the early nineteenth century, it remains to examine the impact of anti-slavery opinion on the outcome. To some extent the answer will depend on the frame of reference.[62] The record of petition campaigns without some other source of leverage was never very encouraging in terms of immediate success. Consider only the three campaigns in figure 2, or the great Chartist petition at the end of the 1830s. Catholic emancipation passed in spite of the fact that a clear majority of the petitioners came out against it.[63] Parliamentary reform passed before slave emancipation although abolitionism produced twice as many petitions in the session of 1830–1.[64] And

Chartism, in 1839, emerged from its first national campaign without so much as a symbolic gesture from Parliament in return for its massive effort.[65] In each of the successful cases one must also consider phenomena extraneous to the public opinion campaign which might have played a decisive role in the precise timing of the outcome. The revolutionary potential of the Irish Catholics in 1829, of the political militants in 1832, and of the West Indian slaves in 1831 can be brought into each political equation in order to argue that something 'extra', even in extra-parliamentary agitation, was necessary to push Parliament to the point of implementing radical legislation, however large the harvest of petitions. The general record of parliamentary responsiveness to non-violent mass requests which also threatened major interests was otherwise rather poor in the short term.

Viewed even in this light, however, the relative success of anti-slavery petitions in achieving some quick positive response from above is impressive. In 1788 the first regulatory bill on the slave trade was passed in the wake of the first large-scale demand for action. In 1792 the House of Commons reversed its almost two to one rejection of the previous year and resolved on the abolition of the trade in 1796, although its will to implement that vote dissolved with the fear of domestic social upheaval. The petition of 1814 apparently was accepted by the Government as a major re-statement of national priorities,[66] and induced it to increase dramatically international pressure on the slave trade. The Government's sponsorship of an emancipation bill in May 1833, shortly after the King's opening speech had neglected even to mention colonial slavery, came not in direct response to the immediate threat of either metropolitan or slave violence, but on the heels of an unprecedented levy of signatures on that issue. Finally, the Government made an about-face on resistance to ending the apprenticeship system after the petition campaign of 1838. Of all the major abolitionist campaigns, only the petitions of 1830–1, when anti-slavery was overshadowed by the constitutional crisis, failed to obtain at least a major symbolic response. It is possible, by looking at the details and compromises of each governmental act, to minimise the role of public opinion. But this is to view public opinion as an instrument for producing details of legislation. Only rarely could public opinion operate in this way and almost never on major questions. Rather than taking the perspective of the parliamentary product, inevitably filtered through very complex stages, we might again profitably consider the impact of public opinion in the broader geographical and temporal perspective of the first section of this essay.

Compared with France, where anti-slavery opinion was never massively mobilised, British abolition was far more cumulative and consistent. Even in the fervour of the early phases of the revolution of 1789 the French National Assembly refused to consider any limitations on the expansion of their colonial slave system. The impetus to the revolutionary emancipation decree of 1794 came almost entirely from colonial developments, including the threat of imminent British conquest and the most massive slave uprising in the history of black slavery.[67] Nor was there any outcry when France revived the slave trade after the peace treaties with Britain in 1802 and 1814. The identification of the British Government with international abolition in the wake of the 1814 petition was far more persistent and determined than that of any other power. Continental action against slavery in general consistently lagged behind Britain's initiatives.

We can consider a few of the implications of this lag, by testing the possible link of popular mobilisation with economic interest theories of abolition. One of the favourite alternative explanations of the timing of emancipation of British colonial slaves emphasises changing economic interests. The argument usually focuses either on the long-term declining value of slave colonies as trading partners before emancipation, or the short-term market situation for British slave-grown products at the time of legislation.[68] Neither the relative nor absolute value of Britain's slave colonies, in terms of invested capital or as trading partners, declined during the crusade against the slave trade 1787–1815. There was a measurable relative decline in some respects between 1815 and emancipation, but the West Indies were no negligible entity even in 1833. Edward Stanley pointedly opened the Government's motion on emancipation by first alluding to 'this question of unparalleled importance – involving a greater amount of property – affecting the happiness and the well-being of a larger proportion of individuals than was ever before brought forward'.[69] Stanley was referring to British commerce, shipping, revenue and capital including the slaves in the West Indies. Although the imperial trading significance of the British West Indies had declined, partly as a consequence of prior abolitionist legislation, it still compared favourably with that of its still unthreatened French counterpart. Figure 3

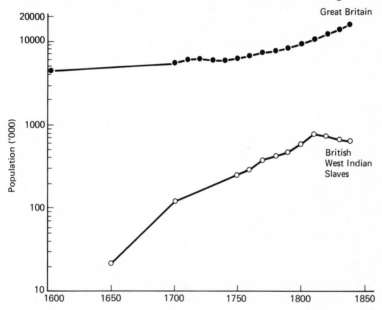

FIGURE 3   Trade of the slave colonies of Britain* and France in the generation before their respective emancipations, as a percentage of the total trade (including re-exports) of each.

*This does not include the British trade with colonies using slave labour in the Eastern hemisphere. The value of the trade of the Cape Colony and Ceylon might theoretically be added to the British figure.

SOURCES: For the British system: B. R. Mitchell and P. Deane, *Abstract of British Historical Statistics* (Cambridge, 1962) pp. 309–11; *Parliamentary Papers* 1831–2, vol. XX; for the French system: *Statistique de la France*, Imprimerie royale, 1835–47 (tables of colonial commerce).

shows the relative importance of the slave colonies of Britain and France as trading partners of their respective metropolises. If one were to measure the slave colonial trade as a percentage of national product rather than of total trade alone, the differential between the British and French colonies would be more than two and a half times greater in favour of the British than is shown in the table. On the eve of their respective emancipations Britain's total trade sector accounted for 18 per cent of its national product. The trade sector accounted for only 7 per cent of the French national product. I have used the less dramatic indicator because contemporaries tended to measure the significance of regional trades in terms of the more accessible figures on overseas trade rather than proportions of national product.

Beyond the significance of slave agriculture as a source of trade lay the crucial question of compensation for legal property in persons.[70] Every European Government was committed to the general sanctity of private property and considered some form of compensation necessary to the erstwhile proprietor.[71] This premise represented the major practical stumbling block to metropolitan emancipation. For parsimonious politicians everywhere, the cost of compensation of itself constituted a capital incentive for indefinitely postponing action. The longer the implementation of emancipation could be delayed after a declaration of intention to emancipate, the lower the price of slaves (and so compensation costs) might fall in anticipation.[72] Correspondingly, if the British public had subverted confidence in slave property its proprietors reasoned that compensation should be calculated largely on the pre-agitation slave market. The Government might accept the premise that the metropolis had undermined confidence in slave capital but it rejected the conclusion. Wary as ministers might be about equating the voice of the people with the word of God, for purposes of liability popular agitation became an act of God. It is important to bear in mind the reluctance of Members of Parliament to disburse large sums of money for which the taxpayer received no certain return beyond the assurance that the juridical status of some inhabitants of the tropical empire was to change.

Since there were more than three times as many British as French colonial slaves, the potential fiscal burden of emancipation in that regard alone was considerably heavier for the British taxpayer than for the French.[73] At the best compensation rate per slave imagined by a Royal commission in France[74] before 1848, the cost of indemnity per British citizen would have been over seven times that of each metropolitan French citizen. Even taking into account the higher productivity of British labour in 1831, each British subject would have paid between five and six times as much as his or her French counterpart, at the best compensation price which the metropolitan élites thought it reasonable to offer slave owners.[75] The French Government dragged its feet despite the knowledge that slave compensation would cost only one third as much, and would represent even less of a burden *per capita*. As it turned out, after emancipation the French Republic allowed its colonists only 60 per cent of the sum contemplated before the Revolution of 1848. The delayed French emancipation therefore ultimately cost the French a quarter as much as the British with a corresponding reduction of *per capita* costs. Insulated from great public pressure for emancipation, French colonial policy moved in a very different direction. The pacification of Algeria, which proceeded during the period of most intense debate over French emancipation in the 1840s, cost France far more than the projected compensation to the French colonial planters.[76]

The weight of public opinion also needs to be viewed in less narrow terms than its immediate effect on the implementation of legislation. The psychological impact of even symbolic parliamentary reaction to petitioning could be quite profound. The West Indian response to the impact of British public opinion was significant even when a tide of petitions was seemingly channelled into a vague resolution for gradual emancipation in 1823. Table I shows the five-year average prices of public sales of slaves in Jamaica from the abolition of the African slave trade in 1808 until just before the emancipation mobilisation of the 1830s. From 1808 until 1822 the average price of slaves remained unusually high, presumably in response to the inevitable consequences of the end of the African supply.[77] After 1823 the average price dropped

TABLE I

Averages of prices per slaves sold for debt in Jamaica 1808–27

Period	Number of slaves sold	Price	Price per slave
1808–11	4452	341,414	76.7
1812–15	5546	402,753	72.6
1816–19	4158	334,886	80.5
1820–3*	4064	317,588	78.1
1824–7	4441	225,760	50.8

* The emancipation compensation figure was computed upon average sale prices of all slaves for the decade following 1822.
Source: *Parliamentary Papers* (1828) XXVI, pp. 25–9.

sharply, apparently responding to the clear knell of metropolitan opinion.

One must also carefully consider the role of colonial slaves themselves in discussing the impact of public opinion on the emancipation process. Historians often treat the large slave uprising in Jamaica immediately preceeding emancipation simply as an external catalyst of the legislation which followed. It is necessary to recall that far more extensive and successful instances of colonial slave resistance did not alter metropolitan determination to preserve the institution. The greatest and most successful slave uprising in history on St Domingue did not deter France from twice restoring its colonial slave empire thereafter. Yet the much less extensive uprising on Jamaica in 1831, perhaps because of its brutal suppression, resulted in the intensification of metropolitan pressures for immediate emancipation. In European imperial terms slave rebellions were not confined to the British colonies before 1833. In assessing the role of the Jamaica uprising of 1831, the prior roles of the abolition of the slave trade and of the increasing communication of abolitionist sentiment to the colonies after 1815 must be taken into account.[78] British public opinion was as communicable to the slave cabins as to the Houses of Parliament, and the nonconformist network of anti-slavery stretched from the working-class chapels of Britain to those of the West Indies.[79]

The long-term impact of opinion is therefore as important as short-term results measured in parliamentary motions and votes at any given moment. Anti-slavery opinion could hardly be regarded by those in or out of power as an isolated wave in an otherwise placid sea of indifference. It was seen as persistent and cumulative. As Francis Jeffrey wrote of the reform agitation of 1830: 'True the cry for reform has formerly subsided; but has it not always revived; and, at every revival, been echoed from a wider circle, and in a louder tone?'[80] Jeffrey articulated the conviction which lay beneath all of these activities, that public opinion was a social force which had to prevail in the long run. Ten years before emancipation, the Baptist magazine urged the people of the Kingdom to press the issue on the legislature in a similar temporal perspective. If it were simply universal enough, 'though for a time . . . unsuccessful . . . the voice of the people could not continually be lifted up in vain'.[81] During the 1830s no other cause could begin to approach the number of petitions submitted to Parliament against slavery and black apprenticeship. Foreigners noted with awe that a British MP could cover the floor of the Commons with these petitions, boasting with the assurance of an Inca ruler that he would fill the whole chamber the next time around if Parliament did not act on those before it.[82]

Anti-slavery involved far more than a downward flow of ideology from élites to a nascent capitalist or evangelical middle class. The movement was, of course, 'shallow' in the sense that there was never, on the European side of the Atlantic, any attempt to intensify the voice of the people by even the hint of an appeal to civil discord. In developing a whole range of agitational techniques and symbolic forms, it primarily expanded the tactics and the social base of non-violent public opinion. It ventured beyond the printed word to the famous mass-produced scheme of the packed slave ship which hung on walls all over Britain. The Wedgwood cameo of the kneeling slave allowed women and children to join the movement through the wearing of emblems whether or not they could sign petitions. The abolitionists initiated the selective commodity boycott of slave sugar to strengthen commitment, and symbolically to strengthen the sense of collective dedication through a dietary taboo. The variety of techniques used to develop a common consciousness was almost endless. Carlisle weavers who saw a fellow worker dressed up 'as an ethiopian in collars and chains' could identify immediately with the victims of overseas slavery.[83] Displays of whips, chains and so on created a dramatic and palpable sense of social distance between the audience and the merchants and planters who used the hardware of slavery as their ordinary instruments of production and trade. Antislavery agitators knew the value of having black lecturers as well as persecuted missionaries giving personal testimony in preparation for electoral and petition campaigns. Popular mobilisation thus aimed not just at arousing the attention of ministers and Members of Parliament, but at forging an alliance which would link innumerable and disparate individuals, including people who had no direct previous role in the national political process. With the exception of a small intellectual counter-tradition, abolitionism institutionalised from one basic symbol a shared activity, a shared vision of the future and, ultimately, a myth of national achievement with more than a grain of truth.

2. The Propaganda of Anti-Slavery

JAMES WALVIN

It has been argued that one of the crucial reasons for the success of the anti-slavery movement in Britain was the unprecedented support it came to acquire in the years 1798–1838.[1] In a society where Government was unaccustomed to the arts of containing and deflecting public pressure, the public demand for abolition of the slave trade and later emancipation of the slaves was not merely more powerful than any comparable movement but, significantly, it was thought by contemporaries to be irresistible. It is easy to take a cynical view of this — to fall back on a deterministic position and argue that no British Government could have contemplated ending so economically important a system as slavery unless flaws had begun to appear in that previously profitable edifice. At the very time the British ended the slave trade in 1807 the slave system was not regarded as unprofitable by contemporaries. Indeed the work of Seymour Drescher has shown that abolition came at a time of economic buoyancy for the slave system.[2] If this is true, and if it is also true that anti-slavery became the political issue which attracted more support from more varied social groups, the time is ripe for a closer examination of the anti-slavery campaign. The purpose of this essay is to examine how the anti-slavery message was conveyed to the British public, to examine the mechanics of abolition propaganda. But it is also important to look at the content of that propaganda and to suggest what lay at the heart of the anti-slavery ideology as it was openly enunciated by its leading spokesmen.

From the early, largely Quaker beginnings in the 1780s,

the anti-slavery movement evolved into a national, highly effective and vocal criticism of, in the first instance, the slave trade. The subsequent campaigns fell into a number of divisions. In the first, roughly 1787–1807, the thrust of the public and parliamentary campaign was against the slave trade, in the hope that this was the most immediately practical first step and in the expectation that an end to the trade would, by cutting the slave colonies' life-line to Africa, oblige slave owners to ameliorate slave conditions. It was hoped that the ending of the slave trade would produce a natural withering away of slavery itself. Given this premise, abolitionists had to wait to see the outcome of abolition in 1807. It was soon obvious that whatever improvements might accrue to the slaves would be slow in coming and difficult to detect. Thus there was launched a new campaign, for slave registration – a census – which yielded the statistical data which commentators could analyse for the results of abolition.

The evidence from registration was not pleasing to the abolitionists and, in conjunction with a growing body of other evidence about the slaves' continuing miseries, it was instrumental in launching a fresh drive, in 1823, for full freedom. The Anti-Slavery Society established in that year and the proliferating provincial groups sought to end slavery throughout British possessions. The arguments raged back and forth: should emancipation be immediate or gradual? And, as time passed and emancipation came nearer, the details of the arguments tended to concentrate on the mechanics of securing freedom and on the sensitive question of compensation to be paid to the planters. Slavery finally came to an end in the British colonies in August 1838. Thereafter the British embarked on their crusade against other slave traders, using the Royal Navy as an instrument of their new-found zeal to curb an institution which they had been so important in shaping for the better part of two centuries.

It had taken half a century between the initial anti-slave trade movement of 1787 and full black freedom in 1838. In retrospect that seems a remarkably brief episode. For those contemporaries involved, however, it was a long drawnout affair. Some spent the whole of their adult life striving in the cause. Yet the methods used to promote abolition remained remarkably constant from first to last and were unusually successful.

The traditional historical emphasis on abolition had been to concentrate on the struggle within Parliament and Government. This was in keeping with a British historical tradition which until relatively recently regarded parliamentary history and the details of high politics as the proper and main concern of the British historian. It was this tradition, particularly in relation to abolition which so incurred the literary wrath of Eric Williams. *Capitalism and Slavery* and the subsequent historical debate shifted historical attention to new and relatively ignored areas of the abolition movement. Yet in the last resort it was Parliament which abolished the slave trade and slavery. As the work of Roger Anstey reminds us, it was the precise chronology of parliamentary debate, ministerial wrangles and governmental decisions which was crucial in the exact progress – or delay – in securing abolition and emancipation. This was true for *any* measure of reform or change which required parliamentary sanction, be it parliamentary reform, Roman Catholic emancipation or factory reform.

Every reforming campaign needed to persuade Parliament of the justice of its case. In this respect abolition was exceptionally successful in its own right and, moreover, was influential on subsequent reforming crusades. The main purpose here is to trace the methods by which this success was achieved outside Parliament, for it was extra-parliamentary pressure, directed to Parliament largely, as Seymour Drescher shows, through the petition, which was instrumental in changing parliamentary and ultimately ministerial minds about the slave trade and slavery.

I THE SPOKEN WORD

The lecture and the public address were crucial in the abolitionist cause. They could, for instance, take the abolitionist word even to those areas of society unable to master the rudiments of literacy. But the importance of the lecture transcends this point; it reached into every corner of the nation, persuaded untold numbers of the abolitionist case and,

remembering that lecturing was an art which both entertained and entranced, often converted and excited. Today,
when entertainment is easily available and often requires
little personal effort, it is difficult to recall the importance
of the lecture in British social and political life, an importance
which survived until well into the twentieth century. Lectures
were an important arena for political debate from the late
eighteenth century onwards and of course much earlier.
Radical organisations in particular were wedded to the lecture
as a means of informing their friends, converting waverers
and attracting a crowd. Indeed the most prominent radical
figures, from the corresponding societies of the 1790s through
to the Chartists, often rose to prominence, and are remembered primarily because they were arresting lecturers and
public speakers. John Wilkes was unusual in being a poor
public speaker who became the people's darling.[3] Just as
parliamentary figures often rose to fame (and historical
attention) by their verbal skills, so too did radical figures
secure for themselves a political fame via their public speaking.

It was in keeping with contemporary political custom
that, in 1787, the abolitionists should launch their attack on
the slave trade by dispatching Thomas Clarkson on a nation-
wide lecture tour. From the first — and long before his reputation preceded him — Clarkson attracted large crowds. In
Manchester he remarked: 'When I went into the Church it
was so full that I could scarcely get to my place'.[4] Naturally,
there were to be disappointments. Yet what is striking is the
number of abolitionist lectures and the size of the crowds
they attracted. Between 1787 and 1794 Clarkson covered
35,000 miles on seven lecture and research tours of Britain.[5]
From first to last, he and other abolitionists attracted vast
crowds to lectures and meetings. In the later phase, when
abolition reached a crescendo in the late 1820s with the
proliferation of local abolition societies and publications,
carefully orchestrated by the Anti-Slavery Society and the
Anti-Slavery Reporter, the number of such meetings proliferated, attracting ever bigger crowds. In April 1830 2000 tickets
were distributed for an abolition meeting in Dublin.[6] Expense
did not seem to deter the audience; a meeting called in Bradford in March of that same year charged 1/- (5p) entrance

fee, yet was 'attended by numerous, respectable and attentive audiences'.[7] In May 1830 the General Meeting of the
Anti-Slavery Society attracted an audience of 2000 with
1500 unable to enter.[8] Much the same story was repeated
wherever anti-slavery societies met — as far afield as Cork.[9]
In Leeds it was claimed that 6000 people filled the local
Coloured Cloth Hall.[10] When in the New Year 1831 a similar
meeting was called in Edinburgh, *The Scotsman* thought it
'one of the largest and most respectable meetings ever assembled in that intellectual city'.[11] Buildings were packed long
before the proceedings were due to start.[12] Exeter Hall,
which came to symbolise anti-slavery, attracted some of the
largest crowds. In May 1832 3000 plus an overflow attended
a meeting which lasted from noon until 7 pm. In August of
that same year yet another vast crowd squeezed into the
hall.[13]

This was not merely an urban phenomenon. In Roxburgh-
shire in 1833 a certain Mr Douglas 'delivered lectures on
Slavery, or addressed at public meetings . . . and had diffused
correct information and just sentiments on the subject throughout the remotest dales of that pastoral district'.[14] In this, the
last phase of abolitionism, the attraction of lectures was
enhanced by the Agency Committee (formed as a radical
breakaway). Wherever their lecturers spoke, the only restraint
on the size of the audience seems to have been the physical
capacity of the building.

If proof is needed of the centrality of the lecture, we need
only recall that the Agency Committee thought that it was
the main means of reaching the public and of arousing the
national conscience about slavery. Dividing the country into
'districts', the Agency Committee appointed an initial group
of five lecturers 'To prepare the way for a general expression
of the public feeling, when the time shall arrive, by widely
disseminating an accurate knowledge of the nature and effect
of Colonial Slavery.'[15] They *assumed* that the mere presentation of 'the facts' about colonial slavery would be enough to
persuade the people that bondage was wrong and ought to
be abolished. To a large extent this optimism was shared by
other contemporary reforming groups who, zealous in the
pursuit of what they understood to be just demands, expect-

ed the nation to be fair and reasonable when confronted by evidence and argument. Indeed, it is characteristic of these years that reason and justice were thought (by reformers of all hues) to be a public force which they could tap and utilise – merely by presenting the facts. These are assumptions which might seem sanguine to the more cynical audience of the late twentieth century.

The Agency Committee lecturers were given detailed instructions on how to broach the question of slavery and which books to rely on. They were urged to do their utmost to have their meetings widely advertised and reported and to have their lecture subsequently published in the locality.[16] Transforming a successful lecture into even more widely available printed format had been a commonplace feature of radical politics since the late eighteenth century.[17] The Agency Committee was unusually successful in providing a national framework of lectures which were, in practically every case, attended by capacity audiences. Reports of these lectures show a recurring pattern of crammed halls, overspill audiences, throngs travelling great distances to attend and of audiences – of all classes and both sexes – waiting patiently for and during the lectures. The St Albans Wesleyan Chapel 'was *crowded* with attentive hearers'.[18] At Woburn, the lecturer reported, 'such an excitement, I am assured, has not been witnessed here for thirty years'. 'The Hall was literally packed'.[19] Often second lectures were hastily arranged for the disappointed overspill crowds. A lecturer reported from Newport Pagnell, 'In this town as in all others, we were compelled to seek more extensive accommodation for the second lecture'.[20] At some lectures there was simply insufficient room for the audience. At Baldock, the lecturer reported, 'about 200 could not get in'. At Hitchin 'the chapel was crowded in every part, the aisles and doorway blocked up'. In Basingstoke 'the Town Hall (by no means of limited dimensions) was thronged'.[21] From Barnstaple, the lecturer reported, 'the Town Hall was quite full (1000 present I suppose)'.[22]

The same story was repeated right across the country. Even bad weather failed to keep the crowds away from anti-slavery lectures.[23] The smallest of villages and towns turned out in force to hear the message. At Hurstmonceaux 400 from a population of 1300 attended; at Folkingham, Lincolnshire, 150 out of 800. At Kirton the lecture 'was attended by about 300 persons; hundreds (I speak truly) went away unable to get in'.[24]

Perhaps as striking as the size of the audience attending anti-slavery lectures was the length of the proceedings. The anti-slavery lectures, continuing for hours at a time, might have proved unbearably long to a modern audience. We need to recall, however, that the lecture was merely the main event in a varied evening's programme. Local dignitaries shared the platform with the guest speaker and the audience was first entertained by local speakers. When the main speaker had finished, there generally followed lengthy question sessions, perhaps further procedural dealings (particularly when a new anti-slavery committee was formed) and protracted fund-raising. They were, quite clearly, crowded activities which seem remarkably like an evening's entertainment, the main attraction preceded by a host of varied offerings. Such meetings were, understandably, protracted affairs. But so too were the guest lectures themselves. The General Meeting of the Anti-Slavery Society in May 1832 lasted from noon until 7 pm, yet still managed to attract 3000 people.[25] When reporting back to London lecturers from the Agency Committee seemed to take pride in the length of their lectures, implying that the quality of their message could be gauged by the time taken to deliver it. One man claimed to have spoken for one and a half hours to a silent audience.[26] At Towcester the lecturer remarked, 'My lecture lasted two hours and a half'. At Olney it took two hours; in Bedford two and a half.[27] In Luton one lecturer reported, 'I last evening lectured . . . from twenty minutes past six to half past nine o'clock'.[28] At Dorking the audience was even more long-suffering: 'I kept my audience from seven until a quarter to ten o'clock, and so interested were they, that I verily believe, they would have sat all night.'[29] At Barnstaple they almost did: 'Our meeting began at seven, and was not over till near eleven.'[30]

In a society where work occupied a substantial part of the waking hours and where there was less free time than today, it was essential that such meetings, like any other public

gathering, should be arranged for a convenient time. The
exigencies of local labour or customs could make it difficult
for people to attend. At Hexham in 1830 an anti-slavery
meeting was organised for 10 am: 'The hour being very inconvenient to the shopkeepers and workmen of all kinds, the
meeting though respectable was by no means numerous'.[31]
A lecture in Bedford was arranged for Friday since Saturday
was 'an inconvenient day for families to attend public proceedings'.[32] None the less, mere convenience of most meetings can hardly explain the amazing popularity of the anti-
slavery lecture. Though they clearly reached a peak of popularity after 1830 (thanks largely to the efforts of the Agency
Committee) the lecture was a consistently attractive feature
of the anti-slavery campaign. Not only did vast crowds flock
to the lectures but, so the activists believed, the lectures
themselves were instrumental in documenting the case against
slavery and persuading ever more people of the need to seek
black freedom.

    The ease with which the anti-slavery lecturers could secure
a meeting place was extremely important. We need only
contrast the lot of anti-slavery with the difficulties encountered by radical pressure groups in securing meeting places to
realise how crucial such access was. It was a standard political
practice of national and local Governments to deny a meeting
place to contentious political gatherings. Informal pressure
(on landlords) or overt pressure from magistrates frequently
denied suitable meeting places to radical groups. Often the
open public place – street, square or field – remained the
last and only radical refuge. Even this could be denied them
by the expedient of limiting the legal size of public crowds.
Between the 1790s and the 1840s corresponding societies,
combinations, reformers and Chartists were effectively denied proper meeting places. This was a fate which anti-slavery
never experienced. From 1787 to 1838 public and private
rooms and buildings were freely available to the campaigns –
a tendency which increased with the passage of time. Churches
were most commonly used. On his first lecture tour Clarkson
frequently spoke from the pulpit to a crowded audience.[33]
Naturally the pioneering Quakers and Wesleyans were de-
lighted to open their doors (and even their homes) to visiting

abolitionist speakers. By the 1820s and 1830s the commitment to anti-slavery had even penetrated the more resistant
sensibilities of the established churches and they too made
their buildings available to the cause. Local Government
seemed no less willing to help and abolitionist lectures were
regularly offered in town, guild and shire halls. Schools too
were a regular abolitionist venue. Indeed from 1828 onwards,
the main criterion of a building's suitability was its size — the
bigger the better. But in all this the experience of abolition
was a remarkable contrast to the more unhappy fate of other
radical campaigns.

II THE PRINTED WORD

To emphasise the importance in abolition of the role played
by the spoken word does not, however, minimise the importance of publications. It is the survival of much of this
printed abolition material, which flew off the presses in vast
and growing numbers, which enables us to reconstruct this
story. Early abolitionists believed that their printed evidence
about slavery would, like the lecture, intrinsically sway public
feeling to their side. Clarkson records how the original committee, 'having voted the Slave-trade to be both unjust and
impolitic, . . . formed themselves into a committee for
procuring such information and evidence, and for publishing
the same, *as might tend to the abolition of it*'.[34] They were
of course able to capitalise on powerful and well-established
traditions of political publishing. Books, tracts, periodicals
and broadsheets were integral to and helped sustain a wide
range of British radical movements, from Wilkes through to
the Chartists. We need to recognise the difficulties in assessing the nature and extent of popular literacy, yet it is surely
persuasive to remember that all radical movements which
set out to win the support of people of a humble station did
so to a marked degree through the printed word. The Wilkes
movement and the corresponding societies built up unprecedented appeal, notably in London, among men who at first
sight might seem to have been denied formal education. In
London exposure to the printed word increased in the course
of the late eighteenth century, and literacy was particularly

important among the artisan trades.[35] Equally, the various dissenting communities were renowned for their levels of education and their commitment to literacy. Not surprisingly (and quite in addition to whatever other religious or ideological motives might persuade people of the abolitionist message) such groups provided a ready-made audience for the massive publication efforts of abolition from 1787 onwards.

The decision taken by the Abolition Society in 1787 to publish cheap tracts and to circulate them among their friends and contacts throughout the country set in train a major and highly successful propaganda campaign.[36] They were copying the well-known and well-proven tactics used so successfully only a few years before by the radical pressure groups, the association movement and the Society for Constitutional Information. With an abbreviated version of a work by Clarkson, the London abolitionists ordered 'two thousand copies of it ... to be printed, with lists of the subscribers and of all the committee, and to be sent to various parts of the kingdom'.[37] In little over a year thousands of tracts and booklets came off the presses and sped to sympathisers across the land. More than £1000 was spent; Clarkson's tract was issued in more than 15,000 copies.[38] And like older reforming groups the abolitionists sought to secure coverage and support in the provincial and national press.[39]

It is difficult to trace the influence and effectiveness of this propaganda which in any case had been preceded by a degree of private and individual effort. But it is surely no accident that a remarkable outpouring of abolitionist publications followed swiftly. Individual authors, correspondents to the press and periodicals turned to the task of undermining the slave trade. In the process they often elevated the black to the level of early Romantic caricature.[40] Poets too lent their skills to the discussion, though much of the anti-slavery poetry which found its way into print was little more than effusive doggerel.[41] It is instructive to recall that many of these Romantic poets were also political radicals, whatever the varied quality and durability of their poems.

The anti-slavery propaganda was challenged by the West India lobby which was able to commit more money, though less powerful talents and arguments, to the task.[42] Tracts and pamphlets poured from both sides and the cumulative result between 1787 and 1793 was a remarkable national propaganda battle through tracts, newspapers and booklets about the benefits or disadvantages, the immorality or the justice, of the slave trade and slavery. Although in the last resort the political battle for abolition could only be won (or lost) in Parliament itself, for six years an unusual battle for the public mind was fought by means of the printed and spoken word. Abolitionists soon felt confident that their efforts were succeeding. In 1790 the minutes of the Abolition Committee recorded: 'The Publick we believe are convinced that there is something both in the principle and conduct of this Trade fundamentally wrong'.[43] Some indication of the degree to which the public was won over to abolition can be gauged in fairly specific details by the nature and volume of abolitionist petitions which flowed into Parliament in apparently ceaseless waves between 1788 and 1838.[44]

By 1793, when war broke out with France, the struggle for abolition had been firmly lodged in Parliament. Thereafter the struggle was primarily parliamentarian − the lobbying of MPs and ministers and the movement of strictly parliamentary support or opposition. Little of this took place in, or indeed needed, the public domain. Moreover the emergence of a fierce popular radicalism after 1791, a radicalism which was itself abolitionist, subsumed the published arguments against the slave trade. Although the strength of popular radicalism initially reinforced the public campaign against the slave trade, the subsequent disapproval of radical politics after 1792 tarred abolition, quite wrongly, with the brush of Jacobinism. When abolition succeeded in 1806−7 it did so as a result of a parliamentary battle.

The power of the printed word in swaying public opinion was revealed in even greater detail in the years after 1823 when the abolitionists renewed their efforts, this time to end slavery itself. These were the peak years of abolitionsim, and printed abolitionist material survives in such abundance that it is tempting to overlook how prodigious this literary effort really was. Of course by this time Britain herself had undergone major transformations through the impact of the war with France, the accelerating process of industrial change and, more especially, of population growth. The attendant social upheavals had in their turn created acute political unrest which was often manifested in printed form. Indeed the demand for the right to argue a radical case in print itself became a major cause in radical politics in these years. Stated crudely, these were years of heightened political awareness and debate on a wide front. But it is unlikely that any contemporary political movement could match abolition for the volume of its printed arguments, the comprehensive national support it enjoyed or the public feeling — among all classes, ages and both sexes — it was able to generate.

Some stark but telling statistics might help to illustrate the case. Between 1823–31 the Anti-Slavery Society published no fewer than 2,802,773 tracts, distributed to their expanding national circle of friends and through their London outlet.[45] In one year alone, 1831, they issued 469,750 tracts. And this was in addition to the massive output of private publications, tracts issuing from local anti-slavery societies, continuous newspaper coverage, reprinted speeches, sermons and local political pronouncements. Men sought to establish their rectitude and sensibility by publishing their views on slavery. Local societies, though guided by the London society, regularly advertised their activities and views.[46] Indeed so extensive was this abolitionist propaganda that it tended to smother the plantocratic opposition and to stifle its arguments. Few men outside the West India lobby could politically afford to deny the pro-black case. By the mid-1820s it was simply *assumed* that, with the exception of the West India lobby, the nation was united against slavery. This was a ploy of the abolitionists — to assert the universality of their support. There is strong evidence to show that this was the case. Although the campaign for full black freedom was only begun in 1823, within two years politicians clearly believed that the abolitionists had overwhelming support on their side. The legislative arguments henceforth were not so much about whether black freedom should be conceded but when and under what circumstances. Speaking at a parliamentary election meeting in York in 1826 a local candidate asserted 'On the gradual abolition of Colonial Slavery, I am happy to believe that there are not two opinions in the Country'. Each of this man's political opponents on those hustings made exactly the same point.[47] Assuming that these opinions were so universal by the mid-1820s, it may seem surprising that slavery was able to survive for another decade. The fact that it did so, and remained resistant to ever strengthening abolitionist pressures, is to be explained largely in terms of parliamentary machinations (and the weight of capital invested in the slave system), in the pressuring of MPs and ministers, the wooing of groups in the Commons and Lords and in interdepartmental manoeuverings.

III WOMEN

Some indication of the unusual pervasiveness of abolitionism can be gauged from the unprecedented role which women played in the campaign. It was rare for women to be involved, or accepted, in the world of late eighteenth century formal politics, though they clearly played important roles in a range of other political activities, notably in food disturbances.[48] Even in the democratic movement of the 1790s and despite the contribution of Mary Wollstonecraft, women were notable for their absence from the corresponding societies. Yet by the mid-1820s women came to play a significant role in the abolitionist campaigns. They flocked to abolitionist meetings and lectures; time and again lecturers remarked on the presence of women in the audience. 'Many of both sexes came from the neighbouring towns' to a meeting in Woburn.[49] At a meeting in Bristol commentators were struck by how many women were in the audience.[50] At such lectures the attending women were often persuaded to form their own female anti-slavery society. Indeed from the mid-1820s onwards the formation of 'Ladies' Anti-Slavery Associations' became a particular abolitionist goal, in the knowledge that the women involved (those of the middle and upper classes) had the spare time to promote important abolitionist agitation: 'By means of such Associations, information may be prepared, printed and diffused; subscriptions may be raised; Petitions to the Legislature, when necessary, may be promoted; the use of sugar, the growth of free labour, in preference to that grown by slaves may be efficiently encouraged'.[51]

It may seem ironic, in the light of the well-known subordination of women in these years, that men should have encouraged female political activism in the interests of the slaves in the Caribbean. There was no hint that this political role ought to be encouraged on more immediate, domestic issues. The political prompting of women was unequivocal:

> We would remind every lady in the United Kingdom that she has her own sphere of influence, in which she may usefully exert herself in this sacred cause; and the effect of that influence, (even if it were quietly and unobtrusively confined to the family circle, or to the immediate neighbourhood), an awakening sympathy, in diffusing information, in imbuing the rising race with an abhorrence of slavery, and in giving a right direction to the voices of those on whom, under Providence, hang the destinies of the wretched slaves . . .[52]

In the eyes of their male peers, these women belonged to and operated within their own separate spheres of influence. It was appreciated that they could exercise great sway over their immediate entourage. Members of the Colchester Ladies' Anti-Slavery Association were urged in 1825 'to endeavour to awaken in the minds of their families, and all those over whom they have influence, a lively sense of the injustice, inhumanity and impiety of Negro Slavery'.[53] They began to have political impact. Supporters in Aberdeen noted that in England 'many amiable and highly-accomplished Females are now directing some of their leisure hours to this object'.[54] Indeed, as early as 1826 the *Anti-Slavery Reporter* was struck by the proliferation of ladies' anti-slavery associations.[55]

It is difficult to assess the effectiveness of this female political effort which was only one aspect of a much wider political movement. There are, however, a number of important indications. Abolitionists, notably in the localities, regularly conceded the important role played by women. This was true, for instance, in towns as diverse and distant as Cork and Hull.[56] When financial donations to the abolitionist cause were reported in the columns of the *Anti-Slavery Reporter* it was clear that a substantial amount of fund-raising was undertaken by local ladies' associations.[57] Moreover when we have specific evidence of female abolitionist efforts, it is clear that women could be exceptionally influential. In 1831 two women alone raised 187,000 names to a petition. In Sheffield, where the local women's anti-slavery society had eighty members in 1825, the women published and distributed thousands of tracts, published anti-slavery poetry and directed their energies 'chiefly among the poor of this town'.[58]

It seems clear that the abolitionist cause was important in providing many women with their first taste of political activity, though it was strictly within the limits determined by their male contemporaries. This ought not, however, to detract from its wider significance. Within the anti-slavery campaign women played a remarkably influential role as fund-raisers, in recruiting names to petitions, and as organisers of meetings and publications. By the mid-1820s they often undertook the tedious, unrewarding but necessary tasks which underpinned so much of the abolitionist campaign.

IV WINNING THE NATIONAL CONSCIENCE

The origins of anti-slavery lay in a feeling of outraged religious sensibility. It was after all the Quakers who took the initial stand against bondage, on theological grounds. Similarly the Methodists added the strength of the growing numbers of articulate congregations to the task of denouncing the slave trade and slavery. Indeed, until 1944 it was traditional for historians to view abolition as a religious (largely evangelical) campaign. Since *Capitalism and Slavery*, however, it has been unfashionable to adopt this view. Yet to read the literature of anti-slavery between 1823 and 1838 is to be struck forcefully by the degree to which opposition to slavery was couched overwhelmingly in religious terms. There is a relatively easy explanation for this. Most churches did turn against slavery and established and nonconformist congregations put their institutional strength behind abolition.

So too did all sorts and conditions of people of varied religious persuasions. By 1830 the great bulk of devout British people regarded slavery as a religious outrage.

This does not, however, answer the prime question, for the most difficult problem about anti-slavery surely lies in the fact that a mere fifty years before (and, of course, much earlier) this had not been the case. By the end of the American War, for example, it was *not* axiomatic among people of Christian conscience that slavery was an offence to their religious feelings. Yet when slavery was abolished it passed away as a hated institution universally condemned as 'a System full of Wickedness, hateful to God, and a Curse and Disgrace to Britain'.[59] This feeling was largely a direct result of evangelical effort in established and dissenting churches.

It was in new areas of the nation, more especially in the newly emergent working-class communities, that so much dissenting (particularly Methodist) effort took place. And it was from these working-class communities that the abolitionist voice was heard no less stridently than from within the propertied circles which historians have previously identified with evangelicalism. Indeed what gave the abolitionist case so powerful a claim was its universality among all classes of men and women. At the lower reaches of society, abolition evolved from two distinct but convergent forces. From plebeian nonconformist congregations (whose wider communities were often engaged in harsh and degrading labour systems and exploitative work) the message came forth that slavery was an outrage. And from working-class radical movements slavery was similarly denounced (though, obviously, in more secular tones) as a denial of social and human rights.

By the mid-1820s three convergent lines of argument came to dominate the campaigns against slavery: slavery was decried as an affront to Christian feelings, as a denial of human rights and, increasingly, as an economic irrelevance. The relative importance attached to these three arguments (which of course were often inextricably intertwined) provides some indication of the changes in abolition which took place in the course of fifty years. It also provides an opportunity of assessing the relative importance and weight which contemporaries came to attach to different criticisms of slavery. If we examine the propaganda which was so assiduously disseminated by the abolitionists over these years we can make an assessment of the basic objections to slavery.

To emphasise the religious objections to slavery offered in the 1820s and 1830s is not to return to the traditional interpretation which saw abolition as a trumph for evangelicalism. Moreover we need to recall that religion itself had been transformed, more especially among the lower orders. And the new religions of many working-class communities, far from being an overwhelmingly conservative force, was in this respect at least an agent for radical change. The voice of working-class nonconformity demanded an end to slavery. There was moreover an even closer link between the slaves and plebeian nonconformity. Slaves and the British working class were both objects of increased activity by missionaries, notably from the Methodist and Baptist churches. The determination to bring religion and salvation to distressed communities (wherever they might be) persuaded those churches to dispatch their missionaries into deprived industrial and urban corners of the Midlands and North as much as to the more obviously neglected reaches of the slave islands. Missionaries from the West Indies were understandably used to telling effect in the 1820s and 1830s, informing parliamentary committees, the public and their own congregations about the daily iniquities endured by the slaves. And of all the messages they conveyed, few things seemed to outrage British opinion more than tales of religious persecution of the slaves and missionaries by a plantocracy resistant to the notion of a converted and Christianised black labour force.[60]

By the mid-1820s abolitionists were also using other criticisms of slavery. They complained, for instance, of the violation of the slaves' social and human rights. Throughout this last decade of the campaign British abolitionists spoke of those rights in a vein which, if uttered in the 1790s about Britons, would have condemned the speaker as a Jacobin. It was commonly held that slavery was 'directly contrary to the natural Rights of Man'.[61] It is some measure of the changes in British society itself that the ideas of the 1790s, notably Tom Paine's 'Rights of Man', should within thirty years have

become the political vocabulary of the abolitionist cause.
Many congregations petitioning against slavery were outraged to learn that one of those rights – the freedom of
religious conscience – was commonly denied. So too, they
believed, was the natural right to enjoy family life. There
was a suspicion (unfounded as we now know) that slavery
was inimical to family life and this suspicion did not stem
solely from the words of returning missionaries. It had been
a commonplace claim about slave societies (and of course
about African life) that both Africans and Caribbean slaves
had no form of family life recognisable to the Western
eye. Now the demographic data, readily available after slave
registration and widely used by the abolitionists, seemed
to add statistical confirmation to this common myth, con-
firming that slavery was unnatural and dehumanising.[62] Thus
there was a conjunction of religious antipathy and secular
feeling which could point to demographic evidence as justification for their criticism of slavery.

Abolitionists also began to offer an economic criticism of
slavery, though this was a relatively minor objection when
weighed in the balance with others. The apparent economic
benefits of the slave system formed the most powerful argument in the plantocracy's case. Planters and their paid
scribes from the 1780s onwards frequently stressed the economic importance of slavery, both to the metropolis and to the
colonies, and how that importance would end with the
abolition of slavery.[63] By the 1820s, however, abolitionists
could counter with a new argument, one born of a new
economic thinking which was more in keeping with changing
conditions, that national self-interest was now best served by
laissez-faire, and demanded an end to the economically
inefficient slave system. In a more general sense the slave
colonies were monuments to an age of mercantilist protection
which, by the early nineteenth century, was contrary to the
nation's changing economic values.

Men with East India interests were among the first to point
out that slave-grown sugar was viable only because of a pro-
tective tariff which was costly to the British consumer and
unfair to other producers (although there was no East Indian
abolitionist 'block'). Some argued that free trade in sugar

would both benefit the consumer (by lowering the cost) and cripple the Caribbean whose sugar would be rendered uncompetitive.[64] Thus by the mid-1820s abolitionists had stood the economic argument on its head. Whereas previously planters had argued that the economic interests of the metropolis and Caribbean were one (and dependent on slavery), abolitionists now argued that those economic interests were divergent and contradictory. And, if only Britain could follow her own economic interests and seek free trade in sugar, slavery would collapse. Free trade would in effect destroy slavery. Thus a neat conjunction of morality and self-interest evolved and it was possible to advance the one without contradicting the other. Within a short time this economic criticism became a commonplace argument in abolitionist lectures and publications. In 1827, when the Chambers of Commerce of Manchester and Birmingham and the merchants and manufacturers of other industrial towns demanded free trade in sugar, it seemed as if the new capitalist order had finally broken with the out-dated economic orthodoxy of the previous century.[65] Yet we need to recall that this argument only effectively emerged in 1822, long after the end of the slave trade and after slave registration. Moreover, though it became an unmistakable theme in abolitionist propaganda thereafter, it was none the less a mere descant to much noisier and more strident arguments. Abolitionist denunciations of slavery were, overwhelmingly, much more concerned with the immorality of slavery, its affront to religious feelings, and its inherent denial of human rights. It was a useful bonus to discover, late in the day, that it was also now contrary to British economic interests.

How far this argument was instrumental in persuading the public of the justice of abolition is difficult to assess. It had not played any significant role in undermining the slave trade and it occupied a much less prominent position in the wider abolitionist debate. If abolitionists regarded the economics of slavery as the central issue involved, they rarely said so. And if we are to rely on their words — in public and private — as a key to the relative importance of the different objections to slavery, the economic criticism was low (and belated) on their list of priorities. However much, in retrospect, slavery seems doomed as an economic institution, it was not as obvious to contemporaries, whether abolitionists or planto-cracy.

What ultimately doomed slavery was the anti-slavery move-ment and the irresistible pressure it exercised, via the public, over Parliament and Governments. Clearly this was a complex matter. But it was above all a political issue, to be decided by Parliament and Government. Just as British slavery and the slave trade had, since their inception, been regulated and shaped by statute law from Westminster, so too were both ended by legislative acts. It is a lasting testimony to the work of Roger Anstey that he has redirected historical attention back to that fundamental fact.

3. 'Our Cause being One and the Same': Abolitionists and Chartism

BETTY FLADELAND

A reader of working men's newspapers and journals for the 1820s and 1830s might easily conclude that the working classes' worst enemies were the members of anti-slavery societies who were dedicated to freeing black slaves in far-off colonies while being blindly insensitive to the exploitation of white workers at home. The anti-slavery movement has been traditionally viewed as middle-class with the presumption that its adherents accepted current theories of political economy which taught that free labour and free trade would follow a natural course toward productive prosperity.[1] Recent histories of the anti-slavery movement have pointed to exceptions, but none has studied the degree to which abolitionists and proponents of reforms for workers recognised their causes to be philosophically and pragmatically inseparable.[2] Although it was initially difficult for many abolitionists to equate wage slavery with chattel slavery, and equally difficult for free British workers to acknowledge the similarity, each group learned from the other. The more the abolitionists publicised the horrid conditions of slavery, the more likely it was that British workers would see themselves as caught in similar circumstances. By the 1830s leaders of working-class movements realised that it would be to their advantage to capitalise on the achievement of the abolitionists in awakening sympathy for the downtrodden, and to do this by copying abolitionist strategy. Workers' cries of enslavement, in turn, forced abolitionist attention to miseries at home.

Of course not all abolitionists were transformed into activists on behalf of workers. Some remained unsympathetic, others were perturbed without doing much, but it is amazing how many became involved beyond the point of simply extending charity to the poor. Analyses of the causes of and solutions to working-class distress varied. Some abolitionists were confirmed Malthusians bent on reducing overpopulation; others advocated emigration and home colonies to make the surplus population self-sustaining on the land; many were dedicated to repealing the Corn Laws which favoured producers rather than consumers. And it is virtually impossible to find a prominent abolitionist who did not advocate increased educational opportunities for the working classes. The most radical of all positions was to endorse publicly the Chartist movement; yet a surprising number of abolitionists took such a stand. In fact, the Chartist movement created a political climate in which the developing arguments about the relationship between black slavery and white wage slavery came to a head. Indeed, a national debate commenced about whether a slave or a factory worker was more oppressed. The immediate result was an intensification of rivalry between abolitionists and Chartists, best exemplified by Chartist attempts to disrupt anti-slavery meetings. But out of these vigorous and often acrimonious exchanges, latent sympathies and a sense of common purpose slowly emerged.

To begin with, one should note that the abolitionist and Chartist movements shared certain common political roots. At the end of the eighteenth century many of the active members of the society to abolish the slave trade were equally involved with parliamentary reform and the extension of the suffrage. Granville Sharp, for example, was well aware of the close connection between black slavery in America and white slavery at home. He argued that as long as slavery remained in the West Indies, working people in general 'would inevitably be involved by degrees in the same horrid slavery and depression; for that *is always the base wherever slavery is tolerated*'.[3] He even feared that black slaves brought to England or escaping there might create an unemployment problem which would threaten the jobs of free labourers who were already 'approaching slavery' because arbitrary legislation had gradually elevated property rights over personal rights.[4] Major John Cartwright, noted as a 'Father' of Chartism, was equally convinced that slavery in any form violated and degraded all of humanity. 'Why the people of England should not stand forward with as much unanimity in defense of their own freedom as that of the negroes, I must be slow to believe. It does not accord with my experience, and is contrary to reason,' he lamented in a letter to Samuel Whitbread.[5] The outlook of these early abolitionist-reformers was well summed up by Thomas Hardy. In a letter to a contemporary who had declared himself for abolition Hardy wrote, 'I inferred from that that you are a friend to freedom on the broad basis of the rights of Man for I am fully persuaded that no man who is an advocate from principle for liberty for a Black man but will strenuously promote and support the rights of a White Man & vice versa.'[6] Between the 1790s and the 1830s abolitionists had enough success in enlisting support from the working classes (chiefly through petition and boycott campaigns) to provide a useful basis for co-operation between Chartists and abolitionists in the 1830s and 1840s.[7]

One can argue that agitation against the Poor Law of 1834 was the first stage of Chartism.[8] It provided a rallying point for those who believed that the working poor were indeed slaves and were no better off in physical or psychological terms than black chattels in the West Indies or the United States. One of the most powerful arguments against the institution of slavery was that it allowed families to be torn apart. Under the terms of the 1834 Poor Law when families went to a workhouse husbands, wives and children were segregated into separate wards. Moreover, the poor, including children, could be sent away from their own parishes to work. Thus English workers, like slaves, lost control over their own family life.   Spokesmen for the working classes naturally made the most of this analogy with slavery. At a meeting in Manchester in 1836 the Reverend Joseph Rayner Stephens waved a document which, he said, illustrated the revival of slavery in Great Britain — a bill of sale for a whole family forced to shift from their home to work in a factory — a proceeding made possible by the Poor Law.[9] *The Operative* reported that a 'Children's Friend Society' had taken English children to South Africa for sale.[10] An editorial in the *Birmingham Journal* satirised the 'liberty' of an English labourer as the privilege of migrating from a parish where he was scantily provided for, to one where he could starve.[11] It was argued that fear of being sent to the workhouse caused the agricultural labourer 'to cringe before his master as an abject slave'.[12] Michael Sadler pleaded with his fellow MPs to give English children at least as much consideration as they gave to adult West Indian slaves. At a public meeting in support of Sadler's Ten Hours' Bill, people carried placards with such slogans as 'No white slavery', 'Sadler and the abolition of slavery at home and abroad', and (copying the famous anti-slavery symbol of the kneeling, suppliant slave) 'Am I not a man and a brother?'[13]

Denunciations of the abolitionists' narrow definition of slavery could quite logically begin with attacks on those anti-slavery leaders who held positions in the Reform Government and had a hand in creating the new Poor Law. Henry Brougham as Lord Chancellor and Nassau Senior, who had a major role in drafting the law, were prime targets along with Harriet Martineau, 'their female assistant', as J. R. Stephens labelled her.[14] All were known to be Malthusians who preached that the working classes must limit their numbers if their situation was ever to improve; it therefore seemed that the provision of the Poor Law requiring the separation of males and females in workhouses was evidence of their clumsy attempt to enforce birth control. Senior advised Brougham that relief work and workhouses should be made as hard and disagreeable as possible.[15] It was no wonder that workhouses were promptly dubbed 'Brougham's Bastilles'. The *Northern Star* thundered that Brougham had now joined the ranks of those peers who lived on the venality and prostitution of the country.[16] In a column headed 'Political Astrology' the *Northern Liberator* predicted, and seemed to hope, that Lord Brougham would die in one of his own bastilles 'of an ossification of the heart'. They were certain that an autopsy would reveal his lungs to be perfectly sound.[17] The *London Dispatch and People's Political and Social Reformer*, published by Henry Hetherington, carried a particularly nasty cartoon depicting a gluttonous Brougham eating a bowl of sprawling, squirming little people – one of them impaled on the fork he lifted to his mouth.[18]

It was unfortunate for the abolitionist image that well-known emancipationists were so closely associated with the passage and defence of the Poor Law. Actually Brougham, and especially Martineau, saw more good in Chartism than they were given credit for. Brougham's relationship with Chartists fluctuated; his long record of support for working-men's education, attacks on the Corn Laws, defence of civil liberties, opposition to flogging in the army and navy, his championing of Queen Caroline, as well as his record against black slavery, all helped to balance his Poor Law and factory legislation sins. He characterised himself as a one-step-at-a-time reformer, although William Cobbett denounced him as 'This great LYING PUFFER'.[19] Even while working with him, Harriet Martineau privately questioned the genuineness of his popular sympathies. She summed up her opinion of his inconsistency most succinctly in the story of his sitting for a daguerreotype. The artist explained that Brougham must be perfectly immobile for five seconds. He 'vehemently' promised not to stir, but moved too soon. The result was 'a blur where Lord Brougham ought to be'.[20]

Yet on several occasions Brougham gave Chartists reason to be grateful. In 1838 and 1839, when agitation for the Charter was at its height, Brougham won the praise of the editors of *The Chartist* and *The Operative* for backing suffrage extension and the ballot. Bronterre O'Brien allowed that Brougham had periods of sanity and hoped he would vote accordingly.[21] To the Chartists' delight, he did support their National Petition. Moreover, on at least two occasions Brougham submitted petitions for leniency or pardon: one for Glasgow spinners sentenced to transportation in 1837, and another for Chartists arrested in the riots of 1839.[22] On such occasions Brougham was something more than a blur.

Oddly enough, the same philosophy that brought Harriet Martineau to the defence of the Poor Law formed the basis for her Chartist sympathies. Her goal was always to help the poor to help themselves, principally through education. Hence her Malthusianism was rooted in optimism that once the working classes realised that their basic problem was over-supply of labour they would limit their own numbers even if it required delayed marriages and sexual abstinence.[23] She was well aware that many families depended on their children's earnings and she therefore saw that the only way to end child labour was to pay adult men higher wages. Moreover, she was capable of learning and flexible enough to change her mind as she gathered evidence. After visiting a coal mine she began to support government inspection of collieries and compulsory insurance. She liked Joseph Hume's proposal for labour arbitration which vested responsibility in the labourers themselves.[24] Although Martineau was loathe to admit that English workers were slaves, her attitude toward their plight was much influenced by her growing involvement in the American anti-slavery cause. While labourers could not legally be sold as slaves, she noted that parish authorities put their labour up for auction to the highest bidder. Recipients of charitable relief, like slaves, developed a 'whining gratitude' – a servile 'Sambo' facade. Her investigations convinced her that English apprentices were treated much like slaves and were equally helpless.[25]

Martineau embraced immediate emancipation on the grounds that slaves could be taught to use freedom wisely only by being freed. Likewise, she concluded, British workers could become independent and self-respecting only by being allowed to exercise their own judgement. In attacking American slavery, abolitionists had made a great deal of the 'higher law doctrine': that principles of humanity must take precedence over fallible, man-made laws instituted by governments clinging to the *status quo*. Slowly this concept was incorporated into Martineau's thinking. If it was proper for governments to take special action to get rid of slavery, why was it not equally proper for governments to act in behalf of any oppressed class? Eventually her own adherence to economic laws and strict principles of *laissez-faire* gave way. 'It is impossible, under the far higher constitution of humanity,' she concluded, 'to refuse attention to the case of the depressed, ignorant and suffering of our peoples.' 'Having permitted a special misery and need to grow up, we must meet it with special solace and aid.'[26]

Given these beliefs, it is not surprising that Martineau saw

Chartism as a valid protest movement, one that demanded
necessary reforms if Britain was to escape violent social revolution. From her point of view it was not Feargus O'Connor
and the Chartists who were to be most feared, but Whigs and
Tories with their bland self-complacency.[27] On one occasion
she wrote: 'Government will stir . . . if urged and supported
by the public voice: not without. Those who wish for the
salvation of the people must petition & petition & petition.'[28]
That, of course, was exactly what the Chartists were doing
and Martineau hailed the Charter as 'a wonderful document'.
But while heartily approving Chartist goals, she deplored the
demagoguery of such 'Tory agitators' as O'Connor, J. R.
Stephens and Richard Oastler, and the actions of the 'torch
bearing Chartists' who led the Newport uprising.[29] It was
during the height of Chartist agitation that Martineau refused
a government pension. She wanted no part of the proceeds of
an unjust tax system for she would 'be haunted by images of
thousands and hundreds of thousands of poor tax-payers —
toiling men who cannot, with all their toil, keep their children
in health of body — to say nothing of their minds'.[30]

Chartists were pleased to discover that there were prominent emancipationists who, using the slave comparison, joined
them in attacking the Poor Law. Edward Baines, editor of the
Leeds Mercury, held forth against separation of husbands and
wives in workhouses.[31] Samuel Roberts, one of the anti-
slavery leaders in the Sheffield area, vented his indignation in
letters to the editor of the *Sheffield Iris*: 'And is England
come to this?' he asked. 'Now is there a country in the world
where SLAVERY like this was ever submitted to?' He
denounced the bastilles for imprisoning 'Freeborn Britons'
for the 'crime' of poverty, and said Poor Law Guardians had
themselves become 'slaves of the vilest tyrants!'[32] Lord
Morpeth's campaign for election to Parliament from the West
Riding included promises to amend the Poor Law. Once
elected, he presented a petition from Bradford spinners
which asked for limitations on working hours, and he later
supported Hobhouse's bills to regulate the cotton mills.[33]

Of all the abolitionists fighting the Poor Law, Richard
Oastler was the most prominent as a spokesman for the
people. His anti-slavery commitment dated back to his youth

when he had worked in the campaign against the slave trade. Later, in the 1820s, he joined the drive for complete emancipation in the West Indies. But it was not until the end of the decade that he was suddenly confronted with the similarity of wage slavery when John Wood, a worsted manufacturer in Bradford, asked him if, when he pleaded for the far-off slave, it did not occur to him that similar evils existed at his own doorstep.[34] Oastler's awakening seems to have been as instantaneous as Saul's on the road to Damascus. He threw himself immediately and with equal zeal into fighting for factory regulation, first publicly appealing to such 'giants of anti-slavery principles' as Lords Brougham and Morpeth to do something about the slavery that existed in their own neighbourhoods in Yorkshire.[35] A public meeting of radicals in Huddersfield as early as 1830 adopted a resolution thanking Oastler for exposing the conduct ' "of those pretended philanthropists and canting hypocrites who travel to the West Indies in search of slavery, forgetting that there is a more abominable and degrading system of slavery at home" '.[36] Oastler did not desert the West Indian slave: 'Willingly lend your assistance to emancipate black slaves;' he argued, 'but *imperatively* require from those . . . who solicit your aid in favour of the blacks, that they shall prove their sincerity, and that they really do hate slavery, by encouraging and signing petitions in favour of "ten hours a day" as the limit of your children's work.'[37] Oastler never officially joined the Chartists, and Samuel Roberts and Edward Baines remained adamantly anti-Chartist, but their contribution, and that of others like them, was that their debates against parliamentary bills and Government policies helped to build up public interest in what Chartism had to offer.[38]

The passage of the Emancipation Act of 1833 gave labour spokesmen an ideal opportunity to contrast what was done for black slaves with the neglect shown white slaves. Two features of the act seemed perfect for Chartist publicity. One was the payment of £20,000,000 in compensation money to the slave owners, and the other was the apprenticeship system set up ostensibly to prepare slaves for full freedom. It was easy for Chartists to point out not only that the Government was doing more for the blacks than for white workers, but

that what was done for the slave was at the British worker's
expense. While Government was the chief villain, anti-slavery
societies and anti-slavery leaders were taken to task for hypocrisy. So, again, as in the case of the Poor Law agitation, the
publicity seemed to put the Chartists and abolitionists on
opposite sides of the barricades.

As soon as the Emancipation Act was passed, the *Poor
Man's Guardian* declared that the compensation money would
be 'exacted from the bones of the white slaves' of Great
Britain.[39] J. R. Stephens took the line that it was the labouring children who were paying the £20,000,000 so that adult
black apprentices in Jamaica could enjoy an eight-hour day.
Abolitionists were willing to exert themselves to circulate petitions for the enforcement of that law, but were unwilling, he
charged, to limit hours for working children in Britain.[40]
Labour publications pointed out over and over again that
apprentices at home, while bound for a fixed period, might
be cast off at a master's discretion. Masters of chimney sweeps
actually bought their climbing boys, beat them and half-
starved them. Men in the army and navy, also, were flogged
as slaves were.[41] After 1833 West Indian slaves had the prospect of complete freedom when the term of apprenticeship
should end, but British workers had no promise of future
improvement in their lot. The impact on labour is evident in
the poignant words of the National Petition promulgated in
1838: 'Our slavery has been exchanged for an apprenticeship
to liberty, which has aggravated the painful feelings of our
social degradation, by adding to them the sickening of still
deferred hope.'[42] 'What have we got for our Twenty Millions?'
Bronterre O'Brien demanded.[43] The *Northern Liberator*
suspected that concern for the West Indian apprentices was
a diversionary tactic of those who 'robbed the starving people
of England of TWENTY MILLIONS STERLING, to put an
end to Black slavery in the West Indies!'[44] The Whigs were
accused of using the slavery issue as a political tactic: 'By
weeping over the miseries of the Blacks they netted thousands
of votes, and, therefore, they determined to weep, and regularly kept an onion in the corner of their pocket handkerchief
for this sole purpose.'[45]

But in their attacks on the Government for spending millions to compensate slaveholders, Chartists found that they had many abolitionist allies who were equally vehement on the point, arguing that it was the slaves who deserved compensation. Immediately after the passage of the Emancipation Act a protest statement to this effect was signed by many prominent abolitionists. Included were Joseph Sturge of Birmingham and his brother John Sturge, George Stephen, the Reverend John Angell James, Captain C. R. Moorsom, Samuel Roberts of Sheffield, John Scoble (later Secretary of the British and Foreign Anti-Slavery Society), James Webb of Dublin, John Wigham of Edinburgh, and many others.[46] In Parliament Daniel O'Connell objected to both compensation and apprenticeship.[47] The Anti-Slavery Society in London published an address 'To the Electors of Great Britain', crying that they had been duped. The Glasgow Emancipation Society passed a resolution declaring that Parliament's duty was to see that all parts of the act were fully enforced before any money was paid out. Similar expressions of opposition emanated from anti-slavery societies throughout the nation.[48] Well-known abolitionists including Joseph Sturge, Daniel O'Connell, Colonel T. Perronet Thompson of Hull, James Silk Buckingham, William and Mary Howitt, and Archibald Prentice were every bit as outspoken against compensation as were Bronterre O'Brien, Richard Oastler or Henry Hetherington. Buckingham, an MP, introduced a resolution in Commons against it. T. Perronet Thompson's article 'The Suffering Rich', which appeared in the *Westminster Review*, revealed an outrage that matched any of the pieces in radical newspapers. In an address to his fellow abolitionists, William Howitt said that the Government had 'purchased' 800,000 black slaves at the cost of £20,000,000 and in doing so had added just that much weight to white slavery, whose victims ought to be the objects of anti-slavery concern as much as if their skins were black.[49] Three months before Bronterre O'Brien's article 'What Have We Got for Our Twenty Millions?' appeared in the *Northern Star*, the *British Emancipator* ran an article, 'What We Got for Our Twenty Millions'. Both voiced the same criticism of the apprenticeship system.[50] Thus, again, it became evident that Chartists and many abolitionists shared common ground.

Widespread public support for emancipation dictated that Chartists must be careful not to go too far in attacking the anti-slavery movement's shortcomings lest they invite the accusation of being pro-slavery. Hence their strategy was to out-flank the abolitionists by demonstrating that they were against all types of slavery everywhere. This was the tenor of 'A Hint to Mr. Buxton, M.P.', which appeared in the *London Dispatch and People's Political and Social Reformer* edited by Henry Hetherington.[51] The editor of the *Northern Liberator* avowed that he hated slavery as much as anyone and blasted the House of Commons for voting to continue it under the guise of apprenticeship, but he was contemptuous of any friend of the black slave who was not a friend of the white worker as well.[52] Bronterre O'Brien, in a letter to the editor of the *Northern Star*, extended his good will even so far as to commend Brougham's stand on apprenticeship, but then went on to recommend that if his Lordship really wanted to end slavery he needed to look nearer home where 'victims of his Malthusian economics' died by the dozens on diets of gruel and water. O'Brien refused to concede that any man abhorred black slavery more than he did, and much of his wrath was focused on the fact that slave masters had been compensated rather than punished for their crime. He took the abolitionist line that it was the slaves who deserved recompense.[53] The *Northern Star* came close to apologising for not playing a bigger role in the campaign to end West Indian apprenticeship immediately, but reasoned that they could not divert efforts from the cause of manhood suffrage.[54] A survey of the radical publications of the 1830s reveals that they all took much the same position: the issue was not a choice between chattel and wage slavery. If, as the editor of the *Northern Liberator* suggested, two eyes instead of one were used, both kinds of slavery could be abolished; or, as Bronterre O'Brien put it, to contrast white and black slavery was to create a 'distinction without a difference'.[55]

Once apprenticeship in the West Indies was ended and anti-slavery activists were free to champion a new cause, Chartists sought to woo them. Richard Oastler made such an appeal in the *Northern Star*, calling for sincere abolitionists now to help British working men, 'our cause being one and the same —

they must now help us'.[56] Oastler was shrewd enough to realise that the momentum of the emancipation movement must not be allowed to die, and he accurately perceived that loosening the shackles of black slaves would inevitably help to loosen the bonds of white workers: 'Every tear which watered the floor of the House of Commons, from the eye of Pease was a sledge hammer acting upon the irons of *his own slaves* in Darlington! Every peal of Brougham's eloquence in the Lords, was a flash of Heaven's lightning *against* his own CODE OF MURDER, *daily executing in his favourite Bastiles.* '[57]

Joseph Sturge, the Birmingham Quaker abolitionist and a power in the British and Foreign Anti-Slavery Society, had led the fight against West Indian apprenticeship and for immediate freedom. He therefore became a special target for appeals. A letter in the *Birmingham Journal* claimed that within one week three apprentices in Sturge's own city had been taken to the magistrate for flogging. Would not Sturge do the same on their behalf as he had for the slaves?[58] Actually, Sturge's involvement in the anti-slavery movement had, as with Martineau, pushed him steadily in that direction, and he eventually admitted to Lewis Tappan, his American anti-slavery cohort, that ' "Our unenfranchised countrymen are *politically* much in the same position as your slaves, and in many of the electors there is nearly as strong a feeling against giving them the franchise as there is with giving it to the slave with you." '[59] Consequently, once West Indian slavery was ended, Sturge was prepared to move toward an alliance to try to attain the Chartist goal of suffrage. He, along with several other abolitionists, was to be in the thick of the manoeuvering in the period from 1838 to 1842.

In examining abolitionists who became Chartists one must also remember that many Chartists had been abolitionists for years and, like Sharp, Cartwright *et al.* before them, were thoroughly cognizant of the inseparability of the issues of black and white slavery. Two such men were William Lovett and John Collins who were among the first to spell out the meaning of Chartism.[60] When Lovett spoke of 'Tyrants [who] delight to crush the yielding, suppliant slave', he conjured up in one sweeping clause mental images of slaveholding planters, factory overseers and upper-class government officials.[61] Lovett, along with Hetherington and others, organised the London Workingmen's Association in 1836 whose 'Address to the Working Classes of Europe' posed the rhetorical question, 'Where, but from the ranks of labour, have the despots of Europe raised their fighting slaves to keep their brother slaves in awe?' And in its address to the working classes in the United States, after bemoaning that democratic America should tolerate legal oppression, reasoned that, 'Surely, it cannot be for the interests of the Working Classes that these prejudices should be fostered — this degrading traffic be maintained.'[62] The refrain was that the same people who perpetuated slavery kept working people ignorant and divided. Collins, speaking at a Chartist rally in Manchester, said that the one stain on the Star-Spangled Banner was slavery which, like the slavery of children in England, did not proceed from her democratic institutions but from vestiges of aristocratic rule. His phrases were the same ones he and Lovett used in their pamphlet which became one of the sacred documents of the Chartist movement.[63]

Other abolitionists appeared at meetings of the London Workingmen's Association (and therefore were connected with the beginnings of Chartism), notably Daniel O'Connell, James Silk Buckingham and Colonel T. P. Thompson. O'Connell's relationship with the Chartists, much like that of Lord Brougham, fluctuated. Lovett credited O'Connell with 'being a party to' the drawing up of the Charter, but the volatile Irishman soon fell out with the Lovett—Hetherington group over the issue of trade unions, though Whig politics also played a part.[64] None the less, O'Connell staunchly defended his credentials as a friend of Chartism and continued to expound on the theme of slavery. 'Yes, you are slaves,' he wrote in the *Northern Liberator*, 'so long as the law allows a "master class" to have political privileges.'[65] James Silk Buckingham believed that if a government could pay to emancipate slaves, it could also pay to provide employment in public works for all who were able-bodied, and asylums for the helpless. Moreover, the Commons should be elected by secret ballot by all literate people — including women — who attained a specific age, were of good character and were employed sufficiently to earn their subsistence.[66] T. Perronet Thompson identified himself with the Chartists from the beginning, and was one of the speakers at the Palace Yard meeting in 1838 which helped to launch 'The People's Charter'. He worked earnestly in co-operation with the Hull Chartists, who backed his election to Parliament in 1841.[67]

The Charter was published in May 1838 and then presented in public meetings to gain mass support. Newspaper accounts furnish evidence that anti-slavery people attended and sometimes played leading roles in such meetings. Glasgow, for instance, was one of the major cities where such Chartist demonstrations took place in the spring and summer of 1838. The first, on 21 May, was chaired by James Turner of Thrushgrove, a long-time anti-slavery advocate.[68] In 1831 Turner had been one of the leading organisers of a Glasgow Political Union that would include all classes, and had insisted that dues must be low enough to enable workers to join.[69] Other members of the Glasgow Emancipation Society involved in planning the Glasgow Chartist meeting were James Moir and John Ure.[70] In the Midlands it was significant that the date for the local demonstration was 1 August, purposely chosen to coincide with Emancipation Day in the West Indies so that orators could capitalise on the opportunity to denounce slavery at home. The main speech was given by Henry Vincent, another Chartist leader who ascribed his motivation to early anti-slavery convictions. As a youth in Hull he heard a lecture by George Thompson which filled him with a 'holy zeal' to fight slavery and the slave trade, thus arousing his sense of personal responsibility for reform.[71]

One of the most important Chartist meetings was held in London in September, in Palace Yard opposite Westminster Hall where Parliament was sitting. Abolitionists in attendance and speaking (besides Lovett) included T. Perronet Thompson and the Sheffield poet, Ebenezer Elliott. Already known as a people's poet sympathetic to both slave and white workers, Elliott's verses often fused the two causes:

> Servant of servants, brow beat by a knave
> Why, for a coffin, labour like a slave?[72]

The Palace Yard meeting helped to thrust into the limelight another Chartist leader who had long been an abolitionist, George Julian Harney. While a boy he watched a political parade in which he saw among the banners the emblem of the kneeling slave who asked, 'Am I not a man and a brother?' 'There needed not the speeches of a Wilberforce or a Clarkson, or the writings of a Granville Sharp, to make me an Abolitionist forthwith', was Harney's testimony to his conversion. His second commitment, to the cause of workers, came through reading the *Poor Man's Guardian* with its criticisms of those abolitionists who neglected the slavery in their own factories.[73] Harney's involvement in the Chartist movement coincided with the growing dispute between the groups labelled 'physical force' and 'moral force' Chartists. He allied himself with the first, the Feargus O'Connor faction, but more of the abolitionist leaders preferred the 'moral force' approach, probably because of their strong religious feelings.

The Reverend Patrick Brewster of Paisley advocated moral force with phrases as aggressive and uncompromising as those William Lloyd Garrison used to attack slavery in the United States. As early as 1820 when the Paisley weavers were engaged in an uprising, Brewster used his pulpit in the fashionable Abbey Church to proclaim his support for them. Shouting that the workers produced the wealth of the country and were robbed of it by the rich (including the church), he 'stirred the artisans to frantic enthusiasm, and roused to malignant anger the nobility and snobocracy of the district'.[74] In a series of 'Chartist and Socialist Sermons' his texts were chosen to reveal the sufferings of the poor and the power of the rich. He declared that having dared to seek justice for African slaves in defiance of vested interests, it was equally the duty of the people to seek justice for their own countrymen. He believed it was Christian influence that had outlawed both slavery and the slave trade and, like an Old Testament prophet or Jesus decrying the hypocrisy of the Pharisees, Brewster denounced the British ruling classes and the laws that maintained unfair privileges. The suffering of slaves, including the white slaves of 'Christian autocrats', was greater in sum total, he declared, than all the suffering which came in the wake of social convulsions and insurrections against despotism. British workers, like black slaves, were subjected to 'Constables, Jails, Bridewells, Stocks, Whips, Collars, and Treadmills' — all instruments of torture. Yet he found hope for white slaves in the fact that 'the sable captive' had already 'hailed the glad sound of freedom'.[75] The day of jubilee would come for white slaves as well. It is hardly surprising that Brewster's Synod suspended him from his pulpit for a year. He held the Edinburgh Chartists to the moral force position (cautioning against armed rebellion because it would only give the Government an excuse for suppressive retaliation). Glasgow Chartists, on the other hand, joined the camp of the Scottish O'Connorite, Dr John Taylor.[76] When Brewster attended one of their meetings and confessed that he was not a reader of O'Connor's *Northern Star*, he was hissed out of the gathering. The ensuing contest for leadership left Scottish Chartists badly divided.[77]

In Birmingham, in addition to John Collins, two other local abolitionists, Joseph Sturge and Captain C. R. Moorsom, became much involved in the Chartist meetings during the summer of 1839. Fearful of an outbreak of violence when Chartist crowds packed into the meeting in the Bull Ring, the Home Office in London sent police reinforcements. There followed confrontation and the arrest of several Chartists.[78] Sturge strongly opposed the presence of outside police, headed a commission of investigation and wrote to the Home Secretary to plead for commutation of the death sentences meted out to three of those arrested. Speaking at a protest meeting he warned the Government of the consequences of treading on 'a smothered volcano'. At the same time he cautioned the Chartists not to fall into the trap of agents who would like nothing better than a show of violence that would provide an excuse for government interference and further arrests.[79] Sturge's public stand in support of Chartist rights was to make him the object of Home Office surveillance for the next four years.[80]

In the wake of the 1839 persecutions, Chartists adopted a policy of 'visiting' parish churches to express their dissatisfaction with 'Christian' attitudes toward labour's problems.

They also began to interrupt Anti-Corn Law League meetings by attending in such numbers that they held a majority and could elect a chairman who would give the floor to Chartist speakers. From the Chartist point of view this was not interruption of a good cause but a method of carrying the cause further than the narrow platform of one issue. By 1840 their disruption tactic was extended to every kind of public meeting that did not give priority to the Charter.[81] The World Anti-Slavery Convention held in London in the summer of 1840 offered an excellent prospect because the enthusiasm it kindled multiplied local anti-slavery societies holding numerous meetings for them to disrupt.[82] For example, an anti-slavery meeting was held in Newcastle with James G. Birney and Henry Stanton of the American and Foreign Anti-Slavery Society present. When the chairman of the meeting tried to deny the floor to a Chartist spokesman, a great uproar ensued. Votes were repeatedly interpreted as unfavourable to the would-be speaker, who then attempted to force his way to the platform by jumping from a gallery. A confrontation was avoided only by extinguishing the gas lights and the subsequent dispersal of those present.[83] At a gathering in Norwich to form an anti-slavery society, Chartists with their wives and children attended in such numbers that 'the men in fustian' dared to stand up to the bishop and other assembled dignitaries. J. J. Gurney, the wealthy Quaker anti-slavery leader, was hissed, as were members of the Norwich clergy. The Chartists failed, however, in their attempt to substitute a resolution against slavery at home for one against black slavery in America.[84]

The biggest disturbance of all developed in Glasgow when Chartists tried to take over the annual meeting of the Glasgow Emancipation Society in August 1840. Lloyd Jones, a 'socialist missionary', presented a resolution to prod manufacturers to end the slavery of children in their mills. A Mr Jack then proposed that while working for the emancipation of American slaves, the GES must also take every opportunity to improve the condition of the people of their own country by urging the government to grant manhood suffrage. According to the *Glasgow Argus* the meeting degenerated into 'a constant howl'. When George Thompson (who was later to join the Chartists) protested against the chairman's rulings and the irregularity of the voting, the meeting was adjourned, against the opposition of the 'large body of Chartists present'.[85] Before the next monthly meeting James Moir announced that henceforth the Glasgow Chartists would interrupt all public meetings that diverted attention from the Charter, including those of the Anti-Slavery Society of which he was a member. Contention in the GES and within the Executive Committee smouldered through the winter months and erupted openly in the spring when John A. Collins, an American abolitionist and Chartist sympathiser, arrived.[86]

Collins believed that Americans travelling in Britain were as much obligated to speak out against class prejudice as British travellers were to attack slavery in America. Support for him and for Chartism then became entangled in abolitionist in-fighting between Garrisonians and anti-Garrisonians. Patrick Brewster and Dr John Ritchie of Edinburgh arrived to support Collins and the Chartists who were demanding that seventeen of them be added to the GES executive committee. For strategic reasons GES leaders William Smeal and John Murray conceded, and the Chartists triumphantly held a great meeting in the Bazaar at which an address to Collins from Glasgow working men was read, and at which a 'pure' Chartist resolution was adopted: ' . . . that the People of this Country are entitled to those rights of Suffrage for which they have been contending . . . & that we pledge ourselves to use every moral and legal means to obtain our own liberty & the liberty of all mankind.'[87] This was the greatest Chartist victory within a particular anti-slavery organisation.

Emphasis on Chartist disruptions has lent credence to the theory of labour/abolitionist rivalry and antagonism. Yet when we recall that disruption was a planned tactic used in public gatherings of every variety, the charge that it was an anti-abolitionist phenomenon is reduced. Abolitionists such as James Moir sometimes led the disruption. While this eye-catching tactic alienated many emancipationists, the ensuing debates led other anti-slavery activists to re-examine their definitions of oppression. Different degrees of hostility or sympathy for Chartism coexisted in societies and families. After the disruption in Norwich, the archdeacon acknowledged the necessity for anti-slavery societies to be aware of needs at home as well as abroad. Yet he admonished the workers to be respectful 'towards those whose bread they eat'. Anna Gurney attempted to counteract Chartist influence in the town by distributing bibles.[88] But another of Norwich's daughters, Harriet Martineau, refused a government pension, 'as they who provide the means have no voice in the appropriation of it to me personally'.[89] The Peases, who were prominent anti-slavery Quakers and also Midlands industrialists, were a divided family. Although Joseph Pease bore the brunt of many Chartist attacks, he was not wholly unsympathetic to their goals. Joseph's brother John was given to writing paternalistic advice to the workers to warn them of agitators and demagogues. He criticised socialists and Chartists as impractical, but was basically most concerned about the irreligious nature of their movements.[90] On the other hand, Joseph's daughter Elizabeth was outspoken in defence of the 'poor oppressed Chartists' who 'ask nothing more than what accords with the grand principle of the natural equality of man'. Arguments against the five points of the Charter were to her 'nothing but a slaveholder's argument — the slave was not prepared for liberty — & the people are not prepared for their rights'. She considered herself to be a Chartist and persuaded William Ashurst, another supportive abolitionist, to send her pamphlets on moral force Chartism which she could distribute. During the summer riots in 1842 she admitted that 'one's whole sympathies go with the disorganizers'.[91]

One of the abolitionists who persisted in what Elizabeth Pease called the slaveholder's argument was Edward Baines, who backed only gradual extension of the suffrage to the 'humbler classes'. He feared that household suffrage and equal electoral districts would destroy the influence of the towns, strengthen the landed aristocracy, and thereby make it impossible to repeal the Corn Laws. It is not surprising that Peter Bussey, a physical force Chartist, labelled Baines's *Leeds Mercury* the 'Leeds poison'.[92] Thomas Babington Macaulay, MP son of the abolitionist leader Zachary Macaulay, objected to the Charter because universal suffrage would result in property confiscation.[93] Another famous abolitionist son, Bishop Samuel Wilberforce, stressed that the franchise was

not an individual privilege but a trust to be exercised for the
good of the community; therefore each person exercising it
must be qualified to act as a trustee.[94] On the other hand,
W. E. Forster, son of Quaker missionary William Forster, was
actively engaged in supporting Chartism. From his position in
the wool-stapler business he had observed with dismay the
widening gap between capital and labour, and was convinced
that it was the power of capital at a time of increasing population which kept the poor from improving their condition. He
supported the Ten Hours' Bill, and was proud of the fact that
his own workers were allowed to tell him how much they
should be paid. On one occasion during an election he led a
foray of 'rough Irishmen and Chartists' to release some Liberals who had been locked up by the Tories to keep them from
the polls.[95] Forster, like Edward Baines Jr, was to be even
more closely associated with the cause of suffrage extension
in 1867.

Many abolitionists were torn by the competing appeals of
Chartism and Corn Law repeal. Repeal had the advantage of
seeming less radical and more easily attained, therefore a
reasonable first step. While many Chartists favoured Corn
Law repeal, their conviction was that it would be only a half-
way measure. Genuine improvement in the workers' lot would
come only when they were fully enfranchised. Several abolitionist leaders were genuine believers in both causes and
sought to combine them. Colonel T. Perronet Thompson
provides a good example, believing that the Corn Laws allowed
landlords to live on the labour of workers in just the way
West Indian or American planters lived at the expense of
slaves.[96] Deeply disappointed in the performance of the
Reform Government, Thompson moved into politics himself
and was in and out of Parliament from 1835 to 1854, backed
by Hull Chartists whom he labelled 'my Radicals'. To his
fellow Anti-Corn Law Leaguer, MP John Bowring, he wrote
that 'It is manifest the Chartist Radicals are coming round, if
anybody will meet them half-way.' 'So I mean to march with
them or not at all.'[97] Yet he argued with them that insistence
on priority for the Charter was not good politics since it
would be much more difficult to obtain than repeal of the
Corn Laws. Despite attacks by the press and the advice of

more conservative friends (notably Cobden), Thompson continued to meet with the Chartists, following his own strategy of joining them in order to win them to his point of view.[98]

It was Joseph Sturge who most directly and personally assumed responsibility for trying to forge an alliance of abolitionists, Anti-Corn Law Leaguers and Chartists, declaring that he had no more fear of giving the vote to the people than he had of giving freedom to the slaves.[99] The Birmingham riots of 1839 pushed him to a more active support of the Chartists and his visit to the United States in 1841 on an anti-slavery mission reinforced this inclination. There he noted the relative comfort and prosperity of workers (other than slaves) and concluded that 'it is quite evident that the statesmen who would elevate the moral standard of our working population, must begin by removing the physical depression and destitution in which a large proportion of them, without any fault of their own, are compelled to drag out a weary and almost hopeless existence'.[100] By the time he returned to England his determination was growing that he would take the lead in a working- and middle-class alliance to gain male suffrage.

Sturge's chance came in response to an opening afforded by the editor of the London *Nonconformist*, Edward Miall, who in the autumn of 1841 published a series of letters on the necessity of bringing the classes into co-operation. An active abolitionist, Miall too saw the analogy between the situations of British workers and slaves. 'Treat men as slaves', he wrote, 'and they will soon betake themselves to the vices of slavery . . . would you fit them for freedom, you must make them free.' If Britain could make the experiment of emancipation in the West Indies, why not make it at home also? Miall's articles were collected in a pamphlet for which Sturge wrote an introduction. In it Sturge admitted that while busy in the anti-slavery cause, he had often felt the pressing — perhaps prior — claim of his fellow countrymen, and he 'freely acknowledged' that both patriots and Christians failed in their duty if they neglected to work against the evils of class legislation.[101]

In resolving to bring the classes together, Sturge faced a situation that would have daunted most leaders. Tensions between the classes had increased in the wake of the Birmingham riots and the Newport uprising of 1839. The middle classes were especially perturbed about physical force Chartism. Even Francis Place, long-time leader of London artisans, criticised the Chartists for raising false hopes as they operated under the delusion that threats could move the Government. He feared that they had no real understanding of what was needed to change society: coalition and moderation. For the same reason, many abolitionists preferred to support the Anti-Corn Law League, or at least used that excuse in refusing to back Chartism.

Interestingly enough, Sturge's chief rival in the competing anti-slavery societies, George Thompson, also decided in favour of coalition with the Chartists. Thompson was the leader of the British wing of the Garrisonians, while Sturge affiliated with the British and Foreign Anti-Slavery Society. Their agreement in principle meant that both abolitionist factions were now influenced by a new spirit of sympathy for and co-operation with the Chartists. In fact, it can be argued that Chartism was the catalyst for bringing the two factions into a new, albeit temporary, spirit of co-operation. Both Sturge and Thompson were members of the Anti-Corn Law League, and Thompson was a lecturer for Joseph Pease's British India Society. As early as 1839 Thompson had suggested that the three groups were backing issues that were all part of one bigger question: 'The enterprises must be wedded and proceed indissolubly together until they together triumph.'[102]

At a breakfast party at abolitionist John Wigham's home in Edinburgh in the autumn of 1841, the consensus of opinion was that the Anti-Corn Law movement could not succeed without the working classes, 'and that to gain them we must wisely choose opportunities of declaring ourselves to be their friends'.[103] But it was not until May 1842 that Thompson publicly joined the Chartists with an apology for his tardiness.[104] In the campaign for the Emancipation Act both Thompson and Sturge had learned the valuable lesson of the importance of public opinion in pushing Government reform. Now both of them, together with Anti-Corn Law Leaguers

Richard Cobden and C. P. Villiers, agreed that they must show the Government 'that the masses are with us, or they will defy and defeat us'.[105]

Francis Place worried that Sturge might be too naive in believing the Chartist assertion that a Parliament elected *by* the people could be trusted to legislate *for* the people; but Sturge had by then taken the high ground of the *right* to the franchise, just as he had accepted the right of slaves to freedom, regardless of how the right might be exercised. This was apparent in the 'Declaration' he drew up to be circulated for signatures. It enunciated the principle that taxation without representation was tyranny, and that the right to a 'full, free and fair' franchise was based on both British and Christian principles.[106] Signatures were gathered, local meetings organised, committees of correspondence began to operate (although illegal under contemporary laws), and a memorial to the Queen was prepared in order to gain publicity. By 1842 a provisional committee based in Birmingham had begun preparations for a great conference in April.[107]

Abolitionists from several quarters rallied to support Sturge. Nonconformist clergymen were among the most active, many of whom were sympathetic to the moral force churches the Chartists had established among the working people. Included in this group were Edward Miall, J. H. Hinton of London,[108] J. P. Mursell of Leicester,[109] J. W. Massie of Manchester,[110] Dr John Ritchie of Edinburgh,[111] Thomas Swan of Birmingham,[112] and Henry Solly of Yeovil. The most noted organiser of Chartist churches, Arthur O'Neill, worked with Sturge in Birmingham.[113] Influential abolitionist ministers from the established church included Patrick Brewster of Paisley and Thomas Spencer of Bath (whose famous nephew Herbert made his political debut in the Sturge movement). Spencer and Solly seem to have had the most direct contact with the working classes. Spencer, like Brewster, was outspoken against the established church's failure to meet the needs of working people, and came under much criticism for his radical activities. He insisted that it was a Christian's duty to be political in the cause of the oppressed, and to that end he spoke at meetings in support of the Ten Hours' Bill, challenged the unjust tax system, the standing army and other vast state institutions. What need was there for slavery, he asked, when taxation did its work so effectively?[114]

Henry Solly was a relative newcomer in the anti-slavery cause, having become interested through the publicity attending the World Anti-Slavery Convention in 1840. Shortly thereafter, while beginning his first Unitarian pastorate, Solly was challenged by John Bainbridge, leader of the Yeovil Chartists, who questioned how one could preach Sunday after Sunday about Christ and yet do nothing to relieve the crushing oppression of the poor. Solly agreed to accompany Bainbridge to a meeting at the Mechanic's Institute and was persuaded by the Chartist arguments. The Yeovil Chartists then sent him to Manchester to speak for the Charter at the ministers' conference in 1841, and again as a delegate to Sturge's Birmingham conference in April 1842. Enthused by Sturge's Complete Suffrage Movement, Solly lectured and wrote for the cause. As a consequence of his rapid rise among radicals, he was forced out of his Yeovil pastorate, but found another with a Tavistock congregation which had working-class as well as middle-class members. Solly's commitment to the Chartist cause was put to a test when Chartists and Sturge-ites broke over the issue of retaining the name, 'The Charter'; Solly was one of the few abolitionists who voted with the Lovett group to retain the name, against Sturge who wanted to discard it.[115]

Scottish abolitionist backers of the Sturge movement included James Moir, John Ure, James Turner and Andrew Paton of the Glasgow area; Baillie Turner and John Dunlop of Edinburgh; and James Adam of Aberdeen.[116] Among the most prominent Anti-Corn Law Leaguers who supported him were Archibald Prentice, P. A. Taylor and Dr John Bowring. Other notable anti-slavery politicians who gave a qualified blessing were Lord Brougham and Daniel O'Connell. And one must remember the Chartist leaders who had long been committed to the anti-slavery cause: Henry Vincent, William Lovett, John Collins and Bronterre O'Brien, all of whom now approved Sturge's Complete Suffrage plans. One of the most surprising absentees was Colonel T. P. Thompson who was sceptical of Sturge's approach. He said the problem reminded him of his experience in Sierra Leone (where he had been sent by Wilberforce and the early abolitionists to be governor). There he had learned to float logs by tying some light ones to heavy ones. But Sturge, he feared, was tying Complete Suffrage to the heavy log of Chartism rather than to the lighter log of Corn Law repeal. It would not float.[117] Edward Baines was also among the missing. He hooted at the idea that such a disparate lot of reformers could ever unite, and refused to join them.[118]

While many Garrisonian abolitionists such as George Thompson, Elizabeth Pease and the Smeal and Wigham families were now turning aside from factionalism to support Sturge, his own BFASS never committed itself to back him. In the May 1842 annual meeting Sturge pleaded for support against slavery everywhere in the world, including 'every kind of oppression in this country', some of which was 'closely bordering on slavery'. He confronted his fellow members with the charge that even they were perhaps guilty of 'a pro-slavery feeling . . . that censured the working class and their advocates when demanding only their just and equal rights'.[119] While the BFASS refrained from taking an official stand on Complete Suffrage, many of its individual members were enthusiastically supportive. Indeed, most of the clergymen mentioned above as participants were active members of the BFASS.

The Birmingham conference in April 1842 launched the Complete Suffrage Union amid high hopes for a successful coalition. Invoking the natural right of suffrage, it demanded the vote for every male aged twenty-one, regardless of property qualifications, called for the secret ballot, annual parliaments and remuneration for MPs. All of this was condensed into a resolution for Sharman Crawford to introduce in the House of Commons. Lord Brougham agreed to present it for consideration by the Lords (even though he had some reservations about its substance), and he agreed also to present the memorial to Queen Victoria.[120] The enthusiasm engendered by the April meeting led to Sturge's nomination to stand for Nottingham in the summer election, and the euphoria of unity was so contagious that even Feargus O'Connor decided to get aboard the bandwagon and campaign for the candidate. Although the contest was close, Sturge lost.[121]

The April conference had adjourned with the intention of reconvening in the autumn; but a summer which saw widespread unemployment leading to demonstrations and violent outbreaks, followed by arrests, made the timing less than propitious. Consequently the meeting was postponed until December. Tensions were still high and the promise of unity which had been so strong in April proved to have dissipated. The irony was that everyone agreed on goals but foundered on naming the document through which they should be publicised. The Sturgeites (or 'Sturgeons', as Cobden dubbed them) were afraid of 'The Charter' because it carried an image of militant radicalism which frightened the middle classes. They wanted a 'Document of Rights' or a 'Bill of Rights'. Chartists were naturally attached to the name that symbolised their long battle and were reluctant to yield to people they considered to be upstarts. After two days of debate Sturge and his group were voted down and withdrew from the convention. The *Birmingham Journal* offered an apt summation: it was the old story of marriage on Monday, quarrels on Tuesday, divorce on Wednesday. The two partners had agreed on their affections but could not agree on a name for their child and so had strangled it.[122]

Sturge's brave but abortive attempt was the high point of abolitionist co-operation with Chartism, both from the standpoint of numbers and the degree of public commitment. But the falling-off was not due entirely to whatever disillusionment abolitionists may have experienced. Chartism itself was on the wane. However, an important point is that while organised co-operation declined, a fairly large contingent of abolitionists, as individuals, carried on the agitation for suffrage extension. Sturge himself continued to tour the country to speak for it, and his newspaper, *The Pilot*, advocated the franchise as basic to other reforms and necessary even to obtain repeal of the Corn Laws.[123] Abolitionist MPs sympathetic to Complete Suffrage and/or Chartism in the 1840s included John Bowring, P. A. Taylor,[124] C. P. Villiers, Edward Miall, William Johnson Fox,[125] George Thompson and

Sharman Crawford.[126] The list of abolitionists who continued to work through local politics, lectures and publications included ex-MP James Silk Buckingham, W. H. Ashurst,[127] Sturge's brother-in-law Arthur Albright and his nephew Charles Gilpin, William and Mary Howitt,[128] W. J. Linton,[129] F. R. Lees,[130] W. E. Forster, Thomas Spencer, Henry Solly, Samuel Roberts of Wales,[131] James Haughton of Dublin,[132] and several Scotsmen: Patrick Brewster, John Ritchie, James Moir, Duncan McLaren,[133] John Dunlop, James Turner of Thrushgrove, and Alexander Duncanson.[134] The Complete Suffrage Union survived in Scotland after it had died out in other areas.

A newcomer to both the anti-slavery movement and Chartism in the 1840s was Joseph Barker of Wortley, near Leeds. A Methodist minister and editor of the *Evangelical Reformer*, he experimented with various religious sects and then forsook institutionalised Christianity. While editing *The Christian* (1844–8) he became acquainted with the views of both Chartists and abolitionists and, with the zeal of a new convert, went further than most abolitionists in his insistence on the need to accept the whole Charter. Like Solly, he defended the refusal to give up the name, even though he saw the result would be abandonment by the middle class. Caught up in the Chartist excitement of 1848, he started a new paper, *The People*, attended meetings, and was arrested as an agitator. Barker declared that the British upper classes made brutes of workers just as surely as did American slaveholders.[135]

Increasing sensitivity on the part of British abolitionists to the justice of Chartist demands is reflected in the degree to which visiting Americans were drawn into the discussions on the similarities between slavery and working-class exploitation, and thus into arguments over where priorities should lie. James and Lucretia Mott, John A. Collins, Charles Remond and William Lloyd Garrison himself were decidedly influenced by what they saw of working-class conditions in the British Isles. Lucretia Mott's diary contains references to visits to mines, mills and the hovels of the poor, and reveals that she 'was not very sorry' when Chartists disrupted the Glasgow Emancipation Society meeting 'to plead the cause of their own poor'.[136] Charles L. Remond, the black delegate from

Massachusetts, was repeatedly confronted with the question of what Americans were prepared to do to help oppressed British workers in return for the help received to abolish American slavery. American free blacks were perhaps in a better position than others to understand the situation of British workers. Caught as they were between complete freedom and slavery, they realised that there was no absolute polarity between the two.[137]

John A. Collins was persuaded that the anti-slavery movement had helped to open eyes to other oppressive systems. He saw British society as resting on a dangerous structure just as American society rested dangerously on slavery. When one element in the population existed in an 'atmosphere of physical, moral and mental unhealth' the master class too was in danger of losing its moral health, and he rejoiced that 'the noble band of Chartists' now opened people's eyes to this truth.[138] William Lloyd Garrison said that it was impossible for him to enjoy fully the beautiful English countryside 'because of the suffering and want staring me in the face, on the one hand, and the opulence and splendor dazzling my vision on the other'.[139] After returning to the United States he wrote a sonnet that reflects the enlargement of his vision:

O! Not for Afric's sons alone I plead,
    or her descendants; but for all who sigh
In servile chains, whate'er their caste or creed:
    They not in vain to Heaven send up their cry;
For all mankind from bondage shall be freed,
    And from the earth be chased all forms of tyranny.[140]

The World Anti-Slavery Convention of 1843 brought to London a non-Garrisonian group of American abolitionists who were more closely in co-operation with the British and Foreign Anti-Slavery Society and therefore easily allied with Sturge's Complete Suffrage movement.[141] While the right to vote was taken for granted by white American males, free blacks were usually denied it. This point was stressed by the Reverend W. J. C. Pennington, a black delegate, who was warmly received when he spoke at the convention. Dr John

Bowring used the occasion to point to Pennington as one of a race not supposed to be fit for the suffrage, yet whose ability was apparent. The same unfounded prejudice, he pointed out, kept British working classes and all women from obtaining the franchise. Joshua Leavitt (a leading free-trade abolitionist) recalled that his grandfather 'lay bleeding at the foot of Bunker's [sic] Hill' fighting for the principle that those who were taxed should also vote. On another occasion Leavitt addressed a meeting of the Complete Suffrage Union, crediting the right to vote in the United States with the right to organise an anti-slavery party — a right he viewed as the most hopeful vehicle for accomplishing the abolitionist goal.[142]

Subsequent years brought an increased flood of American abolitionists to Britain, among them many blacks who were often appalled by the conditions of the British poor.[143] Henry Highland Garnet believed English workers understood that chattel slavery affected them directly because slave labour undercut wages and restricted the market for free labour. He pledged to work to unify the causes of slaves and poor whites.[144] Frederick Douglass, most prominent of all the black abolitionists, specifically called himself a Chartist. He spoke at Complete Suffrage meetings and lectured to crowds of thousands which included working-class people. Like Pennington, he was frequently held up as an example of a man of superior intellect who yet was denied his rights because of pointless prejudice.[145]

In 1846 Douglass, Garrison and Henry C. Wright, all committed to Chartist principles, worked closely with George Thompson, Lovett, Vincent, Bowring, the Howitts and Joseph Barker in England; with Brewster, Ritchie, Alexander Ferguson, John Christie and Andrew Paton in Scotland; and with R. D. Webb in Ireland. They preached in Chartist churches, attended and spoke at both Chartist and Complete Suffrage gatherings.[146] Garrison could see no point in the argument that backing reform in Britain might hold up or injure the cause of the slave in America. 'He who will forget one to aid the other, forgets both, and is true to neither', he told an audience in the National Hall in Holborn, and stirred them by quoting from the American poet John Greenleaf

Whittier:

> Hear it Old Europe! We have sworn
>   The death of slavery — when it falls,
> Look to your vassals in their turn . . . .[147]

By the time Garrison, Douglas and Wright had finished their missions, there seemed reason to believe that the words on the masthead of Garrison's *Liberator*, 'Our Country is the World — Our Countrymen are all Mankind', might be translated into actual help for the British working classes.

During the decade of the 1840s several of the Chartist leaders, notably Vincent and Lovett, strengthened their ties with organised anti-slavery groups. Their names frequently appear in records of committee meetings and at conferences. Both Vincent and Lovett participated in the formation of George Thompson's Anti-Slavery League in 1846, and were active in that group's efforts to pressure the Evangelical Alliance to refuse fellowship to visiting pro-slavery American clergymen. Lovett was named to the League's executive council.[148] Vincent frequently teamed up with anti-slavery lecturers such as Thomas Spencer, Frederick Douglass and H. C. Wright who were willing to fuse the causes of black and white labour.

By the 1850s Chartism was dying, yet those who clung to it sustained an interest in black slavery. This is evident in their protests against pro-slavery policies of the American Government, especially the Fugitive Slave Act of 1850 which so blatantly stained the reputation of democracy.[149] Chartist leaders such as George Julian Harney and Ernest Jones, who became dominant after 1848, led Chartism towards socialism, and, according to G. D. H. Cole, alienated many British workers.[150] But it seems possible that the socialist emphasis on the universal brotherhood of the working classes might have had some influence in sustaining working-class interest in black slavery. Harney and Jones both personally cultivated anti-slavery connections, and during the American Civil War Jones was one of the most active men in Britain for the cause of the Union.[151] In speaking to Lancashire workers in 1863 he reminded them of the unity of the two causes: 'I trust that those who are now struggling . . . for the freedom of the black will join us in every effort for a fresh instalment [sic] towards the Charter of an Englishman's liberty. . . . I trust that we shall find that in establishing liberty universally throughout the American continent we shall be placing the crowning pinnacle on the edifice of freedom here as well.'[152]

By 1863 when Jones gave that speech, it had become common practice for radical and abolitionist lecturers to link black and white slavery, and it was an indication of the degree to which the two causes had influenced each other. The success of the abolitionists in winning their fights for emancipation and against the apprenticeship system had persuaded Chartists to borrow their strategy to gain converts. More importantly, Chartists skilfully adapted the arguments against black slavery for use in their own cause, thus capitalising on abolitionist success in heightening the British public awareness of oppression. Equating the conditions of white workers with those of black slaves was bound to give some people a feeling of guilt, and to inspire a few of them to action. Certainly the Chartists, by equating working-class exploitation with slavery, forced many abolitionists to enlarge their vision, and one could carry this study forward in time to show how many anti-slavery people played important roles in the extension of the suffrage in 1867.

As early as the 1830s Richard Oastler had said that the causes of anti-slavery and Chartism were 'one and the same'. Prior to Chartism the motif of the anti-slavery movement had been the Wedgwood figure of a kneeling slave imploring, 'Am I not a man and a brother?' By the 1850s it surprised no one when the *Anti-Slavery Watchman* published on its cover a drawing of Jesus standing over two figures, one a kneeling black and the other a white workman, and saying, 'I come to break the bonds of the oppressed.'[153] The unlaboured but obvious message was a striking indication of the mutual influence which Chartism and abolitionism had exercised the one over the other.

4. Slave Culture, Resistance and the Achievement of Emancipation in the British West Indies, 1783-1838

MICHAEL CRATON

> The negroes . . . believed that Massa King George had said
> they were all to be free — a term very differently under-
> stood by the negroes and by their advocates on this side of
> the water. By free, a Briton means that the negro is no
> longer to be the property of his master, but situated as
> labourers are in England; that is, he is to work for his own
> and his family's support, or starve. But the word *free* means
> quite another thing in the negro sense; for they tell me
> that it means 'there is to be no masters at all, and Massa
> King George is to buy all the estates and gie them to we to
> live upon'.   (Mrs A. C. Carmichael, 1834)[1]

Like most of her white contemporaries, Emma Carmichael, a
planter's wife who resided in Trinidad and St Vincent between
1821 and 1826, thought very little of the intrinsic qualities
of native Africans. But she set great store by the process of
'creolisation' whereby Africans and their descendants adapted
to the New World, and the 'civilising' effects of what she
regarded as the sounder forms of Christianity. She was therefore as puzzled and disappointed as anyone that a crescendo
of slave unrest occurred during the period between the
ending of the Napoleonic wars and 1832, while the proportion

of Creole (or island-born) slaves rose above 80 per cent and perhaps a quarter of all slaves became at least nominally Christian. This included the three largest and widest-ranging of all British West Indian slave rebellions: in Barbados in 1816, Demerara in 1823 and, climactically, Jamaica in 1831–2. Yet even in other colonies where the plantation system had decayed or never been firmly established, slaves proved more confident and assertive of their rights the more their conditions seemed to have improved.

Familiar explanations for slave unrest had gradually lost their force. The notion that rebellion was a peculiarly African response was vitiated by the slaves palpable creolisation. The well-attested fact that slaves seized on the disruptions caused by wars between the European powers did not apply now that peace was re-established. The planters' fears that slaves would be 'infected' by the ideologies of the American, French and Haitian Revolutions had been found to be greatly exaggerated, and faded almost completely once the revolutionary wars were over. Apart from this, the widespread ameliorative legislation passed since 1783 could be produced as evidence against the accusation that rebellion occurred because of excessive cruelty on the part of the slave-owning class.

Predisposed to ignore their own internal divisions and mismanagement, and unable to give credit to the slaves, the West Indian planters were bound to look to outside forces to account for the actual increase in slave resistance in the period after 1815. At a time when a wave of new philosophical, political and economic ideas was sweeping the imperial metropole, and Britain was also in the throes of a religious revivalism almost equally foreign to the plantocratic style, slaveowners placed the blame firmly on those whom they regarded as ignorant metropolitan liberals and the misguided missionaries who acted as their agents. For the most part they concluded that education and Christianisation were dangerously unsuitable for West Indian slaves.

Though it distorted the truth, there was considerable plausibility in the West Indian lobby's case. As the anti-slavery forces in Britain grew in number and power, infiltrating the Colonial Office and influencing Parliament, publishing hundreds of books and pamphlets and sending out dozens of missionaries to the West Indies, they provided increasing, if rarely direct, encouragement to slaves resisting the system. Borne up by the intellectual and moral certitude that were features of the secular Enlightenment and Protestant revivalism, they were able to paint the planters' denial of education and Christianity to slaves as morally evil as well as a mere socio-political stratagem, loftily ignoring the possibility that the slaves themselves might not want the types of education and religion they would thrust upon them.

Imperial politicians, philanthropists and missionaries alike were eager to claim credit for British slavery's downfall after the event, though their innate conservatism and pusillanimity led them to play down both the effectiveness of slave rebellion in speeding change and their own roles in promoting unrest. This interpretation has been followed — swallowed — by many historians. The sheer volume of the paper debate over slavery, and the fact that it was carried on by white protagonists not slaves, have tended to an attribution of more influence to metropolitan polemics and polemicists than either warrant. If the effect of the rebellions in speeding the process is acknowledged at all, planter contempt for the intellectual capabilities of black slaves, philanthropic conceit and an exaggerated view of the role of pure ideas in shaping history have concurred to maintain that it was metropolitan ideas which mainly stirred up the British West Indian slaves in the late rebellions. On the contrary, we would not only ascribe more influence to rebellion, and its threat, in promoting change, but much more weight to the slaves' own motives and aims. To turn the usual proposition around, slave unrest just as much influenced metropolitan ideas and actions as vice versa.

To assert that slaves actually achieved their own emancipation by resistance would be to overstate the case. The freeing of the British slaves in 1838, in common with the ending of the British trade in slaves thirty years earlier, could only be achieved by parliamentary decree. Parliament did not act until a majority of its members had been convinced that slavery was, at the same time, morally evil, economically inefficient and politically unwise. Yet the outcome would certainly have been delayed and different had the planters been able to convince Parliament that the slaves they owned were all humanely managed, contented and efficient. Instead, through the evidence of day-to-day resistance and the major risings of 1816, 1823 and 1831–2, it became gradually apparent that British West Indian slaves could never be ruled without intolerable repression and would never be contented or make efficient workers while slavery lasted.

The British anti-slavery forces certainly worked the slaves' purposes. Yet they were incapable of recognising the ways in which their ideas and actions were cleverly used by the slaves, not depended upon. While Wilberforce became a synonym for reform, he was no more than a distant symbol to the slaves, an ally of convenience. Even more telling was the slaves' attitude to the King. Though in fact very far from being an anti-slavery advocate, he was flatteringly conflated with the Deity as Big Massa — a kind of *deus ex machina* who, along with the anti-slavery lobby, could be pictured as having the slaves' own interests at heart. In this the slaves may have learned from their white masters, who had cloaked their rebelliousness at the time of the American War of Independence in Loyal Addresses.

Similarly, the missionaries led and guided the slaves far less than they imagined. They congratulated themselves on the way in which the slaves joyfully accepted Christianity in slavery's last phase, but failed to notice how the new religion was shaped by the slaves to their own needs and ends, making it an instrument of political as well as spiritual change. As ever, the ruling class apprehended only the mimetic idiom of slave behaviour and the surface of slave resistance, ignoring their deeper structures. The mainsprings of slave resistance in the last years of plantation slavery, and its most positive achievements, owed little or nothing to metropolitan inspiration or aid and, indeed, ran counter to even the revised interests of the imperial economy.

From the time of the first anti-slavery publications of Granville Sharp, Anthony Benezet and John Wesley between 1769 and 1774, those with an interest in plantation slavery and the slave trade knew that there was a rising tide of opposition in Britain. But it was not until the 1780s, with the formation of the first abolitionist organisations and the publications by John Ady, James Ramsay, John Newton, Thomas Clarkson and William Wilberforce, that the debate spilled over into the West Indies and began to be heard by the slaves. James Ramsay's *Essay on the Treatment and Conversion of African Slaves in the British Sugar Colonies* (1784) was particularly influential. For the author was a clergyman of the established church with twenty years' experience in the West Indies, who argued not only for the abolition of the slave trade but also the advisability of switching from slavery to free wage labour and the need to improve the moral climate of the plantation colonies.

The debates in Parliament and the pioneer parliamentary inquiries into the slave trade and conditions in the plantation colonies were accompanied by a flood of polemical writings which reached its high point between 1788 and 1792. While the French wars lasted the number of new books and the vigour of the slavery debate drastically declined, though so steadily did the arguments of the first generation of abolitionists enter the general consciousness that when the debate revived after 1815 the new wave of anti-slavery works began where its forerunners had broken off. Thomas Clarkson remained one of the most forceful anti-slavery advocates, but was equalled or surpassed by Henry Brougham, Zachary Macaulay, Thomas Cooper, James Stephen and James Cropper. Of the second and greater flood of polemic the influential equivalent of Ramsay's *Essay* was probably James Stephen's magisterial two-volume *Slavery Delineated* (1824, 1830) since, like Ramsay, the author had many years' first-hand experience in the Leeward Islands, and added a crushing weight of legal and statistical evidence to evangelical fervour. He was also a brother-in-law of William Wilberforce and became official legal advisor to the Colonial Office — which made him doubly distrusted by the West India interest.[2]

By the time slavery ended no more than one or two slaves in a hundred were literate enough to read books. Besides, masters kept anti-slavery works from their slaves as being more dangerous than guns. Of far wider circulation were the colonial newspapers, which multiplied after 1783. Many of these were no more than gazettes, publishing government notices and proclamations, shipping intelligence and news randomly brought in by visiting captains, planters' letters, current prices and advertisements. But the better newspapers in the more sophisticated colonies sometimes reviewed anti-slavery books and reported anti-slavery speeches if only to condemn them, gave at least a partial and delayed account of transactions at Westminster, and provided full, even verbatim, reports of debates in local legislatures and vestry meetings.[3] Such papers were eagerly acquired by literate slaves, and read aloud or retailed to their illiterate fellows. But, as perceptive whites realised, the most common way in which political news and views were spread among the slaves was by domestics overhearing and passing on their masters' incautious table talk. In these ways, an ever-widening group of slaves became aware not only that they had friends and allies in the imperial metropolis but that the masters felt increasingly embittered, besieged and desperate.

Change was clearly impending, posing a threat to the masters and hope for the slaves. But *rumours* of change played an even more important role in slave unrest than actual changes, becoming part of a common pattern. After every plot or revolt, from at least 1790 onwards, the planters provided evidence that rumours of impending changes had been circulating among the slaves, usually in the form that actual decrees had been made by the King, the imperial Parliament or the Colonial Office, and withheld by the local regime. By stressing the effect of rumours of change the planters hoped to forestall actual changes. They also hoped that by attributing slave unrest to actual or imagined changes imposed from outside they might draw attention away from local causes, and deflect blame from themselves.

But if they overemphasised the rumours, the planters did not invent them. The rumour syndrome in the late slave rebellions was of far deeper significance than a mere planto-cratic ploy. That the rumours could only be transmitted by the elite of literate and 'confidential' slaves and yet were spread widely and uniformly through the mass of slaves implied not only an efficient network of communication but also a degree of concurrence between élite and ordinary slaves that was deeply disturbing to the master class. Equally disconcerting to them was the consistent form of the rumours and the ways in which their very inaccuracy was of use to the cause of slave resistance. Even the most literate and best-informed of élite slaves were unlikely to be informed with complete accuracy, and the manner of dissemination, with many slaves receiving information at fourth and fifth hand, was bound to lead to exaggeration and distortion. But the facts that the rumours were not only consonant with the wishes of ordinary slaves but of remarkable consistency in the circumstances, suggest that they were intentionally shaped by those who stood to gain most — the potential leaders of a slave revolt. Rumours such that an act of emancipation had been signed by the King in London could neither have been invented by the most ignorant nor believed in by the most literate and informed of slaves. The rumours fulfilled the classic canons of successful propaganda — useful half-truths falling midway between fact and wish.

For the would-be leaders of the slaves the rumours were doubly useful — encouraging the mass of their followers that change was inevitable, with outside help available in the fulfilment of their wishes, and driving the masters deeper into their siege mentality. That they no longer enjoyed the sympathy of the British public and could not any more call upon the unquestioning support of the imperial Government was bad enough for the planters. But what wounded them most was the loss of a dream of aristocratic mastery such as was to sustain the planters of the United States South through a bloody civil war. It became gradually clear that none of the slaves would ever be contented with their assigned socio-economic roles. The most privileged were the least contented. Dissatisfied slaves of all types, far from looking to their temporal masters for justice, bounty and mercy, now looked to 'Big Massa' and to metropolitan leaders hated and distrusted by the planters for support in their resistance. Such was the subversive propaganda message conveyed in the slave ditty recorded by Matthew 'Monk' Lewis in western Jamaica in 1816:

> Oh me good friend, Mr. Wilberforce, make we free!
> God Almighty thank ye! God Almighty thank ye!
> God Almighty, make we free!

> Buckra in this country no make we free!
> What negro for to do? What negro for to do?
> Take force with force! Take force with force![4]

The rapid Christianisation of British West Indian slaves after 1783 clearly had a vital effect on their general consciousness, and an important bearing on slave resistance. But it is far less certain that the missionaries themselves were ever quite the 'Enemies to Caesar' claimed by Dr Thomas Coke, the chief Wesleyan evangelist in the West Indies.[5]

Until 1754 the Anglican church had a monopoly of Christianity in the British West Indies, steadfastly upholding the regime as was the proper function of an established church, and solving any doubt as to the compatibility of Christianity and servitude by neglecting to proselytise the slaves at all. The Catholic church, entrenched in the colonies acquired after 1763, had a more integrating approach, but for that reason was treated with extreme distrust by British planters. Contrary to Protestant legend, however, Catholic planters did seem to enjoy closer and more fruitful relations with their baptised slaves than those enjoyed by Protestant planters with pagans. Consequently, a minority of optimistic British planters — most of them nonconformist converts themselves — came to speculate on the practical as well as spiritual value of allowing missionaries to work with their slaves. Some were completely cynical in their motivation. 'I must in candour own that I am not influenced by religious principles myself in this matter but simply by self-interest', a prominent Jamaican planter told Rev. H. M. Waddell in 1830:

> I have a bad set of people: they steal enormously, run away, get drunk, fight and neglect their duty in every way; while the women take no care of their children, and there is no increase on the property. Now, if you can bring them under fear of a God, or a judgement to come, or something of that sort, you may be doing both them and me a service.[6]

A steadily growing number of noncomformist sectaries proved willing to enter the field but they were tolerated, if at all, to the degree they supported the *status quo*. The Moravians were first – in Jamaica and Antigua from 1754 – and most adaptable of all, having no doubts that slavery was God-ordained. They actually owned plantations and slaves, and two of their earliest missionaries even tried, in vain, to become slaves themselves.[7] The first Methodist missionary went to Antigua in 1778 at the invitation of a prominent white convert, and Methodism greatly expanded under the direction of the judicious Thomas Coke from 1786 onwards.[8] Methodist missionaries suffered more opposition than Moravians, partly because they were not formally structured and controlled by a missionary organisation until 1812, but mainly because of the uncompromising abolitionist statements in John Wesley's *Thoughts on Slavery* (1774). However, as in England, Methodism turned out to be almost a force for conservatism. A quest for respectability led to racial segregation within chapels, or even between them. Much the same was true of the small number of Presbyterian missions, which ministered almost as much to expatriate Scots as to the slaves, and became virtually a second established church in the Bahamas and British Guiana.[9] Such compromises did not occur to anything like the same extent in the chapels founded by the London Missionary Society, an interdenominational body dominated by Congregationalists which began work in 1808, or by the Baptist Missionary Society, which sent out its first pastors to Jamaica in 1814. Their ministers had fewer social aspirations and their congregations were, and remained, almost exclusively black.[10]

Without exception, though, the missionary societies carefully instructed their ministers not to engage in politics or to upset the social order. Count Zinzendorf wrote to a Moravian missionary that he was

> not to work against the police, or regard the government with suspicion . . . . Do not interfere between employer and employed; do not play any part in party politics, but teach the heathen by your example, to fear God and honour the King . . . . The right way with savages is this: you must set them such a dazzling example that they cannot help asking who made these delightful characters . . . . You must labour with your hands until you have won the love of the people.[11]

The LMS instructed the Rev. John Smith on his way to Demerara in 1816 that 'not a word must escape you in public or private which might render the slaves displeased with their masters or dissatisfied with their station. You are not sent to relieve them from their servile condition, but to afford them the consolations of religion.'[12] And another LMS missionary wrote to his superiors from Tobago in 1808:

> I am persuaded that it is neither my business nor in my power to deliver them [the slaves] from the bondage of men. I have always conceived it my duty to endeavour thro' divine assistance to direct the poor negroes, how they may be delivered from the bondage of sin and Satan, and to teach them the pure principles of Christianity, which will not only lead to sobriety, industry and fidelity; but will make them loyal subjects, obedient servants and children . . . . I not only endeavour to avoid any expression which might be misunderstood in this respect but always endeavour to endear them to each other, and particularly their employers, in fact all who have authority over them.[13]

In practice, of course, such instructions and intentions proved impossible to follow to the letter and, wittingly or not, nonconformist missionaries became slaves' allies in resistance. As the planters quickly realised, many of the missionaries came from a class closer to the labourer than to the land-owner. By living godly lives missionaries pointed up a glaring contrast to the lifestyle of the average planter. Not inured to the system by profit or long acquaintance, and living close to the slaves, missionaries found it impossible totally to ignore slavery's manifest inhumanity. 'I felt exceedingly distressed and was scarcely able to rest through the night', wrote one missionary from Jamaica in 1829. 'I thought I would rather, if I could have my choice, be lying in jail as I was last year, than hear as I do now, from day to day, of the sufferings of the poor defenceless negroes.' Similarly, throughout that most poignant and telling of all missionary records, the private journal of John Smith of Demerara, the crack of the punishment whip sounds like an unbidden yet unstillable conscience.[14]

Though, as Madeline Grant has written, 'most missionaries

were political innocents with an unconscious bias towards conservatism',[15] some were less ingenuous and all, in time, came to be regarded as dangerous by the planters. William Knibb, the Baptist gadfly, when giving evidence before the parliamentary inquiry in 1832, made a careful distinction: 'I did not say our doctrines led to implicit obedience; I said we taught it.'[16] And in its own heavily biassed report the Jamaican Assembly declared that

> The preaching and teaching of the sects called Baptist, Wesleyan Methodist, and Moravians (but more especially the sect called Baptist) had the effect of producing in the minds of the slaves, a belief that they could not serve both a temporal and a spiritual master, thereby occasioning them to resist the lawful authority of their temporal, under the delusion of rendering themselves more acceptable to a spiritual master.[17]

By this time, though, the tide of missionary activity and slave conversion was irreversible. By 1834 there were sixty-three Moravian missionaries in the British West Indies, fifty-eight Methodists, seventeen Baptists (all in Jamaica) and perhaps a dozen other nonconformist missionaries; a total of 150. In the nonconformist chapels there were about 47,000 communicating slave members and a claimed total of some 86,000 'hearers or inquirers', about 11 per cent of the total slave population of 776,000.[18] To this should be added perhaps twice as many nominal adherents of the Anglican church, which had long since been goaded into proselytising the slaves on inoculative principles. As early as 1788 the Rev. John Lindsay, Rector of St Catharine's Jamaica, had argued in response to James Ramsay's *Essay* that the slaves should be

> stamp'd with the Seal of Religion. From this Quarter (in times to come) it is that we, or at least many of us, shall be served with Honest, Attentive, Sober, Obliging House Servants . . . . And the Saltwater, Stupid, Selfish, Thieving, Vexatious Pack we are commonly served with will be driven where they ought to be — to the Hoe and Bill.

. . . Negroes are ill adapted to receive Instruction, from a Natural sulkiness, stupidity and prejudice — a want of Natural feelings — of Capacity — and an Unusual carelessness about everything which does not forcibly strike their conceptions. But if there be a possibility to bring Negroes, by a Religious knowledge to be Orderly — Neat in their Persons — Sober and Sensible in their Carriage — Diligent — Faithful — and Industrious . . . . Why may not the British Catechist [i.e. the Anglican] gain them to this, as well as the Moravian or Methodist?[19]

Spurred on not by the words of the egregious Dr Lindsay (whose outburst did not find a publisher) but by the Saints of the Clapham Sect, Anglicans founded the Church Missionary Society in 1799. In 1824 bishoprics were established for Jamaica and Barbados, and by 1834 the number of Anglican ministers in the British West Indies had trebled to about a hundred. Under metropolitan urging, new colonial laws were passed which encouraged slave baptism, church marriages, Christian instruction and sabbatarianism. The Rev. George Bridges, for example, claimed in 1823 to have baptised 10,000 slaves within two years in Manchester parish, Jamaica, though he neglected to mention the fee of 2/6d (12½p) a slave decreed by the Jamaican legislature.[20]

The Rev. George Bridges, who was later the founder of the Colonial Church Union which physically attacked nonconformists and burned their chapels, quite candidly saw the role of the Church of England as to counter the sectaries and defend the social order. But after slavery ended even those missionaries who claimed to have opposed slavery from the beginning disclaimed any part in the rebellions of 1816—32, and all tended to stress the function of Christianity (especially their own particular brand) in 'civilising' the slaves and smoothing over the social transition from slavery to free wage labour. Yet almost universally the white ministers in the West Indies exaggerated their own role in the conversion of a quarter of a million slaves to Christianity within a quarter century, and distorted the slaves' motivation in making the voluntary transition.[21] The part played by Christianity in creolisation and slave resistance can only be truly assessed by examining more closely what Christianity meant to the slaves themselves.

Because of the natural blending of religious elements in Africa itself, and the nature of the African slave trade to the New World, one would expect African religion to have taken on Christian elements during the creolisation process even without active proselytisation. The extent of religious blending in the New World was determined partly by the degree to which the African components were mixed and the extent to which they faded and became generalised, and partly by the degree to which Christianity – or rather, its variants – proved culturally adaptable, assimilable, and attractive to slaves.

There was much in Christianity that was strange to native Africans, if not objectively ridiculous.[22] Two missionaries wrote home from Grenada in 1820 that many slaves were too ignorant to be admitted to chapel membership, being unable to understand the content of the teaching. Yet in the same letter the missionaries listed the following as the subjects on which they had preached to the slaves: 'the Fall of Man, Redemption by Jesus Christ, the blessings of Redemption such as Justification, Regeneration, Sanctification and eternal glory, the Resurrection of the Dead and eternal judgement.'[23]

None the less, there were many more common or transferable elements in European and African religion than is usually recognised, especially by Eurocentric Christian writers reluctant to acknowledge that Africans had any proper religion at all. As has been especially apparent in Haiti, Cuba and Brazil, with their syncretic religions of *vodun, santeria* and *candombe*, many rituals, inconographies and beliefs were more easily blended than separated out. Africans and European Christians alike believed in a supreme creator and a pantheon of saints or personified spirits who proved easily interchangeable. And what is being done at the baptism of a baby, or of an adult by total immersion, or when flowers are carried to a graveside – even to the bedside of the sick – which a native African would not instantly recognise?

From the first crusading period of contact European Christians, with their sacred relics and pilgrimage sites, their mystery-guarding, miracle-working priests and their holy liquids, were far closer to what was disparagingly termed animistic African religion (or 'superstition') than they were prepared to own. Even Protestants, who dismissed Catholic practices along with African as idolatrous or superstitious, retained easily transferable symbols and imagery: the cross, communion wine as blood and sacrifice, the almost talismanic reverence for the Holy Book, the 'Rock of Ages, cleft for me'. Even the solemn oath sanctioned and enforced by religion, which was so vital both to subversive organisation and to its uncovering, was a feature common to Europe and Africa.

Apart from becoming increasingly accessible, Christianity offered real attractions to the increasingly creolised slaves of the British West Indies — social, political and psychological. Conversion was in its nature a sudden hopeful change, though the way in which this change was visualised, and the motivation of slave converts, was distinctly twofold. At the level most willingly recognised by the master class, conversion was a token of at least partial acceptance, in a quest for social respectability. At a deeper level, conversion could signify resistance, even revolution — the most positive manifestation of that reidentification which Peter J. Wilson has called the quest for reputation.[24]

At first — and in some colonies such as Bermuda and Barbados, for a very long time — the established Anglican church had a monopoly of respectability. Only Anglican persons were authorised to baptise, marry or give Christian burial to slaves. At the very end of slavery these privileges began to be extended to sectarian ministers, as long as they were properly ordained and licensed. Far from weakening the hold of respectability this reinforced it by spreading it more widely. Chapels, especially those presided over by white missionaries or what commonly came to be called 'black Englishmen', became almost as proper, conventional and respectable as Anglican churches. This was particularly true of Presbyterians, Moravians and Wesleyans, but even the Baptist church divided into relatively respectable and 'primitive', or 'native', wings in which the ministers remained unlicensed and unordained.[25]

Even in adhering to respectable religion slaves, in the words of E. D. Genovese, were developing a 'most powerful defense against the dehumanization implicit in slavery . . . drawing on a religion that was supposed to ensure their compliance and docility [they] rejected the essence of slavery by projecting their own rights and values as human beings'.[26] Yet the Native Baptists and their equivalents were at least as important in West Indian history and society as the more respectable churchgoers, and far more important in the history of resistance. The strictly relative sense of social worthiness acquired by joining a respectable church became almost a personality change under the influence of the more fundamentalist Christian teaching and practice in the popular churches, combining personal validation with spiritual regeneration. In a memorable passage, the Guyanese historian Robert Moore has analysed the description of slaves' testimonies given in the Demerara journal of the Rev. John Smith. The slaves' sense of sin, wrote Moore,

> was rather a sense of social worthlessness or inferiority than the concept of personal depravity in which the missionaries believed. Services in slave chapels usually followed the pattern of people weeping for their sins, people crying out loudly for their guilt, and then coming away refreshed by a new confidence . . . no longer feeling the peculiar mixture of guilt and unworthiness which characterised the typical Creole slave. Even if the experience of conversion was not followed by baptism or a particularly close adherence to the church the effect seems to have been to change the Creole slave not necessarily into an outwardly less obedient slave but inwardly into a less accepting one.[27]

Quite apart from this, nonconformist chapels with all-black congregations, such as Shrewsbury's in Barbados, Smith's in Demerara and Burchell and Knibb's in Jamaica, provided an alternative society and refuge from the plantation ethos. They were places in which slaves from different plantations could meet regularly, which offered opportunities for self-expression and spiritual release. They also created their own hierarchies independent of plantation society — though for obvious reasons those who became the leaders in chapel were often those who had already emerged as the plantations' slave elite.

In such chapels the black deacons usually had a closer

rapport with the lowlier members of the congregation than did the white ministers — a source of later tension. In a profound sense (in a phrase quoted by Genovese in the United States context) 'The whites preached to the niggers and the niggers preached to theyselves.'[28] This was most apparent in the most popular black churches of all, those founded twenty-five years or more before the first white missionaries appeared on the scene by black 'Loyalist' slaves: the Wesleyan Joseph Paul and the Baptists Frank Spence, Prince Williams and Sharper Morris in the Bahamas, and the Baptists George Lisle, Moses Baker, Andrew Bryan, Prince Hoare and George Gibb in Jamaica. These all had to fight a running battle not only with the colonial regimes and the established church, but also with the official missionaries sent out from England. For example, the bigoted Anglican Rev. D. W. Rose (as quoted by the historian of the SPG) ridiculed the Native Baptists of Long Island, Bahamas, in 1799 as having been

'misled by strange doctrines.' They called themselves 'Baptists', the 'followers of St. John' and were 'not so happy and contented' as in other parts of the West Indies, though 'every indulgence and humanity' were exercised towards them by their Masters.' Their preachers, black men, were 'artful and designing, making a merchandize of Religion.' One of them was 'so ingenious' as to proclaim that he had 'had a familiar conversation with the Almighty, and to point out the place where he had seen Him.' At certain times of the year the black preachers used to 'drive numbers of negroes into the sea and dip them by way of baptism', for which they extorted a dollar, or stolen goods. Previously to Mr. Rose's arrival an attempt 'to check their proceedings' occasioned some of the slaves to 'abscond and conceal themselves in the woods.'[29]

Even more telling evidence can be found between the lines of the Rev. John Clarke's *Memorials of Baptist Missionaries in Jamaica* (1869), which overpraised such white missionaries as Knibb and Burchell but was far more guarded about Lisle, Baker and their numerous following. Besides the inevitable references to the blacks' affection for fervent hymn singing and call-and-response in chapel services, there are clear references to more obviously African practices: to drumming and dance, spirit possession and speaking in tongues. 'Some of them', wrote Clarke,

> thought the old men were to dream dreams, and the young men were to see visions . . . . There was certainly much superstition mingled with their religious exercises; many had wonderful dreams to tell, which they considered as prophetic visions; some excited themselves by fanatical notions, and fell into wild extravagances which they called '*the convince*' in which they had full faith, as much as in Divine Revelation . . . and from others we had learned that they had gone out at night to what they called *the wilderness*.[30]

Another pioneer black preacher, George Gibb, who went to Jamaica from the United States in 1784, practised baptism by triune immersion, at night, in secret, in unfrequented places.[31]

It should not then be surprising that the members of such recessive, apocalyptic churches should predominate in the late slave rebellions of 1823 in Demerara and 1831–2 in Jamaica; that they should be led by élite slaves and chapel deacons such as Quamina, John Smith's chief deacon at Le Resouvenir, and Samuel Sharpe, Baptist head deacon in Burchell's chapel in Montego Bay; or even that several modern commentators should characterise the outbreaks as classic millenarian phenomena. The voluminous evidence from the rebellions stressed the rebel chapel-goers' emphasis on membership and leadership, their fervent, secret meetings, their use of dream, trance and oaths, their almost cabalistic reverence for the Holy Bible, their choice of biblical texts stressing atonement, redemption, regeneration, apocalypse. Then one is easily reminded of the famous five-point formulation of Norman Cohn: like classical millenarian outbreaks these slave rebellions can be seen to have been collective, to be engaged in by all the faithful. They were immanent, to be realised on earth not in heaven, and imminent, coming soon and suddenly. They were, perhaps, to be total, utterly transforming, bringing not only improvement but perfection. Finally, they would be seen as miraculous, invoking God's direct intervention.[32]

Such an analysis is beguiling but too formulistic, and too Eurocentric. Christianity had a vital role where Christian slaves predominated or where the forces of evangelical revivalism were particularly strong, but it was not a *necessary* condition. It seems to have played no part, for example, in the Barbados rebellion of 1816 or the disturbances that upset the Bahamian Out Island of Exuma in 1828–30. What then, in general, did motivate British West Indian slaves, and what did they seek? If we rely on the evidence of the Jamaican slave ditty of 1816 (which, incidentally, Monk Lewis claimed originated from a person whom he described as 'a brown priest'), the overwhelming wish for all slaves was, simply, for freedom. Slavery was a condition so absolute and intolerable that it must be ended, however much it had been mitigated by familiarity, custom and law. Its very mitigation, indeed, made slavery's ending easier, the result, in part, of friendly forces in the metropolis, and resulting in a more sophisticated generation of Creole slaves.

How slaves visualised freedom and the means by which it should be achieved is far less straightforward. Leadership was of crucial importance and the motives and aims of leaders were likely to differ substantially from those of ordinary slaves. The rebel leaders, paradoxically, emerged from those who had gained most from the system of slavery. As in the independence movements of the twentieth century, they knew the ways of the master class, but the superiority which they had gained over the mass of their fellows made them more rather than less frustrated. There is nothing more energising for a rebel leader than, while feeling to be superior to his fellows, to be treated as a second-class person by the master class, especially when close association and privileged information provide a sense that the power of the masters is crumbling. For the members of the slave élite who became the rebel leaders (and in certain cases for free coloureds too) rebellion offered the open-ended extension of what they had already gained. At one extreme this might have meant a complete takeover from the master class: the retention of the factories, great houses and government buildings, and the substitution of black (or brown) for white overseers, owners and plantocratic legislators. At the other extreme, in which rebellion led to a total destruction of the socio-economic machinery of the plantocratic system, the rebel leaders might have entrenched their leadership by a return to an autocratic African style. In the context of the Haitian Revolution these were, broadly, the divergent approaches of Henry Christophe and Jacques Dessalines respectively. Neither was easily applicable in pure form to the British West Indies, the first being unrealistic, the second outdated. A far more realisable scenario lay somewhere in between, with the rebel leaders simply reinforcing the leadership gained in plantation and chapel in a reorganised system, with slavery abolished, the power of the planters curtailed and the black majority free to work for planters or themselves as and when they wished.

These comparatively moderate ambitions had the supreme advantage of consonance with what seem to have been the wishes of the mass of slaves. Leadership was vital but rebellion depended upon a mass following. To win over the ordinary slaves, the rebel leaders used their established authority as leaders on the estates, in the slave quarters and in the chapels, playing on the slaves' dissatisfactions and aspirations. They also relied cleverly on millenarian tactics, employing the Bible, preaching and oaths upon a susceptible people, and used convenient rumours that they themselves knew to have been untrue, unlikely, or half truths. In sum, the rebellions occurred because the leaders were able to mobilise the slaves, harnessing their seething discontent and potential for retaliatory violence, and offering fulfilment for their deepest aspirations.

The chief of these aspirations was, naturally, to be free. Yet the form of that freedom seems to have become visualised as that of an independent peasantry, about which the slaves had quite clear notions and of which, in most cases, they already had considerable experience. As has been notably argued by Sidney Mintz and Douglas Hall, many West Indian blacks were already what might be called 'proto-peasants' well before the end of formal slavery.[33] Besides the ways in which they worked their provision grounds, with their own methods and with minimal supervision, this was demonstrated by the way in which they had developed an internal marketing system quite independently, and managed to enter the cash economy on their own terms. More deeply, the slaves retained and developed concepts of family and kin quite beyond the comprehension and control of the master class, and a concept of land tenure that was in contradiction to that of the dominant European culture. In brief, for ordinary slaves freedom meant being free to be small farmers, working for the plantations, if at all, only for wages and on their own terms. They wanted to live in family units, to have ready access to land of their own, and to be free to develop their own culture, particularly their own syncretised religion. These were their basic aspirations, amounting to an ideology, though varying according to the different conditions in each of the colonies.

In some cases slaves were ready to seize a peasant lifestyle before their masters were ready to grant it; in others they became rebellious because their masters sought to erode what had already been achieved. Only in the very last period was the slaves' drive towards Christianity involved, and even then not in all colonies affected. Probably the earliest example occurred in Dominica in 1791, when the slaves on the windward side downed tools and refused to work unless they were granted half the week to cultivate their own provision grounds. This claim, reported the island merchants and planters, 'occurred in pursuit of what they term their "rights", which in their interpretation extend to an exemption from labour during four days out of seven'.[34] A similar instance happened in Tobago in 1807, when a type of 'industrial action' on the part of the slaves was narrowly quelled short of actual rebellion.[35] But such early cases were mere straws in a wind that rose to a gale and then a hurricane in Barbados, Demerara and Jamaica between 1816 and 1832.

All slave aims and aspirations were most neatly demonstrated, perhaps, in the Demerara rebellion in August 1823 — though our account and interpretation has to be filtered through the words of white officials. On the first day of the outbreak the Governor, John Murray, went forward to speak with a small group of armed slaves, asking them what they wanted. The more vocal called out. 'Our right.' Murray expostulated with them for half an hour, explaining the limits of the recent Bathurst reforms, but was unable to satisfy them. 'These things they said were no comfort to them', he reported. 'God had made them of the same flesh and blood as the whites, that they were tired of being Slaves to them, that their good King had sent Orders that they should be free and they would not work any more.'[36]

Two days later some 2000 slaves confronted the 300 colonial militia and imperial troops as they marched through the plantations. The military commander, Colonel Leahy, spoke with the rebels under flag of truce. 'Some of the insurgents called out that they wanted lands and three days in the week for themselves, besides Sunday, and they would not give up their arms until they were satisfied', wrote one eye-witness.[37] 'At first there was more demand for freedom and three days than anything else', went Leahy's own account, given at the trial of Parson Smith, 'but latterly when I came out again they were all for freedom, and all of them dwelt considerably on going to Chapel on Sunday.'[38] Refusing to disperse, the rebels were mown down with musketry, with 100–150 killed for the loss of one white wounded. Thereafter, Leahy and the troops proceeded up and down the coast, shooting rebel leaders after drumhead courts martial and hanging their bodies in gibbets as an example *'in terrorem'*. The rebellion collapsed with almost pathetic suddenness. But while such barbarity was still necessary to suppress it — and still possible — yet could no longer be concealed from disinterested or antagonistic persons of influence in the motherland, the days of British plantation slavery were surely numbered.

In 1816 the Barbados slave rebellion had made comparatively little impact on Britain at large. In Parliament it reinforced the decision not to impose the Registry Bill on the self-legislating colonies, and it resulted in a successful parliamentary petition to the Prince Regent to declare that slave emancipation was not an immediate object of British policy.[39] The impact of the Demerara uprising and the subsequent destruction of Shrewsbury's chapel in Barbados was far greater. The news, relayed chiefly through the publication by the LMS of the details of John Smith's trial and articles in the *Edinburgh Review*,[40] provoked an uproar among British emancipationists, who seemingly regarded the ordeals of Smith and Shrewsbury as far outweighing the deaths of 250 slaves. Two hundred petitions were delivered to Parliament in April and May 1824, led by one from the LMS, and in June an acrimonious debate occurred on a motion of censure, during which Lord Brougham delivered two of his marathon speeches against the colonial regime.[41] However, the motion was lost by 193 to 146, the majority agreeing with John Gladstone (father of William Ewart, and owner of the estate on which the revolt had centred) that philanthropy was misplaced and Christianity dangerous when dealing with slaves whose only ambition was 'the freedom to live in indolence'.[42] At one level, then, the concurrence of the Demerara rebellion with the policy of amelioration pursued by Lord Bathurst set back rather than speeded the emancipationist cause.

The news from Jamaica in 1832, though, overwhelmed the remaining opposition to emancipation. It came at a time when the political atmosphere was already electric with the debates over and passage of the Great Reform Bill, and was relayed more completely and quickly than ever before. The details of the suppression of the rebellion and of the scale and scope of the rebel trials provoked official inquiry and public censure, but this was nothing to the storm that arose over the retaliatory persecution of the nonconformist missionaries and their black congregations by the Jamaican regime. Most of those in the British Government and many middle-class philanthropists were ambivalent about the exercise of law and order in suppressing rebellion. But quite another and unambiguous matter was the lawless behaviour of ostensibly Christian whites as described in Governor Belmore's despatches, in Henry Whiteley's lurid *Three Months in Jamaica*, or by refugee missionaries like William Knibb and Thomas Burchell in person, before the parliamentary inquiry during the summer of 1832 and on the speaking and preaching circuit in England and Scotland throughout 1832 and 1833.[43]

Once again the missionaries bid fair to steal the martyr's crown, but no longer could they fully disguise who were the true victims and heroes in the conflict. In all, some 200 Jamaican slaves were killed in the fighting and no less than

540 put to death after military or civil trials. Their paramount leader, Samuel Sharpe, was one of the last to die, hanged at Montego Bay on 23 May 1832. By a fitting coincidence, just one week later the House of Commons in London appointed a Select Committee with the significantly-worded mandate, 'to consider and report upon the Measures which it may be expedient to adopt for the purpose of effecting the Extinction of Slavery throughout the British Dominions, at the earliest period compatible with the safety of all Classes in the Colonies'.[44] The Committee heard evidence during June and July 1832 which provided a background for the General Election for the first reformed Parliament, when, it was reported, all successful candidates were bound to give pledges of support for emancipation. The evidence in the Report, ordered to be printed in August 1832, provoked a deluge of petitions that eventually included 1,500,000 names, and when Parliament reconvened at the beginning of 1833, the emancipation debate was its first priority.[45]

Soon debate centred on the questions of compensation for owners of property in slaves, and ways in which the labour of the ex-slaves could be guaranteed in order to sustain the British West Indian sugar plantation system. But emancipation itself had become inevitable. Samuel Sharpe's dying affirmation in May 1832, 'I would rather die on yonder gallows than live in slavery',[46] can therefore stand as the noble if poignant epitaph for all those thousands of mostly anonymous slaves who, fighting and dying with little hope for the right to make a life of their own, in the fullness of time helped bring slavery down.

5. British Opinion and the Emergence of Haiti, 1791-1805

DAVID GEGGUS

The British public by the autumn of 1791 was well-familiar with the topic of West Indian slavery, perhaps even growing tired of it, when on 26 October rumours raced around London that there had been a huge and gory catastrophe in the Caribbean. The campaign to abolish the slave trade was already four years old and was reaching a new climax, after being set back in the spring by news of a brief rebellion on the island of Dominica.[1] Now reports began to arrive from the French colony of St Domingue of a slave revolt far greater than anything the New World had ever known. The great northern plain of St Domingue, the West Indies' wealthiest colony and Europe's main source of both sugar and coffee, had been devastated. Over 100,000 slaves were in revolt, and with firebrands and machetes had taken a terrible revenge on their masters. Hundreds of plantations lay in ashes. Hundreds of whites had been slaughtered, sometimes in the most grisly of circumstances. As lurid tales were told and retold in the coffee shops and counting houses of the City, the price of sugar shot sky high and stocks fell immediately by 1 per cent.[2]

Through early November the Society of West India Merchants and Planters held emergency meetings at the London Tavern to hear the latest news and to petition the Government for increased military protection.[3] The planters feared how their own slaves were going to react but the crisis worked by no means entirely to their disadvantage. Because of the void created in the world market, British tropical produce rose greatly in value and in the next few months was re-exported in large quantities. Moreover, by blaming the insurrection entirely on the abolitionists, the planters found a strong stick with which to beat their opponents. The danger of even discussing abolition, they claimed, was now clearly demonstrated. An absurd story about Wilberforce being worshipped by the slaves of the French colonies appeared in several newspapers,[4] probably planted by the pro-slavery lobby. Many supporters of abolition now had second thoughts about the campaign and wanted to see it delayed for a year. Even Pitt, its most powerful advocate, seems temporarily to have changed his mind at the cost of heated words with Wilberforce. 'People here are all panic-struck with the transactions in St. Domingo', wrote Wilberforce, 'and the apprehensions or pretended apprehensions of the like in Jamaica and other of our islands.'[5]

The press for the most part supported the West Indians' demand for troops, but was not really convinced by their propaganda. 'Occasional insurrections are the necessary evils of slavery', observed *The Times*, which wanted to see Britain annex St Domingue. The revolt came as no surprise, it declared, and had been caused by the French granting political rights to colonial free coloureds. It recognised that such a massive uprising would be difficult to put down but also asserted that any colony where the whites were united need not fear any number of blacks, however large.[6] Both the anti-slavery *Star* and the (usually) pro-planter *English Chronicle* carried letters that attributed the revolt to the slave system itself and not to any attempts to reform it. *The Star* distinguished major causes (the slaves' hatred of slavery) from minor causes (the influence of the French Revolution and free coloured question), and further asserted that abolition would be in the planters' own interest as the slaves considered the most prone to rebellion were newly arrived Africans.[7] Like the planters, therefore, the abolitionists were able to turn the revolt to their own ends, and to adduce powerful prudential reasons (as well as moral ones) for ending the slave trade. On the other hand, the West Indians were quick to claim, the apparent reluctance of the slaves in the British colonies to emulate those of St Domingue seemed to attest to the mildness of slavery in the British Caribbean, even though the slave trade was there reaching a peak. Similarly, while the planters presented the atrocities of the black rebels as proof of their barbarity, the abolitionists viewed the rebellion as a sign of the blacks' humanity, and the vicious response it encountered as further evidence of the cruelties of the slave system.[8]

The St Domingue insurrection thus sharpened the debate over slavery and gave it a new immediacy for the British public. This immediacy was not just one of dramatic images and apparently impending disaster, but also one of sharply increased sugar prices that created great public indigation. Sugar had ceased to be a luxury in England and was considered a household necessity. Revolutionary disruptions in the French West Indies led to increases in the price of sugar which had always been more expensive in England than on the Continent. The price rise focused attention on the shortcomings of the British planters. They ought not to clamour too loudly about their rights to protection, *The Star* suggested on 24 November, lest 'the immense pecuniary loss' they caused the mother country be realised and lead to an abolitionist victory. At first most commentators blamed the high prices on speculating sugar merchants, but by December public opinion was identifying insufficient production by the British planters as the true cause, and public meetings called for a reduction in their commercial privileges. On 31 December even the *English Chronicle* warned that if sugar prices were pushed higher the public might be converted to abolition. It was no accident that abolitionist associations for the abstention from the use of sugar spread across the country as soon as news of the slave revolt arrived.[9] By April 1792, when the abolition motion was brought before Parliament, some 300,000 people were said to have given up sugar.[10] Its rise in price, whatever the logic of the matter, seems to have contributed considerably to the abolitionist petitions then presented.

Despite the doubts of some of his supporters, Wilberforce had decided to fight on and stress that the slave revolt strengthened not weakened the case for abolition.[11] In early 1792 the controversy intensified and in the ensuing pamphlet war St Domingue figured prominently. The French planters' official account of the slave revolution, which blamed it on the British and French abolitionists and dwelled on the blacks' atrocities, went through four editions in English, published presumably by the West India Committee.[12] Thomas Clarkson replied, using the same arguments as had *The Star*. He also cited the Jamaican authority Edward Long, who had stated in his *History of Jamaica* that it was the slave trade that bred insurrections. The MP William Roscoe added that the blacks' savagery was the product of their brutal treatment (as well as of 'native ferocity'), and he quoted a French report of February 1792 that declared that there was now nothing to be feared from the black rebels and that the fighting in St Domingue had been confined to the whites and free coloureds.[13] Hence, when the House of Commons voted in April, it may have thought the slave revolt was near extinction. This might explain its deciding to abolish the trade but not until 1796 – a verdict that ignored both the planters' predictions of disaster and the abolitionists' arguments about the urgent demands of security.

Nevertheless, in the Commons debate almost all who took part felt it necessary to deal with the St Domingue question and the opening speakers, Wilberforce and Baillie, the Agent for Grenada, accorded it special attention. The arguments used were not new. The West Indians spoke of 'rapes . . .massacres . . . conflagrations', 'impaled infants', 'acts of parricide', while the abolitionists attributed these to the example set by the whites and to the natural resentment of enslaved and transported Africans. Pitt, Fox and Wilberforce all cited the testimony of the Negrophobe Edward Long and observed that the security argument was one of the strongest in favour of abolition. If the slave trade continued, similar uprisings could be expected in the British colonies. The Home Secretary, Henry Dundas, agreed, and he proved to be the key figure in clinching the question.[14] He may also have been persuaded to vote against the West Indians by the prospect of rerouting St Domingue's trade through British ports, which was then under discussion.[15]

'Many have been known and heard to exult', claimed Baillie in his speech, 'at the calamities we daily read of.' However, this was specifically denied later in the debate by Samuel Whitbread, and indeed the attitude of most abolitionists towards the slave insurrection would seem rather ambivalent.

It is true they preferred the neutral term 'insurrection' to either 'rebellion' or 'revolt', and presented the insurgents' actions as an understandable revenge against their 'injurious oppressors'. But no major figure appears to have openly approved of violent self-liberation by the blacks. Wilberforce thought them still unready for freedom, however obtained, and he deplored the 'cruel' and 'dreadful' revolt. Fox, too, spoke of the 'heart-rending . . . horrid scenes' that had taken place and, for all his radicalism, did not wish to see rebellion spreading to the British colonies. Nor did *The Star*, which none the less thought slavery both inefficient and unjust.[16] The position of Thomas Clarkson was less clear. He wrote of the slaves asserting 'their violated rights by force of arms' and of 'the unalterable Rights of Men'. William Roscoe was rather more explicit: 'Resistance is always justifiable when force is the substitute of right; nor is the commission of a civil crime possible in a state of slavery.'[17] Even the conservative Edmund Burke, who now put forward a scheme for gradual emancipation, thought the rebels' cause 'infinitely better' than that of the French revolutionaries.[18] However, the most overt expression of approval came from the veteran northern abolitionist Percival Stockdale. '*We*', he wrote, 'are the savages; the Africans act like *men*; like beings endowed with rational and immortal minds; with warm and generous sentiments . . . . [Their] cries . . . against their tyrants, is the *Voice* — their revenge, is the *Act* — of NATURE and of GOD!' More than this, Stockdale appended to his pamphlet a poem he had first published in 1773, which called on the slaves to 'rush with resistless fury on their foes' and 'of their pale fiends exterminate the race!' This, however, was a solitary voice, expecting in reply only 'ridicule and malignity'.[19]

From the spring of 1792 it became clear that the French could not suppress the slave revolution in St Domingue. This may have contributed to the demise of the abolition movement that then set in although radicalism in Britain was inhibited by the changing political climate in Europe and the approach of war. Along with the Africans of the Middle Passage, the slaves of St Domingue receded from view, and public sympathy was doubtless the more diminished when in 1793 British troops began a five-year struggle to conquer the colony and restore slavery. No abolitionist appears to have protested. Charles Fox and the Opposition attacked the West India campaigns but only on military, not moral, grounds. When the French retaliated by freeing all the slaves in their colonies, only the radical abolitionist William Fox applauded; and he criticised his colleagues for continuing to think the slaves unfit for freedom.[20] In 1793-4, however, St Domingue witnessed several more large-scale massacres which served to justify extreme Negrophobe statements and extinguish whatever remained of abolition as a popular movement. 'The Negro race', wrote a correspondent to the *Gentleman's Magazine*, 'are but a set of wild beasts, when let loose without control.'[21]

Although Toussaint Louverture, the brilliant black general, first appears in a British newspaper in November 1794, it was not the remarkable feats of his army of ex-slaves that attracted the attention of Britain's press and politicians so much as the appalling mortality of the British troops in the Caribbean. As early as August, *The Times* had reported public alarm on the subject, and in October, 'men dying as fast as possible'.[22] By late 1796 the obituary columns of the *Gentleman's Magazine* were strewn with the names of officers who had died of yellow fever. In October 1796 it was said in Parliament that every person in the country had lost an acquaintance in the Caribbean campaigns.[23] It was then that Edmund Burke added to the later printings of his *Regicide Peace* the famous line about fighting to conquer a cemetery. Fear of being sent to the West Indies was hindering recruitment into the Army, when in May 1797 the Foxite Whigs forced a debate demanding that Britain withdraw from St Domingue.[24]

The debate centred on strategy and costs, and Wilberforce and Bryan Edwards were the only speakers to pay much attention to the black revolutionaries. The development they had undergone, said Wilberforce, had received little notice: 'They were no longer like the inhabitants of India, too low for the storm that was passing over them; they stood erect, and influenced its direction.' He none the less opposed the motion.[25] Edwards's views were already known from his *Historical Survey* of St Domingue that had appeared a few months before.[26] An 'enlightened plantocrat', he blamed the slave revolt on the planters' huge imports of Africans as well

as on the interference of 'hot-brained fanaticks'. Both influences, he said, would have to be curtailed in the British colonies, if their 'contented and orderly Negroes' were to remain
immune from 'so dreadful an example of . . . triumphant
anarchy'. To the rebels' atrocities Edwards devoted ample
space and his best prose, and in a curious piece of projection
he represented them as providential retribution for the sixteenth century genocide of St Domingue's aborigines.[27] It
was as if the blacks were punishing the cruelties of the con-
quistadors, not those of the planters.

As for the future, Edwards declared that Europe had lost
St Domingue for good. It would become a 'negro colony'
similar to Jamaica's Maroon community, he said, entirely
ignoring its large free coloured population.[28] Though he
would have liked to imagine it evolving into a modern state,
this was impossible. 'Savages in the midst of society', the
ex-slaves would live 'without peace, security, agriculture, or
property . . . averse to labour, though frequently perishing
with want . . . pretending to be free, while groaning beneath
the capricious despotism of their chiefs.' As a prediction, this
was a mixture of acuity and absurdity, certainly propaganda
and perhaps wishful thinking. The *Survey* was immediately
attacked by the Dominguan exile Venault de Charmilly as an
attempt to keep the Government from annexing St Domingue.
It exaggerated the extent to which the plantation regime had
collapsed, and in subsequent editions Edwards had to omit
some statements.[29] Nevertheless, the *Gentleman's Magazine*
gave the work a very long review, quoting Edwards's prediction, as 'an antidote to the violence and virulence' of Abolitionist literature.[30] Edwards was a much respected authority
and the *Survey* was reprinted many times.

In some quarters, however, enthusiasm for the slave rebellion lived on. The radical *Courier* published at this time a
bloodcurdling ode on the subject, in which the planters again
appeared as 'fiends'. As in Edwards's *Ode on seeing a negro
funeral*, the rebels respond to the spirit of Africa crying out
for vengeance. An indifferent poem, it yet achieves a certain
depth in uniting in the central image of a votive fire the slaves'
supernatural beliefs and their collective desire for revenge,
'the spirit of our fire'.[31] Such picturesque celebrations of

'savagery', while asserting the morality of the insurgents' actions, also served to set them further apart from the whites and hence hinder European attempts to empathise. The same was true of the blacks' military successes, which could often be ascribed to their endurance, familiarity with the climate and cunning, that is 'slavish' characteristics. Their immunity to the diseases that slaughtered the European troops, in particular, emphasised racial differences in a most dramatic manner. For Edmund Burke the blacks of St Domingue were a 'race of fierce barbarians' who thrived on the 'poisonous air' that whites could not safely breathe.[32]

For this and other reasons, the military defeat that the British underwent in St Domingue did not oblige contemporaries to adopt more favourable attitudes towards blacks or anti-slavery. Changes none the less did take place. In 1798 the British troops were gradually evacuated, leaving Toussaint Louverture in supreme power in the once wealthy colony. In the annual abolition debate in April, the radical Hobhouse pointed to the French blacks' 'surprising feats of valour' and argued for emancipation, since it had given France a new weapon 'terrible to her foes'. The *Annual Register* also produced a cogent appraisal of the blacks' (and mulattoes') 'rapid progress' in the art of war, and it presented Toussaint not just as a courageous and skilful general but also as a humane and moderate leader.[33] 'Toussaint L'Ouverture', proclaimed the *London Gazette* in December, 'is a negro born to vindicate the claims of this species and to show that the character of men is independent of exterior colour.' 'Every Liberal Briton', it declared, should feel proud of the 'happy revolution' that, with British help (!), had brought the blacks to power in the nominally French colony.[34] The ministerial *Gazette*, however, was being less than honest, and not merely trying to salve national pride. On evacuating St Domingue the British had concluded a commercial convention and non-aggression pact with the blacks. Although alarming for the West Indians, it was considered the best way to deter Toussaint from interfering in the British colonies, and at the same time to alienate him from the French. As long as the war lasted, a black power in the Caribbean would have to be tolerated.[35] By publicising the convention and exaggerating its terms the *Gazette* wished not simply to justify the Government's volte-face but also to envenom relations between France and St Domingue. Its concern for 'the cause of humanity' was to be strictly temporary.

During the 1790s news from St Domingue had to compete with that of more successful British ventures elsewhere in the Caribbean, while the tumultuous events of the Continent and also India, as well as the British domestic situation, dominated public attention. St Domingue became known as a place of massacre and conflagration and as a graveyard of European troops but 'was noticed only as it served the purpose of the retailers of horrors'. 'Toussaint became familiar on the Parade, and St. Domingo was attacked from every coffee house.'[36] Very little was known of Toussaint's character or past at the beginning of 1802 and still less about the internal situation in the colony. 'Its affairs are almost as unknown to Europe', remarked James Stephen, 'as those of any nation in the centre of Africa.'[37] During 1801, as peace returned to the Continent, Toussaint 'first attracted the fixed attention of the world'.[38] While Napoleon Bonaparte had risen to supreme power in France, Toussaint had eliminated his remaining rivals to become ruler of all Hispaniola. Though nominally still obedient to France he now promulgated his own constitution. How was the victorious First Consul going to react, contemporaries wondered, to these ex-slaves in control of France's most valuable possession? The fighting records of both were formidable. Bonaparte gathered in the port of Brest a massive expedition which sailed in December, shortly after peace preliminaries with Britain had been concluded. Its destination was an open secret; some even assumed that the desire to re-establish control over St Domingue was France's main motive in making peace. All eyes turned to the Caribbean.

While Bonaparte's intentions were regarded with some unease in Britain, it was known that the Government had given the French prior approval for the expedition to sail. No one could be sure how much of the old régime Bonaparte hoped to restore. He might merely wish to reassert French authority in the wayward colony, and to humble its leader. The best informed, however, guessed that France's concern with the Rights of Man was at an end and that Bonaparte would attempt to restore slavery.[39] The issue was seen as one of great importance not only for the French economy, and for French seapower, but also for the future of all the European colonies in the West Indies. Three main questions exercised contemporaries' imagination: Who would win? How would the outcome affect Great Britain? And how should the Government respond? Public attitudes to these questions varied in complex ways, reflecting not so much pro- and anti-slavery sentiment, but more fundamental assessments of the nature of slavery, the character of black people and the role of morality and expediency in politics.

The first to capitalise on the upsurge of interest in St Domingue was a captain in the British Army named Marcus Rainsford, who had served many years in the West Indies including some time in one of the recently raised black corps. He had a sketchy knowledge of past events in St Domingue but having spent several weeks there in the autumn of 1798, when he had briefly met Toussaint Louverture, he rushed into print in January 1802 with a pamphlet detailing his experiences and offering his thoughts on the French expedition, then still at sea.[40] Though the slightest of all the works that would appear on the subject, it was to prove in many respects the most accurate. Rainsford had been much impressed by the sight of Toussaint's army on manoeuvres and also by the spirit of equality, unity and self-discipline that now existed in 'this extraordinary republic'. He had no doubt that the French would find it impossible to reconquer. 'Hardened into an *orderly* ferocity', 'impenetrably fortified on the finest territory on earth', the blacks, he thought, would be ultimately unbeatable. He criticised 'received opinions' that classed Toussaint as 'a fortunate Brigand' and presented the black chief instead as peace-loving, 'of great suavity of manners' and unconnected with the previous massacres. Above all, Rainsford thought the 'general alarm' for the safety of the British West Indies unfounded.[41] This point he elaborated further, when a revised and extended version of the pamphlet was published a few months later, profiting from the apparent success of his predictions.[42] Although alarmist and ignorant 'babblers' were prophesying that a black victory would lead to the 'entire annihilation' of Britain's slave colonies, and had influ-

enced 'persons of discernment', Rainsford still insisted that
the British islands need fear neither external aggression from
St Domingue nor the impact on their own slaves of the
Dominguan blacks' example. While the Dominguans, he rightly
foresaw, would want to court foreign allies and be too
occupied with domestic matters to contemplate self-aggrand-
isement, he also argued that the British West Indies were too
strongly defended and that their much maligned planters
were too 'talented' and humane for their slaves to become
vehicles for insurrection. Danger would only arise if the
Government ever decided to free them and teach them the
use of arms. It is ironic that this most sympathetic account of
St Domingue's black revolutionaries should come from a
defender of colonial slavery who blamed the St Domingue
Revolution on the 'imbecility' of well-intentioned abolitionists.[43]

Rainsford was followed into print by the abolitionist James
Stephen. His *Crisis of the Sugar Colonies* was also largely
written while the destination of the French expedition was
still in doubt, though it was delayed in the press until the end
of March. A systematic and learned piece of speculation,
displaying Stephen's powerful intellect and West Indian
experience, it established his reputation as an expert on
colonial affairs. Like Rainsford, he predicted a black victory
in St Domingue. Yet, while he stressed the advantages enjoyed
by the blacks in respect of climate and terrain, and their
numerical strength, Stephen based his case on the nature of
slavery itself and particularly on its mental dimension. Europeans, he argued, knew slavery only as a metaphor and little
understood how harsh it really was and how fiercely, therefore,
its reimposition would be resisted. More than this, however,
he thought that slave regimes rested not on force *per se* but
on the slaves' irrational fears 'fostered by ignorance and
habit'. Without this 'undefined idea of terror', akin to a belief
in ghosts, slavery's survival would be 'wholly inexplicable'.
Once dispelled, on the other hand, it was gone for ever. In St
Domingue, where the flimsy foundations of white power had
been laid bare, the edifice could never be rebuilt. A revolution
had occurred not only in the lifestyles of the blacks but also
in their ideas, and this was the strongest barrier to the re-

establishment of slavery. Even if the slaves were defeated and driven back to work, they would continue to rebel until the French abandoned the colony.[44]

In common with almost all his contemporaries, Stephen suspected that the foundation of a 'negro commonwealth' would prove fatal to the British West Indies. Although he doubted that the Dominguans' example alone would stimulate a revolution, so downtrodden and 'debased' did he think the slaves of the British colonies, it seemed inevitable that an independent black state, if only for its own security, would eventually feel moved to 'break the chains of its sable brethren'. None the less the prospect of a French victory was for Stephen far worse. Whether or not Bonaparte restored slavery in St Domingue, he was certain to move on, using black troops to overrun the British islands. With remarkable disregard for the planters Stephen argued that, in the interests of 'the British Empire at large', it was better that independent blacks destroy the sugar colonies than to allow the French to take them over intact.[45]

The British Government, therefore, had to remain strictly neutral and hope for a protracted war in St Domingue.[46] Although many Englishmen were expressing 'loud' and 'rash' approval of the French expedition, the ministry should not, as some were suggesting, assist in the venture. This would both strengthen Bonaparte's hand and earn the enmity of the blacks. In addition the Government ought to force on the British West Indies colonies ameliorative slave laws, so as to convert their slaves from 'dangerous enemies into defenders'. Otherwise the British planters would face 'revolution or foreign conquest' and it would be 'well-merited'.[47] This was the climax of Stephen's argument, though in the context of his earlier comments such measures might have seemed either unnecessary or useless. It also seems strangely inconsistent, given the obvious dangers of an open slave trade, that he thought amelioration a more effective, or more easily effected, safety-measure than abolition.

Stephen said he was concerned in the book with questions of expediency, not morality. He did state that 'justice to Toussaint' as well as prudence demanded a policy of neutrality, but he appears to have been by no means certain that the blacks' cause was morally superior to that of the French.[48] He apparently regretted that the ministry had allowed the expedition to sail, and he criticised Jamaica's 'bare-faced anulling of its recent engagements with Toussaint'.[49] However, while he appears to have approved of Toussaint's efforts in government, he had unlike Rainsford a low opinion of their success. 'Great indolence', he thought, reigned in the colony, which had become 'almost a neglected waste'.[50]

Most of Stephen's views were also echoed in the *Christian Observer*, a new evangelical monthly edited by Zachary Macaulay. The February issue in advance of news from St Domingue expressed doubts as to the probability of a French success. The effects of its climate on European troops were 'but too well known in this country', and apart from the decade of 'unbounded licence' that the slaves had just experienced, a new generation had grown up which had never known slavery. The Government, it hoped, would not intervene, as this would cause Toussaint to retaliate and so ruin the British West Indies. If left in peace, he could be expected to do all possible not to antagonise Great Britain. While not expressing actual support for the Dominguan blacks, the *Christian Observer* evinced a growing sympathy at least for Toussaint, as he became better known in England. His proclamations regarding religion and morality were cited with approval, French reports of massacres by him were discounted and evidence was adduced to belie 'the ferocity and savageness of manners' that some attributed to him. It agreed with Stephen, however, that once freed the blacks appeared to do little work.[51]

Unfortunately, it is not very clear how far public opinion shared these writers' confidence that, even against Bonaparte's best troops, the blacks would win. They tended to present their ideas as being radical and daring,[52] and initially they probably were. During the spring, when it became apparent that the French were meeting strong resistance in St Domingue, many more people must have been won over. By mid-June, we find the ebullient journalist William Cobbett, who never thought the French would have the slightest trouble in St Domingue, claiming that merely one in a hundred of the population agreed with him. While military men, he said,

were obliged to think the blacks would win, as they themselves had already failed against them through disgraceful
mismanagement, the 'Philanthropists and Puritans' 'prayed
and sighed for the negro' as 'a brother citizen of the world',
and the numerous 'democratical papers' supported Toussaint
'merely because he was . . . a rebel'. He accused pro-ministerial
papers, and the Government itself, of insincerity, claiming
that, though hoping for a French victory, they affected to
fear that the French would be defeated.[53] Cobbett obviously
exaggerated, and seems to have conflated belief in a black
victory with expectations that the struggle would be hard
fought. When he claimed that the Government really wanted
to see Bonaparte beaten in St Domingue, he failed to separate
satisfaction with seeing the French in difficulties from the
desire for a French defeat. It was a matter of a greater or
lesser evil for the ministry, and presumably most Englishmen.
But the hopes for a French victory were genuine, and whole-
hearted support for the blacks would seem to have been very
rare.[54]

'A Black State in the Western Archipelago', declared *The
Times* on 1 January, 'is utterly incompatible with the system
of all European colonisation.' A spirit of insurrection seemed
general throughout the Caribbean, and as long as Toussaint
commanded so large an army, and with such 'skill and energy',
the paper thought, the British West Indies could never be safe.
Its sense of national self-interest seems to have been reinforced
by feelings of racial or cultural solidarity with the French, for
even its favourable portrait of Toussaint, which was not
extended to blacks in general, was tinged with smug assumptions of white supremacy. On 5 April it assured its readers
that Toussaint was no ordinary uneducated slave but had
been sent to France as a child, which was quite untrue, and
had there been taught by 'some of the best masters'.[55]

Although Cobbett, as late as 20 March, was still doubting
whether Toussaint would resist the French, *The Times* had
foreseen over a year before that the black leader was going to
fight whatever forces the French would send against him. It
now predicted a long guerilla war, that would probably be
fruitless. Like the Government it favoured a French victory,
yet was still glad to see Bonaparte's troops tied up in a distant

country.[56] Although Napoleon enjoyed some popularity in Britain at this period,[57] *The Times* never advocated that Britain and France should co-operate in the Caribbean and French reports from St Domingue were invariably treated in the British press with a cynical scepticism. The position of *The Times* was thus rather ambivalent, like that of the ministry which it closely reflected. If lurking desires for revenge were present, they could be directed against both the French and the blacks. A black defeat might avenge the British catastrophe in St Domingue, but a black victory would serve to rationalise or justify it while humbling the traditional enemy. Either outcome might threaten Britain's interests, but both would assuage British feelings.

Toussaint's sudden defeat and surrender in April excited much public controversy and came as a considerable surprise to *The Times*, as to the *Christian Observer*. Both papers guessed that he must have exacted favourable terms from the French, though the former unfairly assumed that these included the enjoyment of amassed personal riches. Everyone concerned for the safety of the British West Indies would be well pleased, felt *The Times*, at the blacks' defeat: 'Europe will, of course, recover in that quarter the ascendancy and dominion which it justly claims from the superior wisdom and talents of its inhabitants, and whatever measures of kindness and benevolence may be extended to the Blacks, they will at least know, that all their physical force, however exerted, cannot succeed in a contest with experienced Generals and disciplined troops.'[58] Evidently it was not just a sectional economic interest that was felt to have been at stake, but ideas of white supremacy and Europe's right to colonise as well.

William Cobbett exuded self-satisfaction at being proved as it appeared right, and he hoped that the French would hang 'the silly, wavering, cowardly Toussaint'. Yet he was not pleased with the campaign's outcome. He was a staunch supporter of slavery and the slave trade, and virulently racist, but he was also fanatically anti-French. He still held the traditional view that the foundation of Britain's power was her West Indian colonies but, unlike the planters, he considered the French to be a much greater danger than the blacks.

In fact, he had mocked those who had feared what he ironically described as 'the Dreaded Black Empire'. Believing slavery
could easily be restored in St Domingue, he was acutely
aware of its potential value to Bonaparte. He had therefore
opposed even allowing the French expedition to sail; like the
Negrophiles (strangely enough) he had reminded the Government of its treaty with Toussaint and even remarked that his
right to rule was better than Bonaparte's. Now he foresaw the
revival of France's 'commercial and naval greatness' and the
conquest within ten years of all the British West Indies. More
dire consequences would follow. The reconquest of St Domingue, Cobbett claimed, was 'one of the most interesting and
important events that ever took place, in any part of the
world'.[59]

With the black army defeated, other Negrophobes felt free
to air their opinions. In August a Colonel Chalmers brought
out an extremely biased account of St Domingue's occupation
by the British. While attributing to Toussaint, 'this boasted
chief', numerous 'shameful' defeats, it represented the blacks
as a 'contemptible foe' 'not of a warlike cast',[60] and the whole
occupation was termed an 'important and splendid enterprise'.
Like de Charmilly, Chalmers accused Bryan Edwards of dis-
honestly exaggerating the difficulties of conquering St
Domingue and the evacuation, he claimed, had been quite
unnecessary.[61]   Already available in England was Louis
Dubroca's scurrilous *Vie de Toussaint l'Ouverture*, of which
an English translation appeared in 1803, as did a second
edition of Chalmers' *Remarks*.

Rather more remarkable, however, was a review of James
Stephen's *Crisis*, published in the opening issue of the *Edinburgh Review* at the end of 1802.[62] It marked the debut on
the slavery question of Henry Brougham, a young Scots
lawyer, seeking to make a national reputation. Also an abolitionist, and concerned no more than Stephen with expediency
rather than morality, he disagreed radically with all the main
points of *The Crisis*. What Stephen considered the slaves'
'instinctive dread' of the whites, Brougham suspected was
really only a rational appraisal of the cost of resistance, and
he thought it common to all systems of authority. Whatever
its nature, he was sure it could not be easily expunged and

that even in the French West Indies slavery would be swiftly restored. This was a rash statement as fighting had flared up again throughout St Domingue, although Brougham was right about Guadeloupe. 'The discipline and policy of the Europeans', he observed, had always overcome 'the vast numbers and ferocious strength of a savage people.' If the French failed, however, he thought all the West Indian colonies would be lost. An independent black state would probably not pose much of an external threat — Stephen had exaggerated the size of St Domingue's population — but it would excite the slaves of the other islands.

'We have the greatest sympathy', Brougham wrote, 'for the unmerited sufferings of the unhappy negroes', but the interests of the British colonists had to be considered. The blacks were the 'common enemy of civilised society', 'more terrible than Tartars or Cossacks'. To save, therefore, 'from all the horrors of negro warfare one of the fairest portions of the habitable globe', all the colonial powers should coalesce and supply France with troops or subsidies. This strange proposal found some favour in the pro-Government press at this time, and more remarkably was repeated in Brougham's major work on colonial policy published later in 1803.[63] There never seems to have been any possibility of the Government taking this advice. In the latter half of 1802 British opinion had become increasingly anti-French, as the two countries moved once again towards war. Hostilities finally broke out in May 1803 and in ministerial calculations the Dominguan blacks were reconsigned to the category of lesser evil.[64] 'Black Jacobinism' had proved itself 'inoffensive', the *Morning Post* put it less equivocally, but 'white Jacobinism' had desolated Europe and now threatened the entire Americas.[65]

British merchants, even so, were believed to have hired shipping to the French for carrying troops and stores to the West Indies, and Wilberforce suspected the ministry of acquiescing in, or encouraging, this breach of neutrality. He felt 'most strongly on the subject', he told Pitt in February, and said he would impeach anyone involved. The *Christian Observer* did not think the Government was implicated but used the same arguments as Wilberforce, though with less moderation. To assist the French, it claimed, would contravene the treaty signed with Toussaint and also break faith with those black troops abandoned in 1798, whom the British had recruited with promises of liberty.[66] With Bonaparte trying to enslave them, its editor added, Britain owed them at least neutrality if not 'some interference' on their behalf. This was two months before war was resumed. Wilberforce, always more practical, reminded Pitt that even a purely selfish policy demanded a neutrality that would allow the French and the blacks to kill one another unhindered. Pitt thought the conflict could have no satisfactory outcome but agreed that helping the French was both impolitic and abhorrent, and he hoped to legislate against the merchants concerned.[67]

While it was mainly France's activities in Europe and the East that led to the resumption of war, events in St Domingue also played a part by encouraging the Government to profit from the French Army's embarrassment and ensure, as *The Times* said, that France lost St Domingue for ever.[68] Similarly, while the changing relationship with France was probably the main factor in altering attitudes to St Domingue, there is no doubt that the seizure and imprisonment of Toussaint, the bravery of the blacks' resistance and the atrocities that the French committed all powerfully affected at least segments of British opinion and prepared it for renewing the battle with Napoleon.[69]

Even *The Times* had expressed compassion when Toussaint was hastily deported from St Domingue on charges it rightly suspected were bogus. The *Christian Observer* called it an act of 'shameful treachery'; the *Annual Register*, an 'eternal disgrace'. Always favourable to Toussaint, the *Annual Register* for 1802 described him as the major public figure of the year, and a great man. For a former admirer of Bonaparte like Samuel Coleridge, the Consul's 'truly Corsican faith to the blacks in St Domingue' seems to have contributed considerably to his disillusionment with him. Writing in the *Morning Post*, he claimed that the imprisonment of Toussaint was mainly motivated by Napoleon's 'personal envy to a hero' who was 'in true dignity of character infinitely his superior'.[70] The most moving comment, however, came from William Wordsworth. His sonnet *To Toussaint Louverture* was probably written in France in August 1802, and was published in the *Morning Post*, as war was approaching, the following February.

> Though fallen thyself, never to rise again,
> Live and take comfort. Thou has left behind
> Powers that will work for thee; air, earth and skies;
> There's not a breathing of the common wind
> That will forget thee; thou hast great allies;
> Thy friends are exultatioṇs, agonies,
> And love, and man's unconquerable mind.

The use of the St Domingue question for propaganda purposes was at its most explicit in the anonymous tract (actually by James Stephen) *Buonaparte in the West Indies*, which appeared shortly after the outbreak of war. Published in three parts at thruppence each, patriotic and vigorously democratic in tone and style, it was aimed at a working-class audience with the object of convincing it that Napoleon was its enemy not its friend. 'Every body has heard of TOUS-SAINT', the pamphlet began, 'the famous Negro General.' His military exploits were well known, and his defeat of the British, painful to recollect. His good character, however, and more recent events in St Domingue needed to be better known. 'What! Are [Bonaparte] and his ruffians to stab and drown all the poor labourers of St. Domingo because they chuse to work as men for wages, and not like horses under the driver's lash; and must Englishmen be kept in the dark about it?' 'It will be seen who are the true friends of the common people . . . . Those who hate, oppress and murder the labouring poor in one part of the world [cannot] really wish to make them free and happy in another.'[71] Of course, this was powerful anti-slavery as well as anti-French propaganda, encouraging British workers to think of West Indian slaves as 'labouring poor' like themselves. Some might argue, however, that parrying the French threat to Britain's political stability and distracting British workers with anti-slavery amounted to the same thing. William Cobbett, meanwhile, was lambasting Britain's 'negro-pampering' upper class and telling British workers to look to their own interests and not those of Africans and West Indians.[72]

Once again at war with France, the Government had few doubts about blockading St Domingue and so assisting the blacks to drive out the French and proclaim their independence. By the time Haiti came into existence, on 1 January 1804, there was general agreement in England that the new state merited friendly, though cautious, treatment.[73] 'On the very first discovered spot of the New World, has a new race of settlers avenged the wrongs of European invasion.' With more poetry than logic, *The Times* echoed the guilt-based sentiments of Bryan Edwards. With total dishonesty, moreover, it now pretended that all along it had thought a French victory would be more dangerous than a 'Black Empire'. Pointing to the Poles that Bonaparte had sent to St Domingue, it hoped that the nations of Europe would now learn a lesson in resistance 'even from the sooty African!' More than Bonaparte's humiliation, however, it seemed to relish the idea that France's revolutionary humanitarianism had grievously miscarried. The 'chimerical projects of fanaticism' of the *Amis des Noirs* had reaped their just reward.[74]

Paradoxically, under the influence of Haitian Independence *The Times* had been brought to espouse abolition, though for purely prudential reasons. It had become 'pretty obvious', the paper observed, that Edward Long's 'brutes' were 'not insensible to the blessings of freedom or to the feelings of humanity'. It was no time, therefore, to be increasing the imbalance between blacks and whites in the British West Indies. To ensure, moreover, that Haiti did not become either a military or an economic threat, it had to be prevented from replenishing its population through the slave trade. Unilateral action would be of no use; international abolition was essential, and without it revolution in the British islands was inevitable.[75] Writing early in 1802, James Stephen appears to have thought that abolition was not a political possibility. As early as March, however, Zachary Macaulay was hoping that the crisis in the West Indies would cause the Government at least temporarily to suspend the slave trade. The planters' blindness, he thought, was amazing. 'Being marked out for destruction', it seemed, 'they are themselves, through the power of a fatal delusion, made the instruments of it.'[76] Brougham, in the autumn, also referred to the British colonies as 'doomed'.

He does not appear to have thought abolition likely for some time, but he repeated the arguments that it would make insurrections less probable both by ending the inflow of resentful Africans and by compelling the planters to improve conditions. The following year he wrote of 'the most obvious demands of a menacing and awful necessity'.[77]

By 1804 the blacks' victory had brought an even greater urgency to the situation, and the election of a new Parliament, new hope. The effective destruction of the French slave trade by the war and the loss of St Domingue must also have done much to allay fears of unilateral action. In February the Lake poet Robert Southey wrote, after conversing with Thomas Clarkson, that 'the blessed success of the St Domingue negroes' gave hope that the measure could now be carried.[78] After a lapse of eight years the Abolition Committee was reformed, bringing together Stephen and Brougham. While Wilberforce tabled a new motion in the House of Commons, Brougham rushed out by way of a manifesto a *Concise Statement* of their case, stressing the 'new motives to abolition derived from the state of St. Domingo'. He still did not think that a 'commonwealth of savage Africans' posed a direct threat to the British colonies, rather that its mere existence exacerbated a thousand-fold the burdens of being a slave. To delay abolition 'for another hour', therefore, was 'worse than insanity'. The choice was between the slave trade and slavery itself. The *Edinburgh Review* fulsomely praised the pamphlet and predicted that the same arguments would also cause the Spaniards and Portuguese to abandon the trade.[79] Wilberforce's bill passed the Commons with a three to one majority and was then only withdrawn because Pitt hinted that the Cabinet would support it the following year 'as a new question, on the ground of the danger of the colonies'.[80]

The *Christian Observer* also praised Brougham's *Statement* but criticised him for his use of the word 'savage' and for referring, inadvertently it thought, to racial differences. The French, Macaulay pointed out, had just shown themselves 'infinitely more savage' than the blacks, while ideas of racial inferiority, he suggested, were now 'nearly confined' to colonial whites.[81] It was too late to talk of blacks as inferiors, exclaimed the *Edinburgh Review*. The Haitian Revolution

had shown that they loved freedom and that they were prepared to pay a high price for it: 'The instructive lesson is
there taught us, that these beings who have been spoken of
and treated as brutes, can not only feel but think; that they
can conceive extensive designs, and adopt just means for their
execution; that they can combine their efforts . . . concert
their measures with prudence and carry them into act with
vigour.' According to James Stephen, Haiti's 'sable heroes
and patriots' could hold their heads aloft. Not only free and
independent, they were victorious and powerful, and had
proved themselves 'unconquerable by the greatest powers in
the civilised world'.[82]

However, not everyone drew the same conclusions. While
The Times had had to acknowledge the slaves' humanity and
their 'force, energy and perseverance', it smugly attributed
their victory largely to the 'splendid' efforts of the Royal
Navy. The Haitian Army it described as 'a handful of half-
disciplined Blacks', incapable of 'the skilfull practice of
modern tactics'.[83] Even the *Annual Register*, which expressed
admiration at the way ex-slaves had become generals and
statesmen 'of consummate skill', thought the blacks would
have been beaten but for Britain's intervention.[84] The blacks'
cause, furthermore, received a considerable setback when
shortly after Independence the Haitians massacred most of
the French whites remaining among them. 'Ferocious bandit-
ti', commented *The Times*. William Cobbett, who had doubted
reports of French atrocities, was quite willing to believe tales
of blood-drinking massacres by blacks. 'The negroes are a
bloody-minded race', he wrote, 'they are made and marked
for servitude and subjection; it is the purpose which they
were obviously intended for.'[85] Although the *Christian
Observer* pointed to extenuating circumstances, defenders of
the slave trade made great capital out of the massacres. Negotiations for a trade treaty were temporarily broken off.[86] At
the end of the year Wilberforce complained to Stephen that
the public and even some ministers were still unaware of how
badly the Haitian blacks had been treated by the French.
Stephen's life of Toussaint had helped somewhat to enlighten
opinion, but reports were continually appearing about Dessalines' cruelties, while 'the provocations he received [were]
either unknown or forgotten'.[87]

Similarly, for Samuel Coleridge 'the Horrors of Saint Domingo' meant blacks killing whites rather than vice versa. He hated slavery and admired Toussaint, but thought the revolution a 'mournful event' which merely demonstrated the already obvious danger of giving full freedom to 'degraded savages'. He saw that slavery 'creates and perpetuates the evils by which it excuses itself', but thought the only solution to this dilemma would be a transition to a forced labour regime. 'Standing on Ground that already murmurs with the Earthquake', the West Indies, he hoped, would come to be supplanted in the imperial economy by Egypt.[88] Just how little attention and sympathy the Haitian blacks attracted from the English Romantics is rather surprising. Wordsworth's sonnet stands alone.

Robert Southey said he would like to go to the new country as a missionary, but only if he were single and French and he was neither. 'Poor wretches!' he wrote, 'I regard them as I do the hurricane and the pestilence, blind instruments of righteous retribution'.[89] While it was normal for contemporaries and particularly abolitionists to see the slave revolution as an act of divine justice, few concluded that slave revolution, or even emancipation, was desirable. All the major abolitionists felt obliged to deplore the violence of the blacks and none was yet ready to advocate emancipation in the British colonies, let alone, like Dr Johnson, drink to the next slave revolt in the Caribbean.

Rare indeed was the enthusiastic response of Samuel Whitchurch of Bath. A Congregationalist ironmonger and part-time poet, his epic *Hispaniola* was a bloodthirsty celebration of 'retribution's holy day',[90]

> Fierce burns the fire of martial strife,
> Fast flow the crimson streams of life;
> Grim horror strides across th'ensanguined plain;
> Lift, son of Ham, thy wrath-red eye,
> Behold thy prostrate enemy
> Where victory stalks o'er mountain heaps of slain!

The blacks' struggle is identified with British resistance to Napoleon, 'the Enslaver of Nations', who is haunted by the ghost of Toussaint. Their victory foreshadows his downfall and also avenges the souls of the vanished Arawak Indians. Nevertheless it is the blacks' destruction of their slavery that is the central theme of the poem, and it is presented as an act of vengeance necessary before the reign of universal peace can begin. In slaughtering without mercy, the slaves merely mimic the French. The author cites Mungo Park to show that blacks behave differently in Africa, where they are not 'goaded to madness by ill treatment'.[91]

> Proud European blame him not –
> Would'st thou act better, if, hard lot!
> Thou like the African wert bought and sold?
>
> When by the voice of freedom hail'd,
> If by the tyrant's sword assail'd
> Would'st thou not march thro' blood to liberty?

However one felt about slave emancipation, violent or otherwise, the future development of Haiti was clearly going to be something of a test-case both for colonial slavery and for ideas about race. 'The experiment of a black nation possessing European skills', noted the *Annual Register*, 'is now fairly at issue.' It was 'of the greatest general interest to Europe and to mankind', for 'if a civilised nation of blacks [could] exist in St. Domingo', the editors mused, it would enjoy much more extensive trade relations with Africa than Europe could have. This might lead, they hinted, to the eventual 'enlightenment' of Africa itself, and so compensate for all Europe's wrongs to the black race. Yet, they concluded, this was mere 'romantic speculation'.[92] *The Times*, however, entertained no such illusions. It thought Haiti's population ignorant and indolent, much depleted in numbers and likely to decline further through internecine warfare. With agriculture neglected and its army ragged, it was unlikely to trouble its neighbours for fifty or a hundred years.[93]

William Cobbett, of course, agreed. So too, however, did Henry Brougham. Although he tended to take a less disparaging view than did James Stephen of slaves in general, his opinion of the revolutionaries was low, and his view of blacks was considerably more pessimistic. All were capable of revolt, he thought, but none were yet ready for freedom. Toussaint was entirely atypical. While Brougham was sure that free labour in the West Indies would be in theory much more productive than the grudging and dilatory work of slaves, he believed that the 'negro character' would upset the laws of liberal economy. Africans had no tradition of wage labour and the legacy of slavery was indolence not industry. Haiti, therefore, was bound for economic stagnation and political anarchy. Emancipation in the British colonies could not be considered for several generations.[94]

Stephen, on the other hand, continued to stress the differences between the 'sable heroes' of Haiti and the 'dulness and stupidity' of those still in slavery. Brougham thought this absurd, but Stephen had lived in a slave society and obviously found it difficult to relate what he had witnessed there to the upheaval in St Domingue. Moreover, in this he was proved right. There was no attempt in the British West Indies to emulate St Domingue and modern historians are perplexed by this.[95] Stephen's view of the freed slave was much more positive than Brougham's, and also less realistic. Like Zachary Macaulay, Stephen had revised his earlier impressions of the economic results of Toussaint's rule and now considered them quite a respectable achievement, boding well for the future. Neither he nor Macaulay thought that slaves were slack workers and he accepted that as free men they would work less hard. However, diminished productivity, he argued, would be offset by a rapidly increasing population. Macaulay held the more orthodox, though scarcely tenable, abolitionist view that slaves were driven hard but would work even harder when free. For all their stress on the harshness of slavery, neither realised that the slave's hatred of the institution would extend to plantation work itself. Stephen was right that the 'superfecundity of unoppressed human nature' would be exemplified by Haiti's population, and this became an important plank in the anti-slavery platform.[96]

Like the British Government, Stephen wanted to see a close commercial relationship develop between Britain and the new state. Haiti was a potentially valuable market for manufactured goods and a military threat. If isolated and bullied, it would build forts instead of sugar mills and become a 'nation of soldiers'. It needed steering in a peaceful direction, and not towards France or the United States. Here

Stephen radically parted company with British opinion. To secure a commercial monopoly and ensure peaceful relations, he argued, Britain must recognise and guarantee Haiti's Independence. The black state, moreover, might then provide a model for eventually handing over power in the British West Indies to the blacks, while preserving the commercial monopoly. Slavery, he said, could not last much longer, but he did not explain why.[97]

In 1805 Marcus Rainsford brought out a full-length history of the 'Black Empire', which maintained his own rather inconsistent stance. While evincing much sympathy for the insurgents and their new state, he continued even to oppose abolition and to assert that emancipation would be cruel to the slaves. Although sure the Haitians would never attack the British colonies, or be re-enslaved, he was uncertain as to their future. They might, as Bryan Edwards had said, descend into anarchy 'without agriculture or property', or they could attain 'a state of grandeur and felicity'. 'The rise of the Haytian Empire', he asserted, 'may powerfully affect the condition of the human race' and yet, he lamented, it was regarded as a mundane matter of battles, atrocities and disease. The previous fifteen years had seen 'a great and polished nation . . . returning to the barbarism of the earliest periods' and 'a horde of negroes emancipating themselves from the vilest slavery . . . enacting laws, and commanding armies'. This merited 'serious attention', but public interest in Haiti had obviously fallen away since the high-point of mid-1802. People refuse to think, Rainsford concluded, about things that 'threaten a violation of their system, or wound a favourite prejudice'.[98]

Then as now, one might conclude, it was the sensational and superficial facts of Haitian life that impinged most on public opinion. The emergence of the new state, none the less, had attracted the 'serious attention' of many commentators. Besides causing widespread alarm for Britain's Caribbean colonies, it had powerfully affected public discussion of the character and abilities of black people and of the nature and future of West Indian slavery. It contributed to both sides of the anti-slavery debate, but its overall impact is not easily judged. Where Edwards, Cobbett and *The Times* saw regression to barbarism, James Stephen derived hope for an orderly decolonisation of the British West Indies, while the *Annual*

Register looked to the Westernisation of Africa. If the destruction of St Domingue obviously hindered the abolition campaign, in 1792 and 1804 it also boosted it, and to an extent not hitherto appreciated. Among the abolitionists, with the exception of a few fringe figures, the black rebels found apologists rather than supporters. Most avoided the question of the legitimacy of the use of violence, and none seem to have spoken out against Britain's brief but traumatic attempt to restore slavery in the colony. Thereafter however, as long as Britain and France were at war, the blacks were guaranteed a certain amount of goodwill in England, though this tended to focus on Toussaint Louverture rather than on the ex-slaves in general. During the War of Independence, attitudes towards the blacks varied in complex ways and did not necessarily reflect pro- and anti-slavery opinion. The response of the British Romantics to this struggle for personal freedom and national self-liberation was surprisingly slight. Although the blacks' resistance won them respect, prejudice persisted and, while fears for the British colonies rapidly subsided, the massacres that followed Independence further alienated British opinion.

6. The Missionary Context of the British Anti-Slavery Movement

C. DUNCAN RICE

There are some well-known points where the history of the British attack on the slave trade and the history of overseas missions intersect. It would have been surprising if they had not, for the tradition of connections between missionary activity and compassion for black people was a long-standing one. Several of the earliest polemicists, like Morgan Godwyn, were interested first in evangelisation and secondly in slavery.[1] The colony of Sierra Leone was founded as much to spread Christianity in Africa as to cut off the slave trade at its source. Both the death of missionary Smith in Demerara in 1824, and the imprisonment of missionary Knibb in Jamaica in 1832, had a major political impact on the campaign against West Indian slavery. The disastrous Niger expedition of 1841, which brought about a revolution in public attitudes to slave trade suppression, was set in motion by the combined force of commercial, abolitionist and missionary sentiment. Even after the Great Exhibition, the 'Africa fever' which smote the British public in the wake of Livingstone's discoveries was fuelled by a combination of zeal for missions and anxiety over the East African and Saharan slave trades.

These mutual reinforcements were more than coincidental. The relationship between the two movements was a genuinely symbiotic one. Their epistemological origins were similar. Both focused on problems of freedom — in the one case, freedom from temporal bondage, in the other freedom of ethical choice, what a modern commentator has called 'the original freedom'.[2] Indeed both were deeply influenced by anxiety over free will. In many respects their psychological background was similar. Ultimately, both missionary and anti-slavery sentiment had crucial roles in crystallising the values of middle-class Victorian Britain. By the latter half of the century, approval of missions and disapproval of slavery, like faith in monogamy, were shibboleths which helped the culture define the ways in which it differed from non-Western societies. Usually, but not always, the two movements mutually reinforced one another. Few Christian abolitionists, if any, were unsympathetic to missions, and few missionaries, if any, were unsympathetic to anti-slavery, at least in principle. On the other side of the coin, the missionary and anti-slavery movements were equally open to the accusation that their interest in overseas abuses was a substitute for, or even a smoke screen to divert attention from, a proper concern over distress and oppression at home.

The last point may be explored first, as a means of setting the missionary and anti-slavery movements in their context in British society. There is a vast and familiar literature on the supposed hypocrisy of the abolitionists — from the tract denouncing Wilberforce for his blindness to pressgangs and flogging, to the polemics denouncing the Duchess of Sutherland for the inconsistency between lionising Harriet Beecher Stowe and evicting her cottars.[3] Precisely those resonances which made it compelling to attack slavery overseas made it politically attractive for those working to improve labour conditions at home to use controversy with the abolitionists as a means for throwing their own concerns into relief. This was done with particular success during the course of the Ten Hours' controversy, where a landed abolitionist like Shaftesbury was unusual in taking the side of factory reformers.[4] Moderate Chartists even had some success in capturing anti-slavery meetings and using them as a platform for their own views, to the discomfiture of all but the most radical abolitionists.[5]

Overseas missions did not give the same opportunity for drawing parallels with conditions at home. The work of the missionaries, like that of the abolitionists, was exposed to the criticism that it was both misguided and a diversion from real ills at home. One argument was that it was Quixotic, and therefore perverse. One early issue of the *Edinburgh Review* was bewildered by the 'misplaced expense' and 'mistaken zeal' involved in 'preaching the most abstruse mysteries of our holy religion, to tribes of [Hottentot] savages who can scarcely count ten'.[6] Another, after demolishing a series of writings on East India missions, concluded that 'there is scarcely a parish in England or Ireland, in which the zeal and activity of any one of these Indian apostles would not have done more good, – repressed more immorality, and awakened more devotion, – than can be expected from their joint efforts in the populous regions of Asia'.[7] These themes are constants in the domestic response to missionaries. 'With some folks', noted *Punch*, 'sympathy, like Madeira, is all the better for a sea voyage.'[8] One of the most telling points about the famous 'telescopic philanthropy' chapter in *Bleak House* is not Dicken's own animus towards the Niger expedition, but the way in which he could assume his audience would accept Mrs Jellyby's squalid house as a paradigm for the disorderly society the abolitionist and missionary front were neglecting at home. Dickens was much more explicit in a less well-known critique of the Niger expedition: 'To your tents, O Israel! But see that they are your own tents! Set *them* in order; leave nothing to be done there; and outpost will convey your lesson on to outpost, until the naked armies of King Obi and King Boy are reached, and taught.'[9]

For practical purposes, to denounce abolitionists was also to denounce missionaries, and vice versa. The British anti-slavery leadership was also deeply interested in foreign missions, from the period of the Clapham Sect to the campaign against East African slavery in 1880. This was not just a matter of joint abolitionist/missionary efforts like the Sierra Leone venture, the Niger expedition, or Zachary Macaulay's less known scheme of sending a group of young Scottish-trained Christian intellectuals to form an academy in Haiti, and redeem the great social experiment from disaster.[10] Starting with Wilberforce, Venn and Thornton, the movers behind the foundation of the Church Missionary Society in 1799, each of the three generations of British leaders – for slave trade abolition, West India emancipation and universal emancipation — included active supporters of missionary work as an end in itself.[11] In 1835, for instance, the thirty committee members of the Edinburgh Emancipation Society included eleven who also served on the committee of a missionary organisation.[12] Another typical provincial leader was Ralph Wardlaw of Glasgow, the congregationalist who had a formative influence both on George Thompson, himself an enthusiast for East India missions, and on the young David Livingstone.[13] Indeed the two causes were mutually reinforcing. For one evangelical the slave trade was postponing the thousand-year reign by excluding Christianity from Africa.[14] Others saw missions in West Africa as reparation for the wrongs of the slave trade.[15]

In fact the commitment to anti-slavery or missionary societies seldom excluded an interest in reform at home. This was true of Wilberforce and his generation of evangelicals, just as it was true of Buxton and his allies in the West India emancipation, of the merchant princes who led the British and Foreign Anti-Slavery Society after 1833, and of their provincial counterparts.[16] As an extremely broad generalisation, however, the political activities of leaders in missionary and anti-slavery societies were channelled into support of measures like the First Reform Act and Corn Law Repeal, which had a demonstrable bearing on the liberties of the business interest. The whole dissenting-evangelical lobby from which missions and abolition drew their support was much less interested in providing political safeguards for the labour force. It was habitually at odds with working-class radicals, and with Tory reformers like Oastler and Cobbett. Shaftesbury was unusual in supporting the Ten Hours' movement. Although individual leaders like Elizabeth Pease of Darlington developed strong radical sympathies, the Garrisonian wing of the Glasgow Emancipation Society was going quite outside normal parameters when it formed an alliance with local Chartists. The supporters of missionary and slavery work characteristically approached the condition of the domestic labour force through evangelisation. Their master plan was to change the cultural assumptions of the unchurched poor by drawing them towards piety, respectability, self-discipline, and thus indirectly prosperity.[17] The limitation on their concern for domestic problems was that they had little interest in giving labour more political liberties, or in protecting it by legislation from the excesses of regimentation associated with factory society.

That this was equally so for supporters of both causes raises the question of the motives for spending energy on issues which were essentially foreign. David Davis has implied that for the early industrialist the onslaught on slavery had the function of reaffirming faith in a paternalistic community which the industrialists themselves were destroying at home.[18] A different form of this hypothesis may be applied to foreign missions. Baptist Noel, the fashionable evangelical preacher, could make what seemed extraordinary claims for the work of missionaries:

> They go to let loose men's imprisoned energies, and to chain up their lawless passions. They go to make property secure, and industry profitable; to secure to the rich man his palace, and to the poor man his cabin; and to spread contentment, domestic affection, and general happiness, where penury, vice, and discord make existence a curse.[19]

To strive for an orderly and pious community overseas may also have been a paradoxical but reassuring response to the problem of working-class irreligion, which was often unmanageable.[20] This attempt to impose ideal constructs outside the society in which abolitionists and missionaries lived is in line with the phenomenon an American scholar has identified in the history of asylums, which were organised along unrealistically orderly lines to provide a blueprint of the social structure the reformers were unable to impose on the unmanageable society around them.[21] In the same way, the standards of sacrifice and piety expected of converts in the field were often higher than those of parishioners at home, just as the attempt to free the slaves from regimentation was at odds with a tendency to impose a new discipline on the domestic labour force. Such plans were in one sense caricatures, in another ideal types. But they could be imposed on the distant worlds of the plantation, the asylum, or the mission field, where neither success nor failure carried any risk, and where the effort itself acted to resolve anxiety over the stresses in day-to-day society at home.

More specifically, the appeal of the missionary movement was connected with changes in the social structure of the clerical profession. The first half of the nineteenth century was a period of increasing professionalisation of the ministry. This was not a factor in the early missionary movement, which began by drawing recruits for the field from the ranks of devout artisans using missions as a means of upward mobility. The first modern missionaries, including Carey, Marshman and Ward, the Baptist pioneers in the East Indies, were self-educated — so much so that the 'chee-chee' sing-song quality of Indian English is said to be the product of their strong Welsh accents.[22] The *Edinburgh* dismissed them as 'a nest of consecrated cobblers'.[23] Many of the early CMS missionaries were actually German Lutherans, for want of available English clergymen. With the exception of the Scots, most early South African missionaries were poorly educated.[24] Even Robert Moffat, the ex-gardener, had to translate the Bible into Tswana without previous linguistic or philological training. Moffat served into the thirties and forties. By then, however, the expansion of seminary education had produced an over-supply of trained clergymen. Many of those who did not find settled parishes were absorbed into the ancillary work of the benevolent empire — as journalists, professional lecturers, or agents of benevolent societies. The relatively modest scale and varying tempo of the British anti-slavery movement prevented more than a handful from being involved in it full time — unlike the American case, where the backbone of the anti-slavery movement was the young men who had taken orders and gone into professional reform rather than being called to a congregation.[25] Even in Britain, however, the field of missions was able to absorb many of the young men coming out of ministerial training. By the fifties, even a relatively small denomination like the United Presbyterian Church, which had about 400 congregations, controlled no less than five theological colleges, which produced thirty young ministers per year.[26] In this and other denominations, overseas missions provided an important means of absorbing at least some of this surplus. Quite a number of missionaries actually were eaten by the cannibals, or perished in less spectacular ways. Whether or not missions shared abolition's role in soothing anxiety over social change at home, they outdid the anti-slavery movement in providing a supplementary career outlet for one of the new élite professions of Victorian society.

The more fundamental connection between the two movements, however, was their common religious background. Most British abolitionists saw the main impetus behind their work as a religious one. George Thompson, who was himself deeply interested in East India missions, spoke for them all when he cried that 'A war of extermination should be waged with the works of the devil, under all their manifold and delusive appearances.'[27] Missionaries saw themselves engaged in the same cosmic battle. Melville Horne, one of the early Sierra Leone evangelists, wailed that 'our adversary sleeps not . . . he makes head against the kingdom of Christ; and . . . wars on the little territory of Jesus'.[28] Baptist Noel was quite specific about the affinity between missions and other reform enterprises, including anti-slavery – the missionaries 'go to set the slave free . . . to substitute everywhere order for anarchy, law for despotism, benevolence for cruelty, and justice for oppression'. His vision for the missionaries was similar to Thompson's for the abolitionists: 'The servants of Jesus Christ go forth to subdue every form of evil . . . they go to turn men from darkness to light, and from the power of Satan to God.'[29]

In view of the religious inspiration shared by the two causes, this commonality of vision was not surprising. The anti-slavery movement drew much of its dynamism from the themes of denominationalism, post-millennialism, sanctification, redemption, and Arminianism.[30] However, the resonances of these conceptions had an impact on other reform causes. It only needs a glance at the list of benevolent organisations in any nineteenth century British city to demonstrate the strength of the denominational loyalty. It had an impact on all the evangelical reform movements, sometimes constructive, often corrosive. Post-millennial assumptions were essential to all the activities of the benevolent empire, on both sides of the Atlantic. Sanctification, too, had broader connotations.

It is impossible, for instance, to look at the lives of Wilberforce, Thornton or Shaftesbury, without being impressed by its force upon a huge range of reform commitments. As for redemption, there is no doubt that slavery carried with it a cultural and psycho-linguistic baggage which intensified the abolitionist commitment to saving the slave, but the Redeemer's central example moulded the whole Protestant reform vision, including that of the missionaries.[31] In the same way, Arminianism had no more effect on the anti-slavery reform than any other, and it had particular force for the missionary impulse. John Wesley himself had found the injunction at the heart of Arminianism: 'Brother, go out, go out and preach the Gospel to all the world.'[32]

These insights on the religious basis of anti-slavery can be applied to middle-class voluntary reform as a whole. When that is done, the particular connections between religious anxiety and abolitionist's commitment become less specific, and perhaps, in twentieth century terms, less technical. One of the reasons why anti-slavery was *primus inter pares* among the causes of the Atlantic benevolent empire was that it best combined domestic concerns with the missionary thrust that was common to them all. Missions were themselves the offspring of Arminianism and the drive to redemption, and they were deeply influenced by denominationalism, post-millennialism and sanctification. It is not surprising that the missionary and anti-slavery enterprises mutually reinforced one another, that so many British reformers supported both, or that so much of the metaphor and iconography of their literature was shared.

Few abolitionists could resist defining their work in missionary terms. Their opponents they cast as opponents to the spread of the gospel. George Thompson could ask an American audience whether it was a wonder that 'there should be darkness in your land, that there should be Popery among you, when you thus debar man of the Bible?'[33] Thirty years before, after the 1807 abolition, Thomas Clarkson had rejoiced that Africa now 'may be in a better state to comprehend and receive the sublime truths of the Christian religion'.[34] Joseph Sturge, too, could conflate emancipation and the triumph of West Indian missions: 'A few years ago, the negroes were

heathen and benighted, now they are to a great extent enlightened and Christian.'[35] For Ralph Wardlaw, emancipation was
a clarion call to missions, which would send a stream of ex-
slave converts to evangelise Africa: 'They need another
emancipation, — the emancipation proclaimed by the Gospel
Jubilee.'[36] At the same time, slavery was itself one of the
touchstones of the barbarism against which the missionaries
were fighting. As an American evangelist once remarked of
the Gabonese, 'they are an amiable people, apart from the
vices that belong to them as heathen, such as slavery, polygamy, superstition, and intemperance'.[37] Baptist Noel, in the
same way, laid great stress on slavery among the Maoris, perhaps particularly because of their willingness to use roasting
and eating their bondsmen as a punishment.[38]

Slavery and irreligion ultimately came to be interlocking
parts of the same system, and the mantle of martyrdom could
equally well be taken on in fighting either. Much of the tension created by commitment could be resolved by exposure
to violence and suffering.[39] For evangelicals, the psychological
strains created by the conversion experience were extraordinary. 'Looking back upon a blank and forward to eternity —
inward to Christian conflict and outward to a world lying in
wickedness I sometimes feel', one of them complained, 'as if
I was weary of life.'[40] To risk martyrdom, real or imagined,
was a fruitful means of releasing such tensions, and a means
without religious hazard. An American scholar had called it
'a spiritual wager: if God granted life, the missionary would
perform miracles in his service. If God willed death, He was
obliged to recognise the sacrifice by conferring salvation.'[41]
It was another version of the wager Pascal placed at the centre
of Christian commitment.

Certainly many of the British missionaries, like the Americans, found the martyrdom they courted. Some, like Williams,
'the martyr of Erromanga', were murdered by those to whom
they brought the gospel. Others died more mundanely on
shipboard, like Henry Martyn, the Anglican translator of the
Scriptures into Urdu. Others fell victim to the spectacular
ravages of tropical disease. Livingstone's demise came to
provide one of the most celebrated scenes in the Victorian
iconography of death. By the middle of the century, the

problem for missionary organisers at home was to winnow
the few qualified candidates from the droves of pious youths
eager for the field. One of the obstacles to selective recruitment was 'the idea that there was necessarily, in mission-work,
a kind of physical martyrdom'.[42] At the same time, however,
the huge literature on missions developed a tradition of hagio-
graphy for each of the main regions of activity.

No martyrdom attracted more attention than that of
missionaries who appeared also to be engaged in the fight
against slavery. Here the martyrdom conception was particularly emotive, in that it conflated abolitionist sufferings with
those of the early Christians, whose primary interest had
been in evangelisation. Harriet Martineau, the Unitarian pole-
micist, assured British reformers that the American abolitionists were 'the confessors and martyrs of our age of the world'.[43]
Yet the martyr complex, whatever its force, seldom impelled
reformers to take the extreme step of proselytising in the
southern United States. Charles Torrey, who died in jail in
1846 after being arrested for helping slaves escape, was an
unusual case – and his British admirers were still remembering
him as a martyr after the Civil War had begun.[44]

In fact British anti-slavery history had its own martyrs,
although the paradox is that they were missionaries rather
than abolitionists. In 1824 and again in 1831–2 incidents in
the West India campaign suggested a British inability to dis-
tinguish between the goals of missionaries and abolitionists,
or between the rights of missionaries and the rights of slaves.
Moravian missionaries had worked in the sugar colonies since
1732, and Episcopalian clergymen also paid some attention
to providing elementary religious instruction for slaves, most
notably through the Codrington estate in Barbados.[45] Activities among the slaves only became seriously offensive to the
planters once Baptist and Methodist missionaries appeared at
the beginning of the nineteenth century. In the face of spor-
adic planter hostility, they continued their work without
major incidents until 1824, when colonial anxieties were at a
height because of an acceleration of anti-slavery efforts at
Westminster, and a series of uprisings among the slaves. The
most important was in Demerara, where John Smith, an LMS
missionary, was thrown in jail and sentenced to death on the

assumption that he was involved in the troubles. He died of fever, and his death caused a public outcry. It became the occasion of the most flamboyant of all Henry Brougham's anti-slavery speeches.[46] From the planters' standpoint, the only advantage of Smith's death was that he could not return to Britain to broadcast his sufferings to the country.

This was not true of the 1831–2 persecutions, where the same combination of anxiety over black insurrections and increasing anti-slavery momentum at home spurred the Jamaican authorities to jail a number of dissenting missionaries. When released, they returned to Britain to influence opinion against the planters. The planters were now the foes of missions, and therefore religion, as well as being the friends of slavery. One of the exiles was Henry Whiteley. His account of his experiences, heavily embellished with stories of atrocities against the slaves, is said to have sold 200,000 copies in the first two weeks after publication.[47]

An even more effective propagandist for what was now a joint missionary and abolitionist position was William Knibb. When he arrived in Jamaica in the year of missionary Smith's death, he saw slave society as exactly the same *daar al harb* as an evangelical abolitionist: 'I have now reached the land of sin, disease, and death, where Satan reigns with awful power, and carries multitudes captives to his will.'[48] He found no reason to change his mind during the eight years of his residence in the Caribbean. At the time of the Christmas insurrection, he was imprisoned along with other Baptist and Methodist missionaries, for inciting the slaves in St James's parish to rebellion. He became much more dangerous than poor missionary Smith, since his escape on a *nolle prosequi* lost him none of the cachet of martyrdom. He was one of the great orators in the nonconformist tradition, and his tours of Britain in the year before emancipation were anti-slavery triumphs. Though his lectures were not as lurid as Whiteley's, they included much standard abolitionist propaganda on the cruelty of slavery. But the British public had been exposed to that before. The crucial theme was that he could tear the mask from the planters once and for all. They now stood exposed to the pious public as the foes of vital religion, and their system as one initiating against the spread of the Gospel.[49] The attack on slavery drew much of its force from purely secular anxiety over social structure, it was supported by simple human compassion for the suffering of black people, and it had plenty of specific religious ammunition of its own — but it is most important that the last stages of the fight for British emancipation came at a time when the abolition and missionary causes were so clearly connected.

This is not to say that all was harmony in the labours for missions and abolition. There were some circumstances in which the preaching and practice of missionaries in the field could have an impact on anti-slavery credibility at home. This only became a problem in the forties when the increasing tactical sophistication of the Garrisonians, and the anti-slavery fragmentation that accompanied it on both sides of the Atlantic, brought a heightened anxiety over absolute consistency in abolitionist behaviour. This raised two questions for missionary societies: first, whether they should receive funds from slave holders, and secondly, whether their workers in the field were obliged to make Christian practice conform to abolitionist belief. In practical terms, the issue on both counts was whether one who owned slaves might be admitted into communion. For the American abolitionists and their British supporters it was technically crucial that missionaries should maintain a simon-pure attitude to slavery, both in the South and in indigenous societies. For the missionaries, however, literal compliance with the technical orthodoxy of anti-slavery ran the risk of seriously slowing the work of conversion. If missionaries were obliged to interfere with slavery, consistency required them to make the same frontal attack on abuses like suttee or polygamy. In areas where such practices prevailed, the effect of such standpoints would be to restrict their capacity to make converts except among those already distanced from their own society. As it happened, it was very much in the tradition of the nineteenth century missions to accept converts only after they had eschewed those anti-Christian practices peculiar to their own culture, but there were some areas in which the problem of slavery presented special complications.

This was always more of a problem in America than in Britain, where the missionary organisation received no income

from slaveholders. In the United States, the controversy over
the standpoint of the congregationalist-dominated Board of
Commissioners for Foreign Missions began in 1839, when
some of its missionaries in the Pacific began to insist that it
should no longer accept money from slaveholders. A few
years later, it was also discovered that missionaries to the
Choctaws were admitting slaveholding Indian converts to
communion. The Board's refuge was the theory of 'organic
sins', which suggested in effect that missionaries had no
obligation to attack slavery – or their converts to abandon
it – if it was well established in the society that they served.
For abolitionists whose task was to persuade Americans that
slaveholding and Christian commitment were incompatible,
this example had horrifying implications. The result was the
foundation of the Union Missionary Society and its successor
the American Missionary Association, which were committed
to excluding converts from communion until they had severed
all connection with slavery.[50] This controversy was closely
followed in Britain, and it was still attracting attention in
British abolitionist periodicals in the mid-fifties.[51]

No British missionary society went through the same travail
as the ABCFM. The only comparable instant was the controversy over the missions of the United Presbyterian Church in
Old Calabar, in the Niger Delta. In 1854 William Lillie, a
United Presbyterian minister from Edinburgh, revealed that
it was accepting slaveholders into communion. Actually
slavery in Old Calabar was a cross between clientage, family
dependency and chattel slavery proper, but American and
British abolitionists rightly thought that the United Presbyterian refusal to maintain its credentials would 'weaken our
hands and obstruct our usefulness'.[52] The controversy continued in Scotland and in the abolitionist press for two or
three years, without changing the policy of the UP Church
on the Delta, or seriously breaking down the unity of the
missionary and anti-slavery public. This does not mean that
the issue was not considered important. One pamphleteer
remarked emphatically that 'organic sins are direct and literal
conspiracies against God'.[53] Unlike the American missionary
societies, however, those in Britain did not have to contend

with income from slaveholders, or converts in their own country, like the Choctaws, who kept slaves.

Organised work against slavery took up a great deal of British reform energy from the end of the eighteenth century until the American Civil War. Throughout this period, the anti-slavery and missionary movements were closely connected, supported by the same people, fuelled by comparable anxieties, and aimed at creating the same religious future. Slavery had peculiarly horrifying resonances, both in religious and social terms. But for the evangelical and dissenting groups who were the mainstay of both movements, it may not be too much to say that the attack on slavery was only one front in the world war of the missionaries. It has often been said that Wilberforce and his friends set out to revolutionise the ruling-class British culture, 'to turn "eighteenth century" gentlemen into "nineteenth century" gentlemen'.[54] The ideal of the Christian gentleman which came to dominate the late Victorian culture is the best index of their success. Whether he was in or out of public service, the positive pole of the Christian gentleman's attitude to the non-Western world was that all decent Britons abhorred slavery and supported missions for the heathen. The negative pole was his view that all sensible Britons were free to exploit the non-Western world economically, and to dominate it politically. This less attractive legacy from the years before Victoria is beyond the scope of this paper.

7. Slavery and the Development of Demographic Theory in the Age of the Industrial Revolution

B. W. HIGMAN

Of the many contrasts between the societies of Britain and her West Indian colonies, one of the most striking was their vastly different powers of population growth. Whereas the population of Britain entered a phase of unprecedented growth in the mid-eighteenth century, almost entirely the product of natural increase, the slave and free populations of the British Caribbean were sustained only by continued replenishment through immigration. After the British census of 1801, and the abolition of the Atlantic slave trade to British West Indian colonies in 1807, the contrast became increasingly obvious to contemporaries, and played an important role in the development of anti-slavery ideology. The absolute decline in the slave population laid bare the anomalous character of the West Indian socio-economic system.

This essay is concerned not so much with establishing the real causes behind these contrasting patterns of population growth, as with investigating the explanations advanced by contemporaries and the use to which they were put in the debate over slavery. It is important to remember that the modern historical demographer has access to a variety of source materials, and methods of comparative analysis derived from decades of census-taking, that were unavailable to theoreticians of the period before slave emancipation. Very often there was no real possibility of proving or disproving the validity of competing theories. Here, an attempt is made to analyse the ways in which contemporary understanding of slave population dynamics contributed to the development of demographic theory in Britain, particularly Malthus's principles of population which dominated the thought of the period. Inverting the analysis, the role of population theory in the attack on slavery and the slave trade is considered. Demographic arguments were implicit to much of the debate over abolition.

I POPULATION GROWTH IN BRITAIN AND THE WEST INDIES, 1600–1838

Before considering in detail the role of slavery in the development of demographic theory, the facts of population growth in Britain and the West Indies, so far as they are known, should be established (figure 4). In the case of Britain, it is agreed that population grew only slowly between 1600 and 1750, faltering in the 1730s, but then grew rapidly and consistently through the following century. It is difficult to be precise about the rate of population growth, since the first official census was not taken until 1801, and civil registration of births, deaths and marriages began only in 1837. Drake suggests that the population 'appears to have grown by about 0.2 per cent per annum in the first half of the eighteenth century, by 0.9 per cent per annum in the second half and by 1.4 per cent per annum in the first half of the nineteenth century'.[1] But if there is general agreement on the broad pattern of growth, there is no consensus on its causes, except that it was the product of changes in mortality and fertility levels rather than of immigration. Essentially, there are two competing hypotheses. The first attributes the sustained growth of population to the reduction of mortality levels (the 'positive checks' of Malthusian population theory) resulting from the changing incidence of epidemic disease, or advances in medical practice, or the declining frequency of subsistence crises, perhaps associated with improvements in living conditions consequent on the Industrial Revolution. The second hypothesis argues that the social changes created

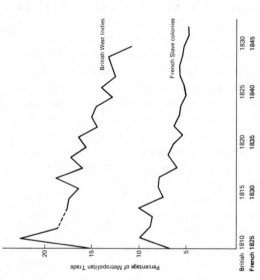

FIGURE 4   Population growth in Great Britain and the British West Indies, 1600–1840 (semi-log scale)

SOURCES: Great Britain: Phyllis Deane and W. A. Cole, *British Economic Growth, 1688–1959* Cambridge University Press, 1969) pp. 6–8; J. D. Chambers, *Population, Economy, and Society in Pre-Industrial England* (London: Oxford University Press, 1972) p. 19.
British West Indies: Richard B. Sheridan, *Sugar and Slavery* (Barbados: Caribbean University Press, 1974) p. 150; Vincent T. Harlow, *A History of Barbados, 1625–1685* (Oxford: Clarendon Press, 1926) p. 338; Lowell Joseph Ragatz, *The Fall of the Planter Class in the British Caribbean, 1763–1833* (New York: Octagon Books, 1963) p. 30; Orlando Patterson, *The Sociology of Slavery* (London: MacGibbon and Kee, 1967) pp. 95–6; T.71 (PRO, London).

by industrialisation and proletarianisation, after 1750, significantly increased fertility by reducing age at marriage and
removing restrictions on the number of children born within
marriage (the 'preventive checks').[2] The nature of the relationship between demographic and economic change remains
controversial.

For the slave societies of the British West Indies, the relationship between population growth and economic change is
equally uncertain. In the first phase of plantation development, during the second half of the seventeenth century, the
slave population multiplied five times. In the first half of the
eighteenth century the slave population doubled, and in the
second half it doubled again. In these periods the British West
Indies matched the doubling of population achieved by Britain
in the first half of the nineteenth century. But, after rapid
expansion in the years preceding the abolition of the Atlantic
slave trade in 1807, the slave population declined absolutely,
so that by emancipation in 1838 it was barely above its 1800
level. The high levels of population growth achieved in the
West Indies before 1807 were not the product of changes in
mortality or fertility levels but resulted from the maintenance
of the slave trade at a high pitch and from territorial expansion. In the seventeenth century the British colonies in the
Caribbean comprised only Barbados, the Leeward Islands,
Jamaica and the Bahamas; but by 1807 these islands accounted for only 500,000 of the 770,000 slaves living in British
West Indian colonies. The others lived in the Windward Islands,
acquired by Britain at the Peace of Paris, and in Trinidad and
Guyana, added to the empire at the end of the eighteenth
century. This long-term pattern of growth followed by
decline in the slave population was matched by very similar
trends in the white population of the British West Indies.

There is no doubt that the growth of the slave population
of the British Caribbean, as a whole, depended on the Atlantic
slave trade, or that its decline after 1807 represented an excess
of deaths over births. But the reasons for the failure of the
slave population to achieve a natural increase are not entirely
clear. There was a significant difference between colonies in
the levels of mortality and fertility they experienced.[3] The
heaviest rates of mortality occurred in the late-settled sugar-

producing colonies of Trinidad and Guyana, while the lowest rates were found in the marginal, non-plantation colonies of the Bahamas, Anguilla, Barbuda and the Grenadines. The latter colonies also achieved the highest fertility levels. Of greater significance is the fact that the slave population of Barbados achieved a natural increase by about 1807, even though the island was fully devoted to sugar culture. Curtin has argued that in the sugar colonies of the Caribbean 'demographic history tended to fall into a regular pattern over time': the ratio of slave imports to Caribbean-born slaves levelled off as the colony reached full production, and then moved gradually to a position of natural increase as distortions in the sex and age structure of the population, resulting from the demographic selectivity of the slave trade, were removed.[4]

In general, it can be argued that the ability of the British West Indian slave population to grow by natural increase was directly associated with the stage of development and prosperity of the plantation economy, with growth occurring in colonies with the least buoyant economies. A similar relationship has been suggested for short-term fluctuations. Thus, Sheridan contends that during the era of West Indian prosperity in the third quarter of the eighteenth century, 'British colonial slavery was apparently harsher . . . than it was in the subsequent period when secular decline was punctuated by wars, destructive hurricanes, and the short-lived prosperity of the 1790s'.[5] In terms of the capacity of the slave population to replace itself by natural increase, Sheridan holds that in the period of prosperity planters believed it more profitable to over-work and under-feed slaves and then purchase new ones from the slave-ships, than to encourage procreation and longevity. After about 1780, however, the masters began to apply a milder treatment to the slaves and adopted a pronatalist policy, initially because of the rise in slave prices and later because of the abolition of the slave trade. This improvement in the welfare of the slave population occurred in a period which has often been seen as characterised by declining profitability to the planter.[6]

If the nature of the relationship between economic change and population growth remains controversial, for both Britain and her West Indian colonies, in the age of the Industrial Revolution, the fundamental contrasts between the metropolitan and colonial cases remain undisputed. In Britain, the great increment to the nation's wealth consequent on the Industrial Revolution occurred at the same time as sustained population growth derived from natural increase, though the extent to which the Industrial Revolution raised or depressed the standard of living of the British working classes between 1780 and 1840 is a highly controversial issue.[7] In the British West Indies, prosperity in the plantation economy was associated with an excess of deaths over births in the slave population, and this congenital demographic crisis was overcome only in areas marginal to the plantation economy or experiencing relative economic decline. Leaving aside the essentially meaningless questions of whether the West Indian slave was better off than he would have been in Africa or had he been an English proletarian, it can be established that there was no positive correlation between growth in the plantation economy and the material welfare, particularly as indicated by demographic health, of the slaves.

II   THE NATURE OF THE DEMOGRAPHIC EVIDENCE

For contemporaries, even the basic facts of demographic change in Britain and the West Indies were open to dispute. In the second half of the eighteenth century controversy raged over the question of whether the population of Britain had increased since the Glorious Revolution, and a resolution was not reached until the publication of the results of the 1801 census.[8] As late as 1820, William Godwin could question the growth shown between the censuses of 1801 and 1811, saying that 'The difference of the two enumerations in Great Britain is not more than may fairly be accounted for from the novelty of the experiment'.[9] For this reason Godwin argued that a better index of the procreative powers of the human race could be found in ancient Rome, since 'The numbering of the citizens of Rome took place seventy-two times in a period of five hundred years', demonstrating 'perpetual fluctuations'.

As Glass said, 'a lengthy debate on the absolute growth or decline of the population of England and Wales could be maintained only because of the inadequacy of contemporary population statistics'.[10] Before the nineteenth century, most population data derived from indirect sources such as poll and window taxes, while vital statistics were available only in virtually inaccessible parish registers or the incomplete Bills of Mortality. But bills introduced to Parliament in 1753 and 1758 for the taking of censuses and the establishment of vital registration were defeated, because of the traditional fear that God's wrath would follow the numbering of the people and protestations of the invasion of personal liberty.

In the West Indies, censuses were taken quite regularly during the seventeenth and eighteenth centuries, but their frequency varied considerably from colony to colony. The most populous colony, Jamaica, took only two censuses in the eighteenth century, though five were taken in the second half of the seventeenth.[11] Thus poll tax records formed the most systematic data available on the size of the slave populations, and these suffered from under-enumeration since the smaller slaveowners were not required to pay the taxes. But the controversy over the slave population of the West Indies was not principally concerned with the question of absolute growth, or even with the question of whether it had achieved a position of natural increase. All the available data demonstrated clearly that absolute growth occurred, and masters and abolitionists were generally agreed, before 1807, that the slave population had failed to achieve natural increase. Rather the controversy had to do with the causes of that failure and whether it applied equally to the African and Caribbean-born sections of the population. To answer these questions much more sophisticated data were required than those found in the censuses or the poll tax records. West Indian ecclesiastical records largely ignored the slave population before about 1820, so that data on mortality and fertility were generally available only in plantation journals kept by individual masters and hence generally inaccessible.

The civil registration of births, deaths and marriages in Britain began in 1837. For the West Indian population at large it did not begin until the 1880s, but for the slave population a system of registration existed between 1813 and 1834 (though the dates varied from colony to colony).[12] Slave registration was intended to prevent an illicit trade in slaves following the abolition of the Atlantic trade to the British colonies in 1807. The initial returns identified each slave by name, sex, colour, age, occupation and birth-place, thus producing a more detailed census than existed for the white population. Subsequent returns listed changes in the slave population resulting from births, deaths, manumission, sale or removal, and slaves who could not then be properly identified were assumed to have been imported illicitly.

Slave registration provided a wealth of relatively reliable demographic data. But only a small part of it was actually exploited by contemporaries. Some of the colonial Registrars of Slaves carried out quite detailed analyses, and more was done at the central registry in London.[13] The data were also used for actuarial purposes. In 1832 G. G. Babington sought permission to analyse the registration returns for Grenada in order to determine the true extent and real causes of decrease in the slave population, and also 'to ascertain whether the principles of life assurance can be applied to the slave population, so that the business of an assurance office with which I am connected may with safety be extended in that direction'. To do this, he said,

it will be necessary to take an account of the slaves, as they stood in the original registry, distinguishing the age, the sex, and the country of each; and afterwards to extract from the subsequent registries, year by year, the births and deaths which have taken place among them. In this way would be ascertained the proportion of births, and also the rate of mortality at each age, with such precision that the results could not subsequently be disputed.[14]

Earlier, in 1828, a London insurance company had collected data (though not necessarily from the registries) on the length of life of predial and other slaves. It was said to offer the masters rates of insurance on the lives of their slaves which were lower than those for Europeans living in the tropics or for most Britons.[15]

If the debate over the abolition of the British slave trade took place in an essentially pre-statistical age, that over emancipation was often formulated around statistical—demographic arguments, deriving from the slave registration materials and, indirectly, from the British census results. Thus, by 1820, the abolitionists were able to use the slave registration data to show that there was no disparity of the sexes in Jamaica, which abnormality the masters had used to 'account for the decline of the black population, without admitting that it had arisen from the mal-treatment of the slaves'.[16] But the masters were not easily moved from their position, and the statistical arguments became increasingly complex. In 1823 William Burnley, a Trinidad planter, observed: 'long and bitter, consequently, has been the warfare; profound have been the essays on puberty, procreation, and the term of child-bearing; registries have been dissected; figures have been heaped upon figures . . . '.[17]

III   SLAVERY AND POPULATION THEORY

The significance of the censuses of Britain for the understanding of population dynamics, including the dynamics of slave populations, lay in the evidence they provided of consistent and rapid growth during the Industrial Revolution. They gave credence to the idea that sustained population growth, dependent solely on natural increase, was in fact 'natural'. Certainly, pre-census theorists had generally taken the view that population growth was the natural state of things, but their arguments must always have seemed less convincing in times when it remained impossible for men to agree that the population of Britain had in fact increased since the Glorious Revolution. More importantly, the alternative argument that population growth was always erratic and faltering did possess considerable validity when applied to pre-industrial Britain, and the steady growth which commenced about 1750 seems ineluctable only from a post-emancipation perspective. The spectre of depopulation retained its credibility across the English Channel.[18] For the understanding of slave population dynamics, the crucial issue for contemporaries lay in the problematic association of population growth and 'liberty'. If it could be shown that the population of Britain had in fact fallen after 1688, in spite of the political condition of liberty, then it would follow that liberty was not the sole factor determining the growth of populations. Had this been so, the slave masters of the British West Indies could have argued that the slaves' lack of liberty was not crucial to the population's failure to grow by natural increase, but that this failure stemmed from adventitious, exogenous causes, or from demographic anomalies over which they had but little control. In an important sense, therefore, it can be asserted that the resolution of the British population controversy, by the beginning of the nineteenth century, gave added cogency to the abolitionist argument, enabling it to link, in a vital and empirical way, morality and material welfare.

If pre-Malthusian population theorists were generally agreed that growth by natural increase was normal, they were divided on the question of whether slave populations were prolific or barren. David Hume, writing in 1752 on the populousness of ancient nations, believed that 'if everything else be equal, it seems natural to expect, that wherever there are most happiness and virtue and the wisest institutions, there will also be most people'.[19] Similarly, the French *intendant* Senac de Meilhan argued in 1787 that population growth was 'an effect of liberty', and therefore most rapid in republics. He, along with the *philosophes* Montesquieu, Condorcet and De Chastellux, believed that slavery had prevented rapid population growth in ancient Europe, and that in modern times it was both depopulating Africa and preventing population replacement among the slaves of the New World.[20] David Hume, who was one of those who believed that human populations had grown since ancient times, held that slaves were barren. His opponent Robert Wallace, on the other hand, thought that slave populations were very fertile and that overall population had in fact shrunk since ancient times. Each of these arguments regarding ancient slave populations found supporters among classical authors, some saying that the decline in the population of citizens was compensated for by the prolific habits of slaves and freedmen, and others that slaves were sterile and not encouraged by their masters to breed.[21] The central issue regarding the ancient slave populations was whether they had grown mainly by natural increase or whether they were dependent on imports. This issue was also central to discussions of West Indian slave population dynamics.

The controversy over the populousness of the ancient world, as represented in the writings of Hume and Wallace, was one of the sources informing the population theory of Thomas Robert Malthus (1766–1834), whose ideas dominated demographic theorising throughout the last years of British slavery. Malthus, of course, believed that population expands according to a geometric progression, unless thwarted by various positive or preventive checks or by moral restraint, whereas food production can be increased only by an arithmetical progression, resulting in constant pressure on resources. His theory was founded on natural law, rather than emphasising the role of social institutions in determining population growth. In the first edition of his *Essay on the Principle of Population*, published in 1798, Malthus argued that 'there can remain no doubt in the mind of any thinking man that the population of the principal countries of Europe . . . is much greater than ever it was in former times'.[22] He said nothing about slave population dynamics in that edition, but confronted the issue directly in the much-revised second edition of 1803, in his chapter on 'The Checks to Population among the Romans'. Malthus argued, with Hume, that the need for a continual influx of slaves was proof of slavery's 'unfavourableness to the propagation of the species in the countries where it prevails'. He developed his argument thus:

To account for the checks to population which are peculiar to a state of slavery, and which render a constant recruit of numbers necessary, we must adopt the comparison of slaves to cattle which Wallace and Hume have made; Wallace, to show that it would be the interest of masters to take care of their slaves and rear up their offsprings; and Hume, to prove that it would more frequently be the interest of the master to prevent than to encourage their breeding. If Wallace's observation had been just, it is not to be doubted that the slaves would have kept up their own numbers with ease by procreation; and as it is acknowledged that they did not do this, the truth of Hume's observation is clearly evinced. . . . It is acknowledged by Wallace that the male slaves greatly exceeded in number the females, which must necessarily be an additional obstacle to their increase. It would appear therefore that the preventive check to population must have operated with very great force among the Greek and Roman slaves; and as they were often ill treated, fed perhaps scantily, and sometimes great numbers of them confined together in close and unwholesome *ergastula*, or dungeons, it is probable that the positive checks to population from disease were also severe, and that when epidemics prevailed, they would be most destructive in this part of the society.[23]

In all of this, Malthus says not a word about modern slavery, even if the parallel was obvious to contemporaries. This apparently curious preoccupation with the ancient world was not peculiar to Malthus but shared by many population theorists of the eighteenth and early nineteenth centuries, and thus may be seen as merely one facet of the hold which classical authors had over the age.[24] What is more difficult to explain is the fact that Malthus derived his geometric principle of population growth from North American experience since European colonisation, without making any serious reference to the slave population of that region. The paradox is even more striking when it is realised that the slave population grew as rapidly as the white population throughout the eighteenth century, in strong contrast to the experience of the West Indies and of ancient Europe, a fact which must have been familiar to Malthus.[25] The demographic calculations of Benjamin Franklin and Ezra Stiles were significant influences on the development of Malthus's thought, as he himself recognised.[26] It was directly from the experience of the United States that Malthus deduced his rule 'that population, when unchecked, goes on doubling itself every twenty-five years or increases in a geometrical ratio'. He related this rule specifically to the northern states, 'where the means of subsistence have been more ample, the manners of the people more pure, and the checks to early marriages fewer than in any of the modern states of Europe'. In the 'back settlements', however, the doubling occurred in fifteen years; while in some towns deaths exceeded births.[27]

Malthus nowhere made clear any distinction between the experience of the slave and free populations of the United

States, or between the northern and southern states. In deriving his geometric ratio from the growth of the northern states he was able to ignore the role of slavery, since slaves had always constituted less than 10 per cent of the population of that region before the Revolution and by the end of the eighteenth century had virtually disappeared.[28] Thus Malthus avoided having to commit himself on the question of growth in the slave population of North America, and avoided having to reconcile his rule with his general statements on the unfavourableness of slavery to propagation.

Critics of Malthus sometimes argued that the population growth of the United States derived chiefly from immigration rather than procreation.[29] Malthus, in defending his position, did not refer to the general tendency for slave populations to depend on a continual influx. But he did discuss the implications of his theory for those areas of Africa affected by the slave trade. Although he noticed a number of factors in African society unfavourable to population increase, particularly among the slaves, Malthus's conclusion was that the slave trade had not depopulated Africa:

> The drains of its population in this way have been great and constant, particularly since their introduction into the European colonies; but perhaps, as Dr. Franklin observes, it would be difficult to find the gap that has been made by a hundred years' exportation of negroes which has blackened half America. For notwithstanding this constant emigration, the loss of numbers from incessant wars, and the checks to increase from vice and other causes, it appears that the population is continually pressing against the limits of the means of subsistence.[30]

This argument was the corollary of Malthus's contention that emigration to the Americas of whites from Britain and Spain had not depopulated those countries. And it paralleled his view that emigration could provide no more than a temporary solution to misery resulting from the pressure of people on subsistence in Britain or Ireland.[31]

Malthus was not noted for consistency, turning his arguments on or off at will. What then would be made of his

general theory, and his few direct references to slave populations, by those who sought the destruction or maintenance
of British colonial slavery? He was used by both sides. But
because the West Indian planters could not point to a natural
increase among their slaves, his theory never became the
central plank of the pro-slavery argument in the way that it
did in the *antebellum* South. For the South, it was argued
that a paternal system of slavery protected the slaves from
the positive checks to growth, and so saved them from a state
of Malthusian misery.[32] No such theoretical defence of slavery
was available to the West Indian masters. Yet demographic
arguments, combining Malthusian principles with more ancient
assumptions, were fundamental to the debate over slavery.

IV   MALTHUSIAN POPULATION THEORY AND
ABOLITIONISM

The earliest explicit applications of Malthus's principle of
population to the defence of the slave trade and slavery seem
to have occurred in William Cobbett's *Political Register* in
1805 and Robert Heron's *Letter to William Wilberforce* of
1806.[33] The argument advanced was that the removal of
slaves from Africa was beneficial because it saved the surplus
slaves from extreme misery, and because for at least a short
space of time the remaining population would enjoy comparative ease and plenty, until the gaps had been filled and
population pressed once again on the means of subsistence.
Malthus expressed astonishment that his principles should be
used thus and published a disclamatory appendix in the 1806
edition of his *Essay*, but this evaded the point.[34] The argument in fact bore a close resemblance to that applied by
Malthus to the British poor and the temporary relief that
might be achieved through emigration and colonisation.

In the parliamentary debates over the abolition of the slave
trade, the planters argued that the continuation of the trade
was essential to the maintenance of the slave population
because the climate of the West Indies was unfavourable to
natural increase. Wilberforce replied to this contention in
1804 by making a comparison with the North American slave
population, though without alluding to Malthus. He observed

that, 'in the 10 years from 1791 to 1801, the American
negroes had increased in such a proportion as to hold out a
fair prospect of doubling their number in twenty-five years'.
And,

> It being ascertained that such a rapid increase was obtained
> in America, he saw no reason to think why our West-India
> negroes might not keep up their numbers, but might posi-
> tively increase to a great degree. The climate of America
> was so far from being more favourable, that the dews and
> exhalations with which it abounded were particularly
> unfavourable to the health of the negroes, accustomed to a
> dry and hot climate.[35]

In the debates of 1807, which culminated in the Slave Trade
Abolition Act, references to Malthus became more explicit.[36]
Thus the Earl of Selkirk, challenging the climatic unfavour-
ability of the West Indies, held that 'In countries where the
means of human subsistence were proportionate to the number of inhabitants, the increase of population had always
been found progressive. This principle had been acknowledged
by all writers on the subject, and had been unanswerably
explained in the able work of Mr. Malthus upon population.'
Selkirk went on to argue that abolition would lead the planters to expect 'moderate profits' and a natural increase in their
slave population, 'whereas the thirst of immediate gain, and
the opportunity of speedily supplying a deficiency of labourers, was, under the present circumstances, a strong incentive
to overwork the negroes, and, consequently, to curtail the
population'.[37]

Malthus's views on the question of whether the slave trade
had depopulated Africa were used by the masters in the
debates of 1807. George Hibbert, representing the Society of
West India Merchants and Planters, contended that British
abolition would not create 'Utopia in Africa'. Although he
did not know Malthus's sentiments on abolition, he said,
'from what I read in his book, I gather no hopes of accomplishing a salutary revolution in the state of society in Africa by
the operation of this bill'.[38] Wilberforce replied that Malthus
had not spoken in favour of the slave trade in his *Essay*, and

reported that 'Mr Malthus had called upon him that day, and expressed his surprise to have learned, that in some publications of the day he was regarded as a favourer of the slave trade; and stated that he had written an appendix to his work, to remove that impression'. Yet a few weeks later Hibbert was able to argue with some conviction that, whatever Malthus's particular statements on abolition,

> the principle he has advanced, and the reasoning he has introduced on this subject, remain unaltered; and when he states that the population of Africa is continually passing beyond the means of its subsistence, and that the condition of the negro nations will experience no amelioration until industry and security of property be introduced among them, these circumstances appear to me to bear strongly upon this question.[39]

Although contemporaries seem not to have challenged his personal stand on abolition, it is worth noting that Malthus and his family in fact had a direct interest in the question. In 1783 Malthus's cousin Marianna Georgina Ryves married William Leigh Symes, the owner of Oxford Plantation in Jamaica. Symes died in Jamaica in 1795. Marianna then married her cousin Sydenham Malthus, the elder brother of 'Population Malthus', in 1799, her children coming into possession of Oxford Plantation. From 1815 until his death in 1821 Sydenham lived in Switzerland and Italy, giving Malthus power of attorney to manage his affairs in England, including the 'troublesome' property in Jamaica. Malthus continued to be directly involved in the management of the plantation until the death of Marianna in 1830, and the property eventually passed into the hands of the Malthus family.[40] This involvement, as much as his religious scruples, may well explain the Rev. Professor Malthus's touchiness on the subject of slavery.

Critics of Malthus objected to his view that the slave trade had not depopulated Africa, and to his tendency to see the West Indian slave population as in some way an exception to his general theory. In his 'refutation' of Malthus, published in 1818, George Ensor developed these points more fully than most. Ensor believed that Malthus's errors arose from 'his want of science; his infinite contradictions; his inhumanity; his loud abuse of the people . . . '.[41] In an effort to achieve consistency, Ensor argued that slavery always resulted in depopulation, of many sorts. It had depopulated parts of Africa, and prevented growth among masters as well as slaves in the ancient world and in the West Indies. Population could not increase where tyranny reigned, for 'liberty is the want of man'. Malthus's argument that populations kept up to the means of subsistence, regardless of tyrannical social institutions, said Ensor, was disproved by the case of West Indian slavery. In St Domingue, the population had decreased in spite of the prosperity of the plantations, but following the Revolution it grew in the face of poverty. In Suriname, the slave population declined while the Maroons increased. But Ensor, like Malthus, adroitly ignored the growth of the North American slave population which fitted his theory even less well than that of his opponent.

According to Ensor, 'Slavery weakens the arms, and bows the body, the mind, the senses; the appetites, except those which injure, are impaired by it; and it is alike destructive both of the oppressed and their oppressors'.[42] In ancient Rome, depopulation went along with slavery, a lack of moral virtue, excessive food and opulence. In the West Indies, the whites were enfeebled by their sedentary habits and so had few children, while the slaves were over-worked and ill-fed, and consequently showed more deaths than births. Ensor concluded: 'Here we have an abstract of the declension of imperial Rome in the perverted progress of a sugar-plantation. Italy had been laboured by freemen, and it was opulent in all productions; but under the culture of slaves it became sterile and effete'.[43]

In the debate over the abolition of the slave trade, the abolitionists generally contended that the slave population of the West Indies need not depend on the trade to maintain its numbers. This argument was advanced, in part to placate the planters, since it implied that abolition would not jeopardise their fortunes or lead directly to emancipation. Thus Lord Howick in 1807 could tell Parliament that 'when the causes were considered that checked the population of the West Indies, there was reason to believe that, by the regulations which the abolition would produce, nature would there, as in other countries, accomplish her own ends, and that the population would maintain itself'.[44] Slavery itself, said Howick, would disappear naturally, as it had done in Greece and Rome. In the meantime, the masters could look forward to a population growth equal to that experienced in North America, since abolition would remove the existing checks and promote the morals and comforts of the slaves.

But, with some notable exceptions, the slave populations of the British colonies were slow to provide evidence of natural growth in the years following abolition, and the abolitionists were equally unimpressed by the evidence of improvement in material welfare. In 1814 Wilberforce stated that 'The object of the friends of the abolition of the slave trade had been in the first place to stop all supplies of slaves from Africa, and then they hoped that the amelioration of the state of the slaves in the West Indies would follow as a matter of course'.[45] The fallacy that slavery was 'created and sustained' by the slave trade,[46] led the humanitarians to seek first the registration of slaves (as a means of blocking the illicit slave trade) and then in the 1820s amelioration. Only after these measures had failed to create conditions favourable to the natural growth of the slave population, did the humanitarians come to promote the abolition of the institution of slavery.

By the 1830s, the abolitionists came to realise that the failure of the West Indian slave population to show a natural increase was an index of the suffering experienced on the plantations themselves, rather than a product of the Atlantic slave trade. Even if the planters' forecast of depopulation consequent on the abolition of the slave trade had in fact proved correct, the abolitionists were able to use this tendency as proof of the slaveowners' failure to promote conditions conducive to natural growth. Thus Thomas Fowell Buxton, giving evidence in 1832 before the parliamentary committee on the state of the West Indies, could state that the decrease in the slave population was 'the best of all tests of the condition of the Negro', and that he had 'always considered it so'.[47] The second test of the slaves' physical suffering Buxton saw as 'the number of stripes which by calculation it appears must be inflicted throughout the West Indies', but he acknowledged the difficulty of making this calculation precisely. Population decline was therefore the best test, for a number of reasons, said Buxton:

> In the first place, because it cannot be liable to the imputation of any excitement of feelings; it was a purely rational argument, it was addressed only to the understanding, it was an arithmetical proposition. Again, I think it is the best of all tests, because the facts we derive from the West Indians themselves . . . : also, perhaps my opinion has been confirmed by seeing that the West Indians themselves, when they wish to establish a case of good conduct upon the part of an overseer, . . . say the population upon that given estate has increased, and that is incompatible with any severe treatment.[48]

On the last point, there is indeed evidence to support Buxton's case, though the planters of the long-settled colonies were the most willing to accept its logic. For example, a group of Barbadian planters, preparing a set of instructions for the management of plantations and slaves in 1786, argued as follows:

> If negroes are fed plentifully, worked moderately, and treated kindly, they will increase in most places; they will decrease in no place, so much as to require any considerable expense to repair the loss, in number or in value. The increase is the only test of the care with which they are treated.[49]

But planters in the newer, expanding colonies were far less willing to attribute decrease to causes which were in their power to control. Thus a Jamaican planter, after pointing out that Italy was depopulated while Rome wallowed in riches, and that the Irish were prolific in spite of lacking adequate food, shelter and raiment, concluded that 'a decrease may arise from a variety of adventitious circumstances having no relation even to the personal welfare of the individuals of a community'.[50] The decrease in the Jamaican slave population, he said, could not be attributed to slavery or sugar cultivation, but resulted from the distorted age structure created by the slave trade, the family structure of the slaves, African debauchery and manumission. Similarly, the Jamaica Assembly reacted to the proposal for slave registration, in 1815, with exasperation:

> After abusing us in detail . . . we are attacked in mass, and told, that although we have refuted the items, the general charge of cruelty and oppression must be just, because the slaves have not increased, but diminished, in number, and a different and natural order of things is not likely to take place.[51]

But, they said, there were special causes preventing a natural increase among the Jamaican slave population which did not apply in Europe: an unbalanced sex ratio, promiscuity and abortion. Thus the decrease should not be imputed to the masters' wanton and improper exercise of power over the slaves. This argument led them to doubt the applicability of any general theory to the case of the slave population. As the Trinidad planter Burnley said:

> Probably, the most difficult of all subjects, satisfactorily to treat, is the theory of population; it presents anomalies at every step; and the conclusions of the most eminent philosopher of the present day on the subject, are so little consoling to humanity, that all are disposed to doubt, though few may be able to refute them.[52]

The abolitionists, of course, were at odds with such nihilism, and accepted at least the bare bones of Malthusian theory. Thus Buxton explained that he 'entered into an examination of the population with an anxious desire to ascertain what was the real condition of the Negro, and to apply the fairest and most unexceptionable test to it', based on the following line of reasoning:

> I take it to be a maxim, as clear and certain as any maxim in political economy, that in ordinary cases population will increase; that this is the law of nature, and that this law is

confirmed by all experience. It is true that the increase
may be thwarted and prevented by certain calamities, such
as war, and pestilence, and famine, and any great convulsions; but where those do not exist, there the law of nature
is clearly for an increase, and that increase can only be
prevented by intense misery.[53]

Buxton attributed the decrease in the slave population to
'the excessive labour attendant upon sugar cultivation in a
state of slavery', especially when coupled with 'the natural
disposition to languor and idleness found to prevail among
those persons'.[54] He distinguished clearly between the positive
checks to growth, associated with Malthus's concept of
'misery', and preventive checks: 'my argument has never been
that there was not a right proportion of births; my argument
has been that there was an undue proportion of deaths'.
Indeed, Buxton did not dispute data which seemed to show
that on certain Jamaican plantations the birth rate of the
slaves was higher even than in England, since he contended
that, in Jamaica and Demerara, 'instead of having a population
likely to decrease, you have a population which ought, under
common circumstances, to increase rapidly, not only more
rapidly than it does, but greatly more rapidly than it does
in England, inasmuch as there is a greater proportion between
the marriageable ages'.[55] The preventive check, therefore,
was not crucial.

James Stephen, too, saw the 'excess of labour' associated
with sugar cultivation under slavery as the depopulating cause.
Like Buxton, he began with the proposition that 'The best
criterion of the good or bad condition of the labouring classes
in any country, may be found in the increase or decline of
their numbers'.[56] Although Stephen acknowledged that
population increase could occur alongside privation ('as I
fear is too much the case, in many parts of England at this
period'), he held that bad conditions could be inferred decis-
ively wherever absolute decline existed. Emigration, famine
and war might create exceptions to this rule, he said, 'but
from these causes of depopulation, the slaves in our sugar
colonies are pre-eminently exempt'. In spite of this relative
immunity, the decline in the predial slave population of the

West Indies exceeded 'any measure of the same calamity, that is elsewhere to be found, under ordinary circumstances, in the history of mankind'.[57]

It is perhaps surprising that the West Indian planters rarely employed the catastrophic interpretation of slave population dynamics, the view that the demographic crisis was a product of exogenous 'visitations' embodied in hurricane, famine, epidemic, volcanic eruption, or war. Generally, they accepted the position of Stephen and Buxton that the slaves were not subject to such calamities to any great extent. In part, the masters' reluctance to employ this argument arose from their desire to portray the slave system as paternal, the material welfare of the slave being fully provided by the owner. Yet it must be remembered that the demographic history of pre-industrial Britain was characterised by intermittent subsistence crises and epidemics, resulting in elevated mortality. Harvest failures, consequent on abnormal weather patterns, were common during the 'Little Ice Age' that lasted from about 1550 to 1850. Although major mortality peaks ceased to result from famine after 1750, the last great subsistence crisis of Western Europe did not occur until 1816–17, ten years after the abolition of the slave trade.[58] And the Great Famine that devastated Ireland in the decade after emancipation formed a grim reminder of the pre-industrial Malthusian pattern. Bubonic plague in its epidemic form disappeared from England by the end of the seventeenth century, but persisted in south-eastern Europe into the nineteenth century; epidemics of typhus and relapsing fever followed the British harvest failures of 1816. The first modern pandemic of Asiatic cholera swept through Europe and North America between 1826 and 1837, hitting Britain with fearful severity in 1832. But, in spite of these reminders of the cyclical demographic crises of pre-industrial society, the catastrophic interpretation of population dynamics became increasingly less credible in the face of the rapid, consistent growth shown by the censuses.

The most widespread 'subsistence crisis' to affect the West Indian slave population occurred between 1775 and 1786, a product of the American Revolution which cut off traditional sources of imported foodstuffs, and of droughts and hurricanes (which were unusually frequent in the 1780s).[59] Yet the crisis mortality ratio experienced in this period was fairly low relative to ratios associated with epidemic disease in pre-industrial Europe. After this crisis the planters shifted to a system of greater self-sufficiency, either allocating provision grounds to the slaves for the independent cultivation of food or, as in Barbados, planting food crops on plantation lands previously under cane. These alternatives to imported food supplies were vulnerable to harvest failure. But only in the isolated, salt-producing island of Anguilla is there evidence of actual starvation among the slave population in the years after the abolition of the slave trade, resulting from prolonged drought during the 1820s. In spite of this crisis, Anguilla's slave population continued to show a positive natural increase as late as 1830, and its crude death rate never approached that experienced in the sugar colonies.[60]

The important point here is that the normal mortality levels of the slave populations of the sugar colonies were consistently high and, while the abolitionists could relate this experience to persistent malnutrition, the masters could not account for it by pointing to catastrophic fluctuations in mortality attributable to erratic subsistence crises arising from external causes. Nor could the number of slave deaths directly attributable to hurricanes, earthquakes or volcanic eruptions, account for any more than an insignificant quantum of the total mortality experience. The impact of epidemic disease remains somewhat less certain, but it seems not generally to have operated at a colony-wide level, so that the effects were diffused rather than producing catastrophic mortality peaks.[61] The whites, concentrated in the towns, and particularly subject to yellow fever and malaria, probably suffered more than the slaves by epidemics. The cholera pandemic of 1826–37 did not touch the British Caribbean, thus saving the slave population from what, the experience of the 1850s was to show, would have been massive mortality.

It may be concluded, with Stephen, that the West Indian slave population's decline was not obviously a product of calamitous causes. Rather, the population was in a state of permanent crisis. To this extent, it is not after all very surprising that the masters rarely resorted to the catastrophic interpretation of population dynamics.[62] It was a theory through which they could hardly seek exoneration from blame, since they had taken charge of so many vital areas of the slave's life. The masters felt much more comfortable when they shifted the blame for the failure of the slaves to achieve a natural increase from the positive to the preventive checks to growth. In so doing they transferred the blame from themselves to the slaves.

V SLAVERY AND OVERPOPULATION

The evidence that some British West Indian slave populations did achieve quite high levels of natural increase was disquieting to both planters and abolitionists. For the abolitionists, it created a theoretical difficulty in their comparative argument. Whereas absolute population decline constituted irrefutable proof of extreme suffering and privation, it was not so easy to demonstrate that an increase was evidence of unusual hardship, rather than of improving welfare, in spite of the theoretical apparatus provided by Malthus. Thus, when they demonstrated the relative sufferings of the British West Indian slave population by reference to the rapid natural increase in the United States, the abolitionists faced problems in attributing this contrast to the slave system rather than exogenous factors. For example, after showing that the slave population of the United States was growing as rapidly as the free (proof of 'the great natural fecundity of the African race, when unsubdued by a pernicious excess of labour'), Stephen felt obliged to add: 'for that the state of slavery is, even without this destructive species of oppression, unfriendly to the multiplication of our species, cannot admit of a doubt'.[63] The latter argument fitted well enough with Malthus's statements on the ancients, but necessarily ignored the experience of slave populations in the United States, Barbados and the marginal colonies of the British Caribbean.

In 1804 Wilberforce told Parliament that the West Indian planters followed the system of the ancients, as described by Hume, depending on slave imports. Pointing to the rapid increase in the United States, he argued that the West Indian decline 'must be owing to something radically wrong in their management'. Slaves in the United States got three times as much food as those in the West Indies, and were employed on a taskwork basis, he said. But he then complicated his argument with the general statement that 'When men are happy and comfortable, they naturally increase'.[64] He told the planters that the United States slave population 'doubled in 20 years', and so long as they adopted the American system the result would be the same in the West Indies.[65] Indeed, the beneficial effects of the abolition of the slave trade would be almost boundless, said Wilberforce:

> It would make it the obvious interest of the master that the slave should be kept with as much care as possible, because his place could not be supplied; that after this, means would of course be adopted to take care of the health of every negro, and also of his moral improvement; encouragement would be given marriage, and other legitimate objects would be pursued, by which they would become populous, industrious, intelligent, moral, and happy; by which we should have a powerful, though laborious and obedient peasantry; instead of a degraded race of beings, actuated only by a brutal impulse . . . .[66]

Thus Wilberforce saw the abolition of the slave trade ameliorating the effects of both the positive and the preventive checks to population growth, creating a 'happy and comfortable' community of labourers with the potential for a very rapid increase.

For the West Indian planters by the early nineteenth century, however, the prospect of a slave population doubling its numbers every twenty years was a nightmare rather than a vision of paradise. This was so for two main reasons. In the first place, such a rate of increase constituted the Malthusian spectre in an exaggerated form. Many of the tiny island-colonies of the British Caribbean would be hard pressed to provide subsistence for so prolific a race. And the individual master, unable to sell his slaves or to manumit them because of legal hindrances, would be faced with the same problem on a small scale. Secondly, the doubling of the slave population every twenty years would mean that the whites would become an increasingly small minority, since their numbers were already dwindling. Hence the masters were faced with the possiblity of a society in which they would be heavily outnumbered and in which Malthusian misery stalked the land. Such a situation they saw as highly conducive to slave rebellion and a threat to their very lives, regardless of Wilberforce's vision of a 'laborious and obedient peasantry'.

That these fears never reached a high peak had to do chiefly with the failure of the slave population to grow at the rate predicted by Wilberforce. Not surprisingly, the threat of over-population was discussed most fully in Barbados. In 1812 a committee of the Barbados Agricultural Society reported on 'the regulation of plantations with a particular reference to the treatment of slaves', couching their observations in a somewhat garbled version of Malthusian theory:

> The power by which a population is maintained is so amaz-ing that, as has been demonstrated in an admirable treatise by Mr. Malthus of Cambridge, mankind will always increase in proportion to the means of subsistence, unless prevented by one or other of two checks termed by him the 'positive' and the 'preventive', that is either by moral restraint, or by vice and misery.[67]

After noting that the climate of Barbados was conducive to the health of the Negro, and that the island's soil was fruitful and capable of supporting a growing population, the com-mittee went on to display clearly their confusion of the 'positive' and 'preventive' checks, making the interesting observation that 'that positive check which operates with more civilised beings, the fear of lowering their condition in life, and of not being able to support a family, we know to have no operation on slaves'. On those rare estates in Barbados where a decrease did occur, said the committee, it stemmed from those 'two preventive checks, excess of labour and insufficient food'. Although reference was also made to the truly 'preventive' checks of vice and promiscuity, the com-mittee argued that 'the decrease of our slaves for the most part is owing to the maladministration of individuals in their private and public capacities', thus emphasising the paternal role of the master. So long as the slave was well fed and 'by being encouraged to realize a comfortable peculium of their own, feel themselves to have an interest at stake and a regard for home', a healthy population increase could be expected. Yet, the committee reassured the Barbados planters, 'there can be no apprehension that the population will under any circumstances increase upon us in any dangerous degree'.[68]

In the early 1820s some planters moved their slaves from the Bahamas to Trinidad, arguing that the rapid increase in the population together with the collapse of the cotton planting economy in the islands meant that they would soon be unable to feed and clothe them properly.[69] But when in 1828 a Barbadian planter sought permission to move slaves to Trinidad, on the grounds that it would benefit their welfare, the Privy Council of Barbados responded by saying that 'we cannot in candour pretend that the population has yet arrived at that degree of density which renders such removal "essential to the well being of the slaves" '.[70] (There were 500 slaves to the square mile in Barbados at that time.) The very fact that the Trinidad slave population decreased while that of Barbados increased, said the Privy Council, demonstrated that the Barbados plan of ration-feeding was preferable to the provision ground system.

By 1833, however, a Barbados newspaper was prophesying that Malthus's 'principle of population' would be verified in the island, it being 'already overpopulated'. The paper questioned the fate of nine-tenths of the population in twenty years time, when the pressure on the means of subsistence would be excessively great, and called for permission to send the surplus to the fresh, fertile soils of the United States.[71] Emancipation, removing as it did the planter's direct responsibility for the welfare of the population, created a situation in which an abundant, low-wage labour force was to the advantage of the employer, and it was not until the 1860s that the Barbados government gave any encouragement to emigration from the island, when Malthusian pressures threatened to burden the public revenue.[72] But where the plantation was not dominant, as in the marginal islands of Barbuda and Anguilla, for example, rapid population growth in the last decades of slavery was followed by heavy emigration after emancipation, activated by drought and unemployment.[73]

It is clear, then, that fears of overpopulation never concerned the West Indian masters as deeply as fears of depopulation. Overpopulation remained a nightmare. It was relegated to the remote future as a causative factor in slave rebellions. And the planter's material bankruptcy was thought much more likely to result from his inability to command sufficient numbers of slave labourers than the need to support an excess.

VI   SLAVERY AND POVERTY

It would be wrong to suggest that an appreciation of slave population dynamics played a significant role in the development of demographic theory in Britain between 1780 and 1838. Rather, there was a tendency to ignore slave populations, or to refer only to the classical examples of the ancient world. There were several reasons for this apparently paradoxical lack of interest in modern slavery. Malthus thought of slave populations as exceptional, believing that the problem of the British poor should be kept completely distinct from West Indian slavery.[74] His theory was deeply rooted in the demographic experience of pre-industrial Britain, in which slavery could be viewed as an archaic institution, of little moment for future population prospects and increasingly a 'colonial' problem. Again, the patently rapid increase of the United States slave population raised disturbing theoretical problems which Malthus sidestepped by focusing on ancient Rome, whose decline and fall, and depopulation, were obvious to all. Malthus might readily have incorporated the demographic experience of the United States slave population into his geometric principle of growth, seeing it as no more than an extension of his general rule, but he chose to ignore it because it contradicted the classical and West Indian models, and because he had no desire to be seen as a defender of slavery. Another reason for the relatively minor role given slave populations in the formulation of universal demographic theory lay in the fact that many of the assumptions applied to population growth in industrialising Britain also informed discussion of slave population trends. These ideas included the beliefs that the poor were everywhere prolific while the idle rich were not, and that the husbandman was more fertile and healthy than the townsman.[75] Since West Indian slaves were obviously poor, and husbandmen, their failure to replicate the growth shown by their counterparts in Britain and Ireland made them aberrant.

If the demographic experience of West Indian slaves was little more than a disturbing element in Malthus's theory of population, there is no doubt that demographic theorising, generally grounded in Malthusian principles, played a significant part in the debate over slavery and the slave trade. It has been the burden of this essay to illustrate the ways in which general theories were used to explain the variable patterns of increase and decrease displayed by West Indian slave societies. Modern historians are not agreed on the real causes of these patterns, but the comparative study of slavery continues to have a strong demographic focus, and the factors referred to by abolitionists and masters during the early nineteenth century debate continue to be emphasised. Although the positive (mortality-increasing) checks associated with the heavy labour demands of sugar cultivation and poor nutrition seem to explain variations within the British Caribbean, and the contrast between Britain and her colonies, recent research suggests that preventive (fertility-depressing) checks may have been central to the contrast between the West Indies and North America, particularly differences in marriage and family patterns, child-spacing intervals, and lactation practices.[76] Malthus tended to see the operation of the positive and preventive checks as mutually exclusive, but it seems likely that they in fact worked together in the British West Indian slave population. In comparing West Indian slaves and the British poor, however, Stephen and Buxton were certainly correct in emphasising their different mortality experience.

Early nineteenth century discussions of social welfare policy affecting the British poor often made reference to West Indian slavery. As David Brion Davis argues, there are striking 'parallels between the rise of anti-slavery and a profound transformation in attitudes toward the English poor, a transformation that reflected the growing contradiction between paternalistic traditions of local charity and the demands of a free-market economy'.[77] Yet the comparative references were frequently only symbolic (the slave bearing the most degraded and despised status in society), or emphasised the moral and material state of West Indian slaves, rather than differences in population dynamics.[78] The main reason for this focus, of course, was the great gulf which separated the demographic experience of Britons and West Indian slaves. If population growth was the best test of the condition of the labouring classes, as Stephen asserted, then there could be no doubt that the British poor were better off than the West Indian slave population.

Malthusian population theory broke the alliance, which had existed in the early stages of the Industrial Revolution, between art, science and political economy, imbued by a common humanism.[79] Thereafter, there were in Britain two competing models of social policy. The first, advanced by the political economists and rooted in the concept of natural law, held that sound social policies must adhere to universal, long-term principles, even if they might seem to create immediate suffering. The second model, that of the humanitarians, argued that men should act to relieve human suffering wherever they saw it. But the amalgam of humanism, utilitarianism and *laissez-faire* economics which pervaded anti-slavery ideology meant that the tension between these alternative models was at a minimum in the debate over slavery. Malthus's harsh view on the British poor (that 'they are themselves the principal authors of their own poverty, and the means of redress are in their own hands alone') was not extended to West Indian slaves, even though the poor had no more power to choose their parents than did slaves.[80] The Poor Law Amendment Act of August 1834, a product of Malthusian population theory, sought to establish a self-regulating population reacting only to natural laws, just as the Slave Emancipation Act of August 1834 sought to permit natural population growth by establishing freedom.[81] Indeed, abolitionist thought sometimes made a direct connection between slavery and the Old Poor Law, since the abolition of both would make hunger the principal spur to labour, and create the possibility of a new moral economy.[82] In freedom, the West Indian population would be free to press against the means of subsistence, free to bargain for wages and rents, free to inherit the poverty of their parents.

8. Abolitionist Perceptions of Society after Slavery[*]

DAVID ELTIS

While the point might be argued for the eighteenth century, there can be no doubt that in the nineteenth British influence over the West Indian colonies was considerably greater than that of the West Indies over Britain. The abolition of first the slave trade, then slavery itself, and finally the sugar duties were only three events which shaped colonial development. Yet we should not allow this to obscure the fact that the slave colonies had important effects on the British perception of their own society. Reversing the traditional direction of examination of nineteenth century cause and effect makes it possible to gain new insights into the attitude of mind which resulted in abolition. It also allows us to highlight some of the contradictions inherent in the world view of the metropolitan propertied class of the early nineteenth century — contradictions which eventually brought about changes in that world view.

Emancipation in both Britain and the United States may be viewed as one society successfully imposing its view of morality, justice and social relations on another. Since the mid-1970s interpretations of British abolition have tended to emphasise the ideological shift which made slavery, for centuries an integral part of European-based economic systems, appear as unjust, immoral and unprofitable.[1] Wilberforce

* The author wishes to thank Stanley L. Engerman for valuable suggestions both before and after his reading of an earlier version of this essay. The remaining errors are of course the author's own.

commented in 1823 that 'it is unquestionably true that the path of prosperity rarely diverges long and widely from that of integrity and virtue'[2] and anti-slavery literature, letters and speeches are replete with similar comments usually emphasising the inefficiency of slavery. In short the religious and intellectual origins of the anti-slavery belief evolved together with the conviction in the economic superiority of free over slave labour. Thus, if in the anti-slavery view abolition of both the slave trade and slavery could only improve the welfare of Britain and colonies, then the old debate on whether abolition resulted from motives of economic interest or humanitarianism appears less relevant.

Three facets of British anti-slavery are particularly striking down to the 1830s. First was the universality and homogeneity of the anti-slavery viewpoint in early nineteenth century Britain. In comparison to its United States counterpart the movement appears almost monolithic. Although there were relatively few active abolitionists, the conviction that slavery was anomalous was widespread:[3] the West Indians found almost no defenders outside those who had a stake in the slave system. Even Cobbett, bitterly critical of Wilberforce as he was reluctantly supported abolition during his brief sojourn in Parliament.[4] Within the movement, moreover, there were no significant ideological divisions. Inconsistencies are apparent in the works of, say, Cropper and Hodgson as well as between the early and later writings of James Stephen; there was also the well-known disagreement on tactics which resulted in the Agency Committee operations. But on fundamentals there was unanimity; even the transition to immediacy occurred without serious discordance.[5] Sir James Mackintosh, Stephen Lushington and Henry Brougham might see slavery primarily as the most basic infringement of human rights; Joseph Butterworth, Zachary Macaulay and the host of missionaries examined by the parliamentary select committees of the 1830s could see abolition as a confirmation of their evangelicalism; Harriet Martineau might write of the inefficiencies of slavery in her popular tracts on political economy; but none of these positions were mutually exclusive. For most activists, particularly men like William Allen, James Cropper and Buxton himself, emphasis on one of these elements at the expense of the others produces at best a partial insight into their anti-slavery beliefs.

The second striking facet is the utter certainty and self-confidence of the mental attitude which generated the anti-slavery impulse. When Melbourne grumbled on his way out of a cabinet meeting that he wished he was as certain about anything as Thomas Babington Macaulay was about everything, one feels that it was Melbourne rather than Macaulay who was the exception. From the abolitionist homilies on how to run a plantation in the slave trade debates of the 1790s[6] to Richard Madden explaining in a personal interview with an astounded President Jackson that he should seize the opportunity of supreme office and proclaim emancipation,[7] one perceives the sort of absence of self-questioning which is a normal prerequisite of a group bent on changing the structure of other people's societies. That the abolitionist position was often at odds with the empirical evidence serves only to strengthen our appreciation of that certainty. For example, given the record of institutionalised Christianity it is hard to grasp at first sight how anyone at the beginning of the nineteenth century could serenely affirm that slavery was incompatible with Christianity.[8] Yet few of the spiritually aware in Britain thought otherwise. Similarly the abolitionist economic critique of slavery which concluded that the planters were behaving irrationally was surely inconsistent with the *laissez-faire* emphasis on self-interest which the abolitionists fully accepted. Indeed in the early nineteenth century colonial context it is the anti-slavery group who appear as irrational, and the planters who emerge as the true economic men.[9] Even James Stephen, who understood the West Indian economic system better perhaps than anyone else, was unable to reject totally the conviction in the superiority of free over slave labour for Caribbean plantations.[10]

The third and perhaps most remarkable facet of the British movement are the parallels apparent in the approach of its supporters to colonial problems on the one hand and domestic tensions on the other. Many have stressed the dichotomy in abolitionist attitudes to domestic workers and colonial slaves. Coupland entitled his chapter on Wilberforce's behaviour towards manifestations of British social upheavals 'The

Shadow', though it is not clear whether this refers to the
threat of revolution hanging over Britain or to Wilberforce's
inhumane and illiberal response to this threat.[11] The radical
press, such as the *Black Dwarf*, the *Political Register* and the
Republican, certainly emphasised these differences and
claimed that the slavery issue was designed to divert attention
from tensions between classes in Britain – an interpretation
which some have discerned in a recent major work.[12] There
were, as we shall see, some nice distinctions in the abolitionists' approach to colonial and metropolitan societies, but
essentially the anti-slavery group presented the same solution
to the two situations. At home the move to a freer labour
market had been combined with an increasing emphasis on
labour incentives and productivity, an emphasis which con-
trasted strongly with the coercive overtones of an earlier
mercantilist era.[13] But recognition that increased rewards
induced increased quantities of labour did not preclude the
coercion of idlers who refused to respond appropriately. The
slaves, we should note, became apprentices the same year
that the New Poor Law was passed. An understanding of this
point will emerge from the answers to two questions: what
kind of society did the abolitionists expect to see in place of
slavery, and how did they react when the expected outcome
did not occur?

As we might expect from the above comments a long-term
decline in sugar output was not part of the anti-slavery scenario. As immediate abolition became more likely and discussions of anticipated consequences less theoretical, abolitionist
leaders were prepared to countenance a temporary drop in
production as employers and labourers adapted to their new
roles.[14] But that a system based on free labour should be less
productive than one based on slave labour was inconceivable,
and the Wesleyan missionary who believed 'that it is very possible there might be a state of society in Jamaica far happier,
and the exports fewer than they are now'[15] was very much
the exception. Perhaps the key difference between metropolitan and the larger colonial societies was the availability of
unsettled land in the latter. The abolitionists had long been
aware of this, indeed they were instrumental in putting the
most recently acquired Caribbean territories beyond the

reach of the slaveholders in 1797 and 1805. There was some questioning of the slave's desire to work on the estates after liberation and the possibility was admitted that smaller production units, perhaps even smallholdings, would emerge, but all were expected to produce for the market and in particular the export market.[16] None doubted that in one way or another the ex-slave should be pressured into such work if necessary.

Behind this attitude there lay not so much a dedication to maximising GNP or profits *per se* as a conviction that the alternative production mode of self-sufficiency could only be antithetical to civilised society. After their trip to the West Indies Joseph Sturge and Thomas Harvey wrote:

Few will be prepared to dispute the advantages which the division of labour and combination of labour under the direction of capital and skill, offer in comparison with that simple condition of society, in which each individual supplies all his various wants with his own hands. It is therefore desirable that the cultivation of the great staples of the colonies should go on with uninterrupted success.[17]

Such sentiments echoed a Colonial Office memo written when that avowedly abolitionist institution was casting around for an emancipation plan:

A state of things in which the negro escaped the necessity for such labour would be as bad for him as for his former owner. He would be cut off in his mountain hut from civilizing influences, would have no incentive to better his condition or to impose any but the slightest discipline on himself. Thus he might well become a more degraded being than his ancestors in Africa.[18]

It is not surprising that though the Baptist missionaries devoted much of their resources to the establishment of free villages after the ending of apprenticeship, they ensured that the individual lots were small and the villagers themselves within easy reach of the plantations. The villages were perceived as 'reservoirs of labour enabling them [the planters] to employ many or few hands according to their actual wants'[19] as much as devices for protecting the workers against low wages. And even where waste lands were scarce as in Barbados, some anti-slavery supporters argued, the effect of slavery on the work ethic was such that coercion, or at least education, would be necessary to ensure as many potential workers as possible would respond appropriately in the post-abolition labour market.[20] In short, although in the final year of the campaign the demand for immediate abolition was often linked and even merged with a demand for unconditional abolition, few of the abolitionist leaders were prepared to support the latter.

For the abolitionist spokesmen at this time, who were of course drawn exclusively from the propertied classes, emancipation meant above all equality before the law. The possession of property rights, the right to give evidence in court, to select employers, freedom from arbitrary punishment and all the other normal privileges of freemen stemmed from this central concept. The major issues in all but the last two years of the abolition campaign were not directly about slavery but about outrages perpetrated in West Indian law courts, usually against missionaries, which would not have been possible if the principle of equality had been recognised. Perhaps the main imperial initiative towards the West Indies in the 1820s was the commissioning of a comprehensive study of colonial law and legal practices and the most substantial and sophisticated abolitionist publication of the period was an examination of West Indian slave codes liberally sprinkled with metropolitan comparisons.[21] This principle of equality was explicitly elevated above the satisfaction of basic material wants. Lord Nugent was loudly cheered when he told a Buckinghamshire anti-slavery meeting that the English peasant had 'enjoyments few, comforts few, hardships many and difficult to endure, but rights . . . which may look the proudest oppressor in the face'.[22] On the eve of abolition Charles Stuart wrote that

> the misery of the slave is . . . that he depends for all his present comforts, and future hopes on earth upon . . . the life of a fellow sinner. The happiness of the free labourer is not that he has abundance, for he is often in want – but

that he is dependent mainly upon God and his own exertion.[23]

Such a conception allowed abundant room for ensuring that if the ex-slave was to have the rights of the English labourer he was also to work like the English labourer. To maintain 'due subordination on the plantations without invading the right of individuals'[24] one could always rely on the fear of want which would replace the dread of the lash or as the *Anti-Slavery Reporter* put it, the 'promotion of industrious habits by their only effectual spring, a sense of self interest',[25] but even in England experience had shown that this was not always enough. Abolitionists usually expected that colonial societies would follow one of two broad routes after emancipation. The first, which may be traced to Brougham's model,[26] involved an evolution to the English system with the landlord, yeoman farmer renting land of varying acreages, and labourer replacing the plantation system. Sugar mills would be set up by capitalists as in the East Indies or after the pattern of saw mills of North America, but a much wider range of produce would be grown for export. An infinite gradation of classes would replace the rigid two-class structure and presumably the white supervisors would no longer be able to claim 'there may be living hundreds at your very door and you do not know what they feel or what they are going to do'.[27]

The second, more favoured by the anti-slavery leaders, looked essentially for a continuation of the plantation system. Supporting evidence was culled from the experience of St Domingue under Toussaint Louverture, the Barbados experiment carried out by Joshua Steele of paying wages to the slaves, and more fancifully the labour background of industrial Britain. The approach received its clearest exposition in Buxton's evidence before the House of Lords committee of 1832. Starting from the general proposition that 'it may be extremely necessary for the state to introduce laws for protecting persons from living in idleness to the detriment of the state',[28] he argued first, that all those without visible means of support should be required to enter an estate labour contract; secondly, that occupation of the provision grounds be conditional on working on the estates. For the latter Buxton drew the rather inappropriate parallel of his brewery workers occupying company houses. Thirdly, he argued that a strong police force and an independent magistracy should enforce contracts and eliminate vagrancy. Offences were to be penalised with imprisonment and corporal punishment. As evidence Buxton offered a version of the Haitian Code Rurale not much different from that which had been approvingly published and examined in the *Anti-Slavery Reporter* a few years earlier.

These two proposals or expected outcomes were not of course mutually exclusive: the first was more suited to areas where unused land was scarce and the second to the relatively undeveloped parts of the British Caribbean. Moreover there was a suggestion that the first would eventually replace the second even in Trinidad and Demerara. While both plans anticipated a rapid population rise and increased use of labour-saving machines after emancipation, both incorporated vagrancy laws which were more or less Draconian. It is remarkable that all the pro-abolition witnesses examined by the parliamentary select committees of 1832 wanted large police forces with broad powers created before emancipation. While this suggests a view of labour more appropriate to the early mercantilist period than to an industrialising society, one should note that in Brougham's analysis the colonies would develop like Europe from villeinage to freedom, only at an accelerated pace, and that a 'mercantilist' intermediate stage was to be expected. Both plans also allowed for smallholdings which were proposed even for those areas where provision grounds had not been customary during slavery. The function of these, however, was seen first, as giving the labourer a stake in society; secondly, as already noted, to permit easier adjustment to the plantations' seasonal demand for labour; and thirdly, to allow employers to take advantage of the slave's well-known attachment to his plot of land: occupation of the latter, all agreed, should be made conditional on the ex-slave working for the planter.[29] Finally, and somewhat paradoxically, almost all the abolitionists exaggerated the malleability of the labourer's character. It was, of course, an article of faith that slave culture was degenerate and that the slave system was utterly destructive of initiative. However, Clarkson's conclusion after a survey of post-slave societies of the early nineteenth century that the 'negroes yielded themselves to the will of their superiors so as to be brought by them with . . . ease and certainty into the form intended for them'[30] still appears sanguine. The response of the ex-slave meant that severe police measures were to be a temporary feature of post-emancipation society, at least where the missionary influence was strong.

It is perhaps too easy to see the shadow of contemporary British labour issues in the discussions. Indeed in many cases one feels that the subject was explored more frankly precisely because it concerned a society somewhat removed from the British milieu. Some urged the planter to use the free labourer because unlike the slave he could be laid off at no cost to his employer when not required, a somewhat dubious argument for a humanitarian to make.[31] Others, especially missionaries, urged the creation or rather continuance of a labour aristocracy which would influence the rest of the labour force.[32] This could be combined with the right touch of condescension. A special magistrate devoted several pages of his diary to a planter who asked to use the snuff box of the head boiler on a visit to the boiling house. This he argued was 'one of the legitimate arts of drawing the heart of a poor man towards his master' and one of the hallmarks of trouble free labour—employer relationships in a civilised society.[33]

Abolitionists thus had little doubt that the British experience was relevant for a West Indian society. Yet there was nevertheless a definite awareness of the potential conflict between on the one hand development strategies aimed at producing a marketable surplus and the resulting benefits of 'civilization', and on the other the actual development pattern of newly settled areas with self-sufficient production predominating. The *laissez-faire* approach and the full application of the associated principle of equality before the law would probably have resolved the issue in favour of self-sufficiency, as the Wakefieldians were beginning to point out at this time in a different context. In England such policies could be used precisely because of the absence of waste lands and the fact that the labouring population were demanding goods and services which could only be obtained in the market place. For the West Indies there was some doubt on both these issues and two persistent themes in the questioning by the 1832 select committees as well as in anti-slavery literature were first, whether the ex-slaves would leave the estates and secondly, the level of effective demand for goods and services to be expected from a freed Negro population.[34] The emancipation plans and associated legislation proposed by abolitionists and British government alike constituted an attempt to recreate in the West Indies conditions which would ensure that the English development strategy would succeed.[35] That they came perilously close to violating the first principles of *laissez-faire* is indicative of the priorities of the strategists. Modernisation, the latter expected, would in the end provide a happy, prosperous, deferential, church-going labouring population. If this also suggests the perpetuation of inequality of condition, the expectation that the free labour market would create a community of interest in place of the adversary system of slavery, and a reduction in the more obvious class barriers, then that also is a reflection of the contemporary attitudes of the British propertied class.

The major post-emancipation trends in the West Indian colonies are now well-known though it should be noted that thanks to some high quality contemporary works there was no shortage of information at the time.[36] In common with most societies which have undergone emancipation, the British West Indies experienced a decline in the labour force participation rate, a drop in labour productivity, and of course a shift from production for export to production for home consumption which resulted in a sharp decrease in the former. In the years immediately after the ending of apprenticeship females withdrew from the labour force and by the mid-1840s, at least in the colonies where unoccupied lands existed, labourers of both sexes were leaving the estates in increasing numbers.[37] The productivity trend is less well-established, unlike that for post-emancipation America, but for Jamaica and British Guiana seems solid enough. Of the output figures there can be no doubt. Exports of plantation produce rose only in Barbados and some of the smaller islands. Sharp declines were apparent in British Guiana, Trinidad and Jamaica, with recovery occurring only because of massive inflows of indentured labour or in the case of Jamaica only after the lapse of a century. For the British West Indies as a whole average annual sugar output went from 204,000 tons in 1830—4 to 126,500 in 1840—4.[38] The development of extensive internal markets for locally grown and consumed produce would suggest that self-sufficiency was never as widespread as some abolitionists might have expected given the large export declines, but this was nevertheless not the kind of market society which they associated with civilisation.[39]

The planter response to this was immediate, as we might expect from a group whose predictions of the consequences of abolition prior to 1833 were reasonably accurate. Even before the termination of apprenticeship a mass of legislation and ordinances from the different colonies had descended on the Colonial Office for approval. They covered master and servant relationships, combinations amongst labourers, ejections from provision grounds, trespassing, vagrancy, policing, immigration (and, for Barbados, emigration), land sales and taxation of foodstuffs. The Jamaican House of Assembly demanded a 'rural code' modelled on the Haitian experience. At the local level many planters made provision grounds and houses available rent free on the basis that to accept rent would imply a right of occupancy independent of the tenant working on the plantation. The proposals and practices varied with conditions and planter needs and the diversity of the British West Indies constantly imperils generalisations, but the common intent was to secure a plantation labour supply. Jamaican planters who had spent their lives in hostility towards wage labour of any kind suddenly became enthusiastic supporters of derivations of Wakefield's theories.[40]

The abolitionists fought for the ex-slaves' rights against the planter after abolition,[41] but nevertheless the parallel between what the planters proposed after emancipation and what the abolitionists prescribed before is obvious. It should not surprise us, however, when we remember that though motives differed somewhat planter, abolitionist and metropolitan Government all had commitments to increasing or at least maintaining pre-abolition levels of exportable output. The opposition of the British Government and the anti-slavery group to most of the planters' proposals occurred because most of the latter came down on the wrong side of the fine line the abolitionists drew between attempts to re-establish slavery on the one hand and to guarantee a continuous supply of estate labour on the other. Nevertheless one feels that some proposals might have been acceptable if they had come from groups with anti-slavery credentials. During the 1830s abolitionists other than missionaries visited the West Indies in increasing numbers, and perhaps first-hand knowledge of the situation, not a major foundation of earlier abolitionist positions, generated a more moderate stance on the coercion issue. The abolitionist perception of apprenticeship which saw the latter not as coercion so much as continuation of slavery may have pointed in the same direction. In any event after 1839 the Colonial Office did not gain abolitionist support for allowing a number of West Indian measures, the total effect of which was to put labour under a much greater degree of coercion than existed in contemporary Britain.[42]

The initial anti-slavery post-apprenticeship response was that the system, within the framework of these measures it should be noted, was working reasonably well. Almost all believed that the planter was trying to sabotage the operation of the free labour market, an approach incidentally which recent research has tended to support. John Scoble, William Knibb, John Candler and others demanded that the provision grounds be rented separate from any involvement by the worker in estate labour – in direct contradiction of the typical abolitionist position before emancipation.[43] Wages were also felt to be below market equilibrium rates. Such behaviour, however, could be attributed to attitudes carried over from slavery and would disappear when the planter realised the advantages which could be derived from such a market. The ex-slave also had to adjust and even the special magistrates on the spot expected that the smallholder would leave the estate only long enough to establish his plot of land before returning to supply the labour the planter wanted.[44] Declines in output in the early years had been a part of the abolitionist prognosis, and the severity of the decline in Jamaica after 1838 could be assigned to the special circumstances of drought years in 1839 and 1840. West Indian sugar output had always varied widely from one year to the next.

It was the continuation of the decline and the emergence of the sugar duty issue which put unbearable strains on the anti-slavery movement. Indeed perhaps the significant fact is not that the abolitionists continued to oppose the planter after 1833 despite having similar goals, but that by the later 1840s much of that opposition had evaporated. The Government, the planter and, as we shall see, a significant section of the abolitionists were prepared to countenance a range of measures which coerced West Indian labour as well as to tolerate the entry into the British market of slave-grown foreign sugar from Brazil and Cuba. The divisions amongst the humanitarians in the 1840s have been well charted though less well for Britain than for the USA. The most radical British group with close connections with the American Garrisonians had a strongly individualist middle-class work ethic which was an integral part of anti-slavery beliefs of the pre-1833 period. But after 1833 the logic of the position was pursued: personal liberty meant political and religious liberty as well as an emphasis on the universal brotherhood of man. A commitment to the free market was not only consistent with the elimination of exploitation and misery but would itself lead to it. Freedom for the slave should be matched by universal suffrage and the ballot both at home and in the colonies. 'Why are not the abolitionists of Great Britain Chartists, Repealers and ultra Democrats', wrote the Garrisonian E. M. Davis. For his correspondent Elizabeth Pease, who equated Toryism with the 'slaveocratic spirit', there was no reason.[45] While the group was always in the minority it had significant support in the provinces and could claim George Thompson amongst its ranks.

From the standpoint of this, the most doctrinaire wing of the anti-slavery movement, the implication of the abolitionist free labour position from Ramsay down to Cropper and beyond was not only that free should be allowed to compete with slave labour but that this in itself would be enough to vanquish the latter. Free labour production in India was expected to replace the plantations of the Americas and even in the 1840s it was still possible to argue that the southern cotton planter needed to be shown that he would benefit directly from replacing his slaves with free labourers.[46] The British Government's efforts to reduce the duty on foreign sugar, which also happened to be slave grown, were thus to be supported rather than opposed. The tariff

> by encouraging an unremunerative produce will leave the black to the mercy of his employer . . . [it] enriches bitterest enemies, forces capital out of its natural channels and depresses labour below the level it would find in the development of its inherent resources . . . . It is the slave's question in the same sense as the corn-law is the labourer's question.[47]

If the West Indies could not compete then its resources would shift to other crops or, in the case of labour and capital, move out of the region altogether. Indeed by 1848 George Thompson was proclaiming that the West India interest was doomed.[48]

A vote for abolition of the sugar duties was not so much putting free trade principles above humanitarianism as C. Duncan Rice implies,[49] but rather an affirmation, albeit rather blinkered, of one of the central tenets of abolitionism. Thompson supporters moreover did not object to British Government plans to allow the immigration of indentured labour into Trinidad and Guiana, although Thompson himself had reservations. But British attempts to suppress the slave trade could be viewed as wrong because it was not possible to abolish so lucrative a trade until the market itself was removed through abolition of slavery: attempts to fight the symptom thus resulted only in increased mortality, a position shared by the London Committee itself.

When results of such *laissez-faire* policies failed to meet expectations then the adjustment argument could always be relied on as a last resort. As Earl Grey pointed out in a not untypical example of government assertion of ends over means, equalisation of the sugar duties was a 'great advantage to the *permanent* welfare of these colonies'.[50] Yet the major impression from reading the correspondence of this group and comparing the minutes of say the Garrisonian Bristol and

Clifton Ladies' Anti-Slavery Society.[51] with the mainstream British and Foreign society is that West Indian issues were not major concerns. '[T]here is nothing anti-slavery in it', said J. B. Estlin, writing of the latter's campaign on behalf of the ex-slave. 'I wish the British and Foreign Anti-Slavery Society would concentrate their energies more upon American slavery until the negroes there are as well off as those in the W. Indies.'[52] Perhaps the ideological limitations which prevented the American Garrisonians from co-operating with the Irish in the United States campaign also prevented their British counterparts from taking effective or indeed any action on behalf of the West Indian freedman.[53] But such a position implied no abandonment of the goal of production for the export market and reaping the accompanying benefits of a humane and civilised society. On the contrary, free trade, immigration and a free labour market were the surest ways of reaching that goal and the level of marketable output, which in practice means sugar exports, continued to be an acid test into the 1850s.[54] There was considerable irony in Wendell Phillips's claim, which at one level is indisputable, that Garrison and his cohorts undertook

> to forget interest and remember only justice . . . [they] undertook to look at the slave question as the negro looked at it. Clarkson, Wilberforce, Lushington and Buxton looked at the slave question for thirty years as the white man looks at it. They piled Blue Books mountain high to show that Bristol and Liverpool would not suffer in trade, that sugar would be as cheap and rum would be as plentiful after emancipation as before. They proved that the white man could *afford* to be just . . . .[55]

The main body of British abolitionists did not follow this route and their concern with the plight of the ex-slave has been amply documented.[56] Yet their position on the future of the West Indies was not radically different. Some missionaries in Jamaica excluded, they were not opposed in principle to immigration but merely to the lack of safeguards. The opposition of the British and Foreign Anti-Slavery Society to equalisation of the sugar duties, designed of course to keep

West Indian marketable output as high as possible, was not conceived as permanent. It would last only so long as slavery existed in Cuba and Brazil or until the British West Indies had recovered from the special circumstances which were preventing the assertion of the natural superiority of free over slave labour. These included the baneful influence of slavery carried over into post-emancipation society, absentee ownership, capital shortages, the lack of a hard-working middle class and many more.[57] Yet the short-term could not be extended indefinitely and while Charles Buxton's 1860 book provides a marvellous restatement of this 'infant industry' argument the humanitarian defence of West Indian developments did become quite muted. In 1866 the British and Foreign Society were warning Jamaicans to be 'honest, industrial and peaceful lest they lose the sympathy of the English public'.[58]

One line of argument more plausible than most stressed the impact of the continuing transatlantic slave trade in lowering the costs of Cuban and Brazilian sugar producers. The slave trade was branded as inhuman and therefore no more to be included in the usual economic calculus than say murder or theft. Suppress the slave trade, it was argued, and the superior efficiency of the free labour British West Indies would become immediately apparent.[59] Two trends supported this reasoning. First, much of the exodus of labour from the estates came in the second half of the 1840s when the influx of 'slave trade' sugar attendant on equalisation of the sugar duties was beginning to lower wages.[60] It was thus not completely clear whether the ex-slave was giving priority to his aversion to plantation labour or whether, like any market-oriented individual, he was simply offering a lower quantity of labour in response to a lower price. Secondly, despite Cuban competition 'free labour' Trinidad and British Guiana successfully maintained their share of the British sugar market throughout the second half of the century, this despite the fact that these were the colonies with the most waste lands available for smallholding activities. Such a position, however, conveniently ignored the question of how free was indentured labour in Trinidad and British Guiana as well as the fact that the original abolitionist critique held that free labour could out produce even slave-trade supported slave labour.

The mainstream abolitionist vision was simply inappropriate for a post-emancipation society. Such a vision incorporated the Herman Merivale axiom that the free labourer should be 'by a law of nature dependent on capitalists'. It was the nature of the 'artificial means' which Merivale thought should be used, if necessary, to ensure this state of affairs which caused dissension, perhaps because few, with the exception of Stephen, picked up the critical Merivale qualification that 'slave labour is dearer than free wherever abundance of free labour can be procured'.[61] By the 1840s and 1850s the abolitionists had largely abandoned the coercionist views of Clarkson, Thomas Fowell Buxton and the earlier generation: the ex-slave was expected to be treated the same as the English worker.[62] Unfortunately, giving the West Indian the same rights as the latter produced an outcome quite different from that in England: measurable output would tend to fall, not rise, as the labourer exercised his right to abandon the estate.[63] Many, from missionary to colonial governor, urged a reduction in the average size of the sugar producing unit to something closer to the acreage of the English mixed farm, as well as the introduction of alternatives to sugar, and while both trends occurred nothing could put a stop to the dramatic drop in aggregate sugar exports. Measures which might have allowed the abolitionists to reach their goals by a different route such as, say, massive state education, state-assisted development strategies[64] or even the imposition of full political equality, were no more possible for the West Indies than they were for contemporary Britain. But while in terms of measured output this mattered little for the stage contemporary Britain had reached, for the West Indies the long-term implications were altogether more serious. The ideology which generated anti-slavery also prevented effective abolitionist and indeed imperial intervention after abolition.

There were, of course, compensations for the abolitionists but these simply added to their dilemma. Even the most doctrinaire had to concede that while things were not as they should be, the general welfare of the black population had improved substantially. The 1842 select committee on the West Indies acknowledged the improved condition, morals and 'the rapid advance in civilization' of the black population:

'. . . unhappily there has occurred simultaneously with this amendment . . . a very great diminution in the staple production of the West Indies'.[65] Though this, it should be noted, was before the depressed sugar prices of the later 1840s. The committee then went on to explore ways to augment the prosperity of both planter and labouring population more in line with abolitionist thinking before 1833. But the message of these years was clear. Improvement in terms which the abolitionist could recognise was possible without increasing or maintaining staple output, and description of these improvements became of course one of the main themes of the abolitionist defence of British emancipation. Indeed, the smallholding option began to receive appreciative notices once more from some quarters, though it was assumed that the peasant would produce a marketable surplus.[66] In any event the ex-slave had ensured the end of the abolitionist's strident certainty and of course shattered the unity of the abolitionist movement.

Two tentative conclusions on larger issues emerge. Perhaps the conviction that other countries, with a modicum of assistance, would follow the British ideal and move the world into 'the millenium of peace, brotherhood, and free trade'[67] received its first check not in the East or in Africa, but in one of the oldest parts of the imperial domain. Certainly this was the first British experience of other races failing to react in the expected manner to what both sides in the transaction saw as an act of benevolence. It clearly did nothing to inhibit the development of a respectable intellectual base to racism[68] or the move to expand the formal empire in the second half of the century. Secondly, the history of anti-slavery after 1833 throws light on the elusive connection between abolition and industrialisation. What the abolitionists did in addition to what they did not do after emancipation suggests that anti-slavery was simply a facet of the predominating view of social relations, property and morality which emerged with the industrialisation process. The '*laissez-faire*, individualistic and localistic definition of freedom' which Ronald Walters argues was the common denominator amongst American abolitionists[69] was also the common bond of their British counterparts by the 1840s. This in itself does not explain why some who accepted this world view became active abolitionists while others did not, but it does offer a more promising approach to the link between the two phenomena than that achieved by an earlier generation of economic determinists. For the British movement, as for the American, we now need to ask not only what was unique about abolitionists but also what it was about them that was bourgeois and early Victorian.[70]

Notes and References

LIST OF ABBREVIATIONS

BL	British Library
BM	British Museum
CO	Colonial Office
EcHR	*Economic History Review*
EHR	*English Historical Review*
HJ	*Historical Journal*
HO	Home Office
PD	*Parliamentary Debates*
PP	*Parliamentary Papers*
PRO	Public Records Office

Note: the place of publication is London unless otherwise stated.

INTRODUCTION *James Walvin*

1. See for instance, D. B. Davis, *The Problem of Slavery in the Age of Revolution, 1770–1823* (Ithaca, 1975); Winthrop Jordan, *White Over Black: American Attitudes Towards the Negro, 1550–1812* (Chapel Hill, 1968).

2. R. R. Palmer, *The Age of the Democratic Revolution*, 2 vols (Princeton, 1969 edn).

3. M. Craton, *Sinews of Empire. A Short History of British Slavery* (London and New York, 1974) ch. 1.

4. See in particular the debate in Christine Bolt and Seymour Drescher (eds) *Anti-Slavery, Religion and Reform* (Folkstone and Hamden, 1980).

5. For the details of the slave trade see P. D. Curtin, *The Atlantic Slave Trade. A Census* (Madison, Wisconsin, 1969) and H. S. Klein, *The Middle Passage* (Princeton, 1978).

6. David Eltis and James Walvin (eds), *The Abolition of the Atlantic Slave Trade* (Madison: University of Wisconsin Press, 1981).

7. Franklin Knight, *The Caribbean. The Genesis of a Fragmented Nationalism* (Oxford, 1978) ch. 5.

8. James Walvin, *Black and White. The Negro and English Society, 1555–1945* (1973) ch. 3.

9. R. S. Dunn, *Sugar and Slaves* (1972) ch. 7.

10. On Granville Sharp see Walvin, *Black and White*, ch. 7.

11. Ibid., ch. 9.

12. Roger Anstey, *The Atlantic Slave Trade and British Abolition, 1760–1810* (1975) chs 4–5.

13. Albert Goodwin, *The Friends of Liberty* (1979).

14. Add. MS. 27, 811, fo. 9.

15. M. D. Conway, *The Life of Thomas Paine*, 2 vols (New York, 1892), vol. II, pp. 417–18.

16. Douglas Hall, *A Brief History of the West India Committee* (Barbados, 1971).

17. James Walvin, 'The Public campaign in England against slavery, 1787–1834', in David Eltis and James Walvin (eds) *The Abolition of the Atlantic Slave Trade* (Madison Wisconsin, 1981).

18. F. O. Shyllon, *Black Slaves in Britain* (1974).

19. Thomas Clarkson, *The History of the Rise, Progress and Accomplishment of the Abolition of the African Slave-Trade by the British Parliament*, 2 vols (1808) vol. I.

20. Anstey, *Atlantic Slave Trade*, pp. 264–6.

21. See the essay by Seymour Drescher in this volume.

22. Paul Edwards (ed.), *Equiano's Travels* (1977 edn).

23. M. Craton, *Testing the Chains, Slave Rebellions in the British West Indies 1629–1832* (Ithaca, forthcoming).

24. David Geggus, *The British Occupation of Haiti* (University of York, D. Phil., 1979).

25. See the essay by David Geggus in this volume.

26. Seymour Drescher, *Econocide. British Slavery in the Era of Abolition* (Pittsburgh, 1977).

27. Barry Higman, *Slave Population and Economy in Jamaica, 1807–1834*, (Cambridge, 1976); Michael Craton, *Searching for the Invisible Man* (Cambridge, Mass., 1978).

28. See the essay by Michael Craton in this volume.

29. Ibid.

30. A. D. Gilbert, *Religion and Society in Industrial England* (1976).

31. On Eric Williams and his critics see D. Eltis and S. Engerman, 'Economic Aspects of the Abolition Debate', in Christine Bolt and Seymour Drescher (eds) *Anti-Slavery*, pp. 272–93.

32. Roger Anstey, 'Religion and British Slave Emancipation', in David Eltis and James Walvin (eds), *Abolition*.

33. See the author's essay below.

34. P. Knight, *Knibb 'the Notorious', Slaves' Missionary, 1803–1845* (1973) p. 112.

35. Quoted in M. Craton, J. Walvin and D. Wright, *Slavery, Abolition and Emancipation* (1976) p. 343.

1. PUBLIC OPINION AND THE DESTRUCTION OF BRITISH
COLONIAL SLAVERY *Seymour Drescher*

The research for this essay was undertaken during a Guggenheim Fellowship in 1977–8. I wish to express my gratitude to the Rockefeller Foundation's Bellagio Study and Conference Centre, for the residency, during the summer of 1980, in which this essay was written and to James Walvin for his helpful editorial suggestions.

1. See *inter alia*: Thomas Clarkson, *History of the Rise, Progress and Accomplishment of the Abolition of the African Slave-trade by the British Parliament*, 2 vols (1808); David Brion Davis, *The Problem of Slavery in Western Culture* (Ithaca, 1966) and *The Problem of Slavery in the Age of Revolution, 1770–1823* (Ithaca, 1975). For recent trends see Roger Anstey's 'The Historical Debate on the Abolition of the British Slave Trade', in R. Anstey and P. E. H. Hair (eds) *Liverpool, the African Slave Trade, and Abolition* (Liverpool, 1976) pp. 157–66.

2. S. Drescher, 'Capitalism and the Decline of Slavery: The British case in Comparative Perspective' in Vera Rubin and Arthur Tuden (eds), *Comparative Perspectives on Slavery in New World Plantation Societies*, of the *Annals of the New York Academy of Sciences*, CCXCII (1977) 132–42.

3. Roger Anstey, *The Atlantic Slave Trade and British Abolition 1760–1810* (Atlantic Highlands, NJ, 1975). Five very rough draft chapters to Anstey's sequel to the above volume were completed before his untimely death. Although they are too incomplete for separate publication, they are the product of extensive research and contain important insights on a broad variety of themes relating to anti-slavery between 1823 and 1833. I will refer to them as Anstey, 'Emancipation' (MS.).

4. James Walvin, 'The Rise of British Popular Sentiment for Abolition, 1787–1832', in Christine Bolt and Seymour Drescher (eds), *Anti-Slavery, Religion and Reform* (Folkestone and Hamden, 1980) pp. 149–62; Walvin, 'The Impact of Slavery in British Radical Politics: 1787–1838', in Rubin and Tuden (eds), *Comparative Perspectives*, pp. 343–55; Howard Temperley, 'Anti-Slavery', in Patricia Hollis (ed.), *Pressure from Without in Early Victorian England* (1974) pp. 27–51; E. M. Hunt, 'The North of England Agitation for the Abolition of the

slave trade, 1780–1800' (University of Manchester, MA thesis, 1959).

5. For the early period to 1807 see Anstey, *Atlantic Slave Trade*; for the period from then to emancipation see P. F. Dixon, 'The Politics of Emancipation: the Movement for the Abolition of Slavery in the British West Indies, 1807–1833' (Oxford, D. Phil., 1970); for the post-emancipation era see H. Temperley, *British Antislavery 1833–1870* (1972).

6. S. Drescher, 'Two Variants of Anti-slavery: Religious Organization and Social Mobilization in Britain and France, 1780–1870', in Bolt and Drescher (eds) *Anti-Slavery*, pp. 43–63.

7. Temperley, *British Antislavery*, Epilogue.

8. *The Record*, 14 Oct 1830.

9. Dixon, 'Politics of Emancipation', p. 213; Anstey 'Emancipation', ch. 5.

10. Temperley, *British Antislavery*, esp. chs 7 and 8.

11. See, for example, the *Manchester Times*, 4 May 1833.

12. On the difficulties of organising a national petition, see the account of the reform petition of 1793 in Albert Goodwin, *The Friends of Liberty: The English Democratic Movement in the Age of the French Revolution* (Cambridge, Mass., 1979) pp. 279–80.

13. John A. Phillips, 'The Political Nation, Political Awareness, and Popular Participation in Late Eighteenth Century England' in MSS., kindly provided by the author.

14. See E. P. Thompson, *The Making of the English Working Class* (1968); Gwyn A. Williams, *Artisans and Sansculottes* (1969).

15. On the Catholic emancipation petitions, see G. I. T. Machin, *The Catholic Question in English Politics 1820 to 1830* (Oxford, 1964) pp. 144–9.

16. The adult male population over fifteen for each country was estimated using figures from B. R. Mitchell and P. Deane, *Abstract of British Historical Statistics* (Cambridge, 1962) p. 11, and B. R. Mitchell, *European Historical Statistics* (New York, 1975) pp. 20, 24, 35, 52 and 53.

17. See Drescher, 'Two Variants', p. 52.

18. See Peter Fraser, 'Public Petitioning and Parliament before 1832', *History*, XLVI (1961) 195–211.

19. From an estimate compiled from *PD* (1829).

20. I have checked campaign speeches in *The Times*, and checked more closely from newspapers in the industrial North, including Manchester, Salford, Preston, Leeds, Bolton, Sheffield, Halifax, Blackburn, Carlisle, Whitehaven, Liverpool, Bradford, Stamford, Nottingham, Birmingham and Leicester.

21. *Leeds Intelligencer*, 24 Jan 1833; The *Christian Advocate* 29 Dec 1832.

22. Stephen, *Anti-Slavery Recollections*, letter XI.

23. *Manchester Courier*, 15 Dec 1832.

24. *The Tourist*, 19 Dec 1832.

25. On political symbolism and the control of discourse see Seymour Drescher, David Sabean and Allan Sharlin (eds), *Political Symbolism in Modern Europe*, Introduction (forthcoming).

26. Stephen, *Antislavery Recollections*, letters X and XI.

27. *Liverpool Courier*, 5 Sept 1832; *Manchester and Salford Advertiser* 18 Aug 1832.

28. *Sheffield Iris*, 29 Jan 1833; *Manchester and Salford Advertiser*, 18 Aug 1832.

29. *Manchester Courier*, 29 Sept 1832; *Manchester and Salford Advertiser*, 9 July 1833.

30. Stephen, *Antislavery Recollections*, p. 196.

31. 27 Apr 1833.

32. 18 Aug 1832.

33. *The Baptist Magazine*, Jan 1833, p. 3.

34. Edith F. Hurwitz, *Politics and the Public Conscience: Slave Emancipation and the Abolitionist Movement in Britain* (1973) p. 44. Roger Anstey's *Atlantic Slave Trade* emphasises the primacy of the evangelical impulse in the launching of abolitionism although he allows for a conjuncture of interests and idealism in accounting for at least one abolitionist victory, the termination of the British foreign slave trade in 1806: ibid., ch. 8.

35. Drescher, 'Two Variants', pp. 45–9.

36. Stephen, *Antislavery Recollections*, p. 160.

37. Donald G. Mathews, 'Religion and Slavery: the Case of the South', in Bolt and Drescher (eds), *Anti-slavery*, pp. 207–32.

38. See the historical squibb on anti-slavery in the *Sheffield Iris*, 29 Jan 1833. Anstey refers to the growing role of the Methodists in anti-slavery in the 1820s in his 'Emancipation', ch. 1, p. 6, and at greater length in the very incomplete second chapter: 'The Methodist Paradox and Slavery Emancipation'.

39. Dixon, 'Politics of Emancipation', p. 118.

40. See *Minutes of the Methodist Conferences, 1825–1837*, esp. VI, pp. 51, 514–15; VII, pp. 67, 175; *The Baptist Magazine*, XXII (1830), 343, 480–4, 524; (1833) pp. 10–12, 226–9; *The Record*, 14 Oct 1830.

41. Hurwitz, *Politics and the Public Conscience*, p. 44.

42. Drescher, 'Two Variants', p. 47. *The Record*, 1 Nov 1830, claimed 6000 petitions from the Methodists alone.

43. Drescher, 'Two Variants', pp. 54–7.

44. G. M. Ditchfield, 'Repeal, Abolition and Reform: A Study in

the Interaction of Reforming Movements in the Parliament of 1790—6', in Bolt and Drescher (eds) *Anti-slavery*, pp. 101—18.

45. The chief religious petition issues in the 1830s were: the admission of dissenters to the universities, sabbath enforcement, and the abolition of church-rates.

46. 9 Mar 1833.

47. *The Record*, 10, 16, 23 and 27 Jan and 4 July 1833.

48. See *inter alia*: Hurwitz, *Politics and the Public Conscience*, pp. 48, 79 and 81 (although there is a later statement that all strata supported emancipation, p. 83); D. B. Davis, *Problem of Slavery*, vol. II, pp. 357, 361—5, 385, 421 and 450; Dixon, 'Politics of Emancipation', pp. 208—11; Williams, *Capitalism and Slavery*, p. 181; Patricia Hollis, 'Anti-slavery and British working-class radicalism', in Bolt and Drescher (eds), *Anti-Slavery*, pp. 294—313. Howard Temperley, following E. M. Hunt, emphasises the fact that the constituency of popular abolitionism in the early period at least 'drew its support from a broad range of social classes'; see his 'Anti-Slavery' in Hollis (ed.), *Pressure from Without*, p. 33.

49. Stephen, *Antislavery Recollections*, pp. 158—9.

50. Vol. I, no. 1, 17 Sept 1832.

51. See n. 4 above.

52. Hollis, 'Anti-slavery and British working-class radicalism', pp. 294—302.

53. Drescher, 'Two Variants', pp. 48 and 58, Tables II and III.

54. *Manchester Guardian*, 8 Sept 1832.

55. Dixon, 'Politics of Emancipation', p. 230 and note.

56. *Manchester Courier*, 16 Dec 1832.

57. On Blackburn see Hollis, 'Anti-Slavery and British working-class Radicalism', p. 302. On the motivation of the Leicester abolitionists, see the *Leicester Herald*, 10 Apr 1833. On the Birmingham Political Union's petition see the *Birmingham Journal*, 20 Apr 1833. At a Nottingham rally the *Nottingham Review* (7 Dec 1832) observed 'a more complete admixture of classes' than it had witnessed for sometime.

58. *The Times*, 1 June 1826.

59. *Preston Chronicle*, 15 Dec 1832.

60. *Manchester Times*, 22 June 1833.

61. On French working-class petitioning see Augustin Cochin, *The Results of Emancipation*, tr. M. L. Booth (Boston, 1863) p. 73; and Drescher, 'Two Variants', pp. 57 and 63n. On the English tradition in American working-class abolitionism in the 1830s, see John B. Jentz, 'Artisans, Evangelicals, and the City: A Social History of the Labor and Abolitionist Movements in Jacksonian New York', (City University

of New York, Ph.D., 1977) pp. 208 and 217. See also Eric Foner, 'Abolitionism and the Labor Movement in Antebellum America', in Bolt and Drescher (eds) *Anti-slavery*, pp. 254–71.

62. For example, Reginald Coupland, *The British Anti-slavery Movement* (1935, 1966) p. 111; E. M. Howse, *Saints in Politics: The Clapham Sect and the Growth of Freedom* (London, 1953) ch. 8, esp. p. 179; Anstey, *Atlantic Slave Trade*, pt 4. On Anstey's general model of the limited scope of the popular phase, see 'The Pattern of British Abolitionism in the eighteenth and nineteenth centuries' in Bolt and Drescher (eds), *Anti-slavery*, pp. 19–42.

63. G. I. T. Machin, *The Catholic Question in English Politics* (Oxford, 1964), pp. 144–8.

64. Figure 1 and Roger Anstey, 'Emancipation', draft ch. 3, 'Reform and Anti-Slavery, 1830–32', 4th and 5th pages.

65. John Cannon, *Parliamentary Reform, 1640–1832* (Cambridge, 1973) p. 214 n; J. T. Ward, *Chartism* (1973), pp. 113–17.

66. Diplomatic note of Castlereagh to the Spanish Ambassador, in Chester New, *The Life of Henry Brougham to 1830* (Oxford, 1961) p. 138.

67. C. L. R. James, *The Black Jacobins*; Augustin Cochin, *L'Abolition de l'esclavage* 2 vols (Paris, 1961) vol. I, ch. 1.

68. For the decline thesis in general, see S. Drescher, *Econocide*, ch. 1; for the period after 1815 see W. L. Burn, *Emancipation and Apprenticeship in the British West Indies* (1937, rpt 1970) pp. 51–2 and 73.

69. *PD*, 3rd ser., XVII (1833) cols 1193–4. The West Indians were able to muster well over 1800 signatures against Stanley's plan, and 'no city meeting was ever more numerously attended, or more zealously watched, than the assemblage of the West Indian body', in responding to the plan (*The Times*, 28 May 1833).

70. See Stanley Engerman, 'Some Considerations Relating to Property Rights in Man', *Journal of Economic History*, XXXIII (March 1973) 43–64.

71. It was with the West Indians, not with the abolitionists, that continuous negotiations took place once it was determined that an emancipation bill would be introduced. See *CO* 318/116 and *Grey Papers*, 3rd Earl, Box 147, item 53, printed minutes of proceedings between Government and West Indians 16 Jan–2 May 1833, cited in Anstey's 'Emancipation', ch. 5, n. 55.

72. In France, the cost of compensation was the principal barrier to emancipation during the July Monarchy. See S. Drescher (ed.), *Tocqueville and Beaumont on Social Reform* (New York, 1968) p. 172.

73. On the eve of their emancipation the number of French colonial slaves was estimated at 250,000, of British at over 770,000.

74. Report of a committee on slavery, named on 26 Mar 1840, and presided over by the duc de Broglie, who wrote the report.

75. The productivity per capita in Britain and France was estimated from J. Marczewski, *Introduction a l'histoire quantitative* (Geneva, 1965) pp. 134 and 135.

76. See Adolphe Gueroult, *De la Question coloniale en 1842. Les colonies francaises et le sucre de betterave* (Paris, 1842).

77. *PD*, new series, IX (15 May 1823) cols 257−360. The West Indian estates themselves were described as unsaleable by 1831: *Report of the Select Committee on the Commercial State of the West Indies* (evidence), question nos. 69, 282, 752, 848 and 989 (*PP* 1831−2, XX). The Committee report itself emphasised abolitionist initiatives as a principal, if irremediable, cause of West Indian distress (pp. 5−6 of the *Report*).

78. B. W. Higman argues convincingly that the Jamaican slave revolt was an unforseen consequence of the abolition of the British slave trade in 1807 in his *Slave Population and Economy in Jamaica, 1807−1834* (Cambridge, 1976) pp. 231−2.

79. Dixon ('Politics of Emancipation', p. 203) characterises the revolts as setbacks to abolition, except as failures. One must, however, separate the impact of a long-term series of pressures from individual events. Anstey, ('Emancipation', 3rd ch., 21st p.) also remarks in passing on the negative impact of the Jamaica uprising itself until the results of the repression began to be known. Other accounts treat the uprising itself as more central, the 'decisive factor' in the abolition process. See W. A. Green, *British Slave Emancipation: The Sugar Colonies and the Great Experiment 1830−1865* (Oxford, 1976) p. 112.

80. Francis Jeffrey, 10 Oct 1831, quoted in Cannon, *Parliamentary Reform*, p. 245.

81. *The Baptist Magazine for 1823*, XV, 283.

82. Dixon ('Politics of Emancipation', p. 341) concludes, 'and it was indeed the strength of opinion that ended slavery'.

83. Ibid., pp. 341−2. The abolitionists were themselves frequently astonished at the explosions of popular excitement during the anti-slavery campaigns. See Z. Macaulay to Lord Brougham, 13 May 1833, Private, Brougham, MSS. 10544 reprinted (but, according to Anstey, wrongly dated), in M. J. Knutsford, *Life & Times of Macaulay* (1900) p. 70.

2. THE PROPAGANDA OF ANTI-SLAVERY *James Walvin*

1. James Walvin, 'The public campaign in England against slavery', in David Eltis and James Walvin (eds), *The Abolition of the Atlantic*

Slave Trade (Madison Wisconsin, 1981); and the essay by Seymour Drescher in this volume.

2. Seymour Drescher, *Econocide. British Slavery in the Era of Abolition* (Pittsburgh, 1977).

3. John Brewer, *Party Ideology and Popular Politics at the Accession of George III* (Cambridge, 1976) p. 166.

4. Thomas Clarkson, *The History of the Rise, Progress and Accomplishment of the Abolition of the African Slave Trade by the British Parliament*, 2 vols (1808) vol. I, p. 418.

5. Roger Anstey, *The Atlantic Slave Trade and British Abolition, 1760–1810* (1975) p. 265.

6. *The Anti-Slavery Monthly Reporter* (afterwards *Reporter*) May 1830, 213.

7. Ibid., supplement, May 1830, p. 225.

8. Ibid., Jun 1830, p. 229.

9. Ibid., Sep 1830, p. 388.

10. Ibid., 5 Oct 1830, p. 405.

11. Ibid., 5 Jan 1831, p. 31.

12. Ibid., p. 58.

13. Ibid., 1 Sept 1832, p. 274.

14. *Anti-Slavery Record*, 18 Apr 1833, p. 169.

15. *Report of the Agency Committee of the Anti-Slavery Society* (London, 1831) pp. 3–4 (afterwards *Agency Committee*).

16. Ibid., pp. 4–5.

17. This is particularly true of John Thelwall, whose lectures to the London Corresponding Society were later issued in published form. See Albert Goodwin, *The Friends of Liberty* (1979) pp. 473–4.

18. *Agency Committee*, p. 8.

19. Ibid., p. 8.

20. Ibid., p. 20.

21. Ibid., pp. 12–13.

22. Ibid., p. 15.

23. Ibid., p. 16.

24. Ibid., pp. 18–19.

25. *Reporter*, May 1832, p. 137.

26. *Agency Committee*, p. 8.

27. Ibid., p. 11.

28. Ibid., p. 12.

29. Ibid., p. 12.

30. Ibid., p. 16.

31. E. Hughes (ed.), *The Diaries and Correspondence of James Losh*, 2 vols (Publications of the Surtees Society, 1962–3) nos. 171, 172, vol. II, pp. 97–102.

32. *Agency Committee*, p. 11.

33. Clarkson, *History*, vol. I.

34. Ibid., pp. 276—7.

35. V. Neuburg, *Popular Literature. A History and Guide* (Penguin, 1977) p. 105.

36. Clarkson, *History*, vol. I, pp. 277—8.

37. Ibid., p. 279.

38. Abolition Committee minutes, 12 Aug 1788, Add. MS. 21 255.

39. Anstey, *Atlantic Slave Trade*, p. 257; Clarkson, *History*, vol. I, p. 125.

40 W. Sypher, *Guinea's Captive Kings* (Chapel Hill, 1942).

41. John Thelwall, 'The Negro's Prayer', in *The Vestibule of Eloquence* (1810); James Montgomery, *The Abolition of the Slave Trade* (1829).

42. Anstey, *Atlantic Slave trade*, pp. 292—6.

43. Minute book of the Society for the Abolition of the Slave Trade, Add. MS. 21, 256, 20 July 1790.

44. See Seymour Drescher's essay in this volume.

45. *Accounts of the Receipts and Disboursements of the Anti-Slavery Society* (n.d. covers the years 1823—31).

46. *First Report Annual of the Swansea and Neath Auxiliary Anti-Slavery Association* (Swansea, 1826); *First Report of the Suffolk Auxiliary Society for the Mitigation and Gradual Abolition of Slavery* (Ipswich, 1825).

47. *Speeches and Addresses of the Candidates for the Representation of the County of York in the Year 1826* (Leeds, 1826) pp. 26, 52, 355 and 99 [York City Library].

48. J. Stevenson and R. Quinault (eds), *Popular Protest and Public Order* (1974).

49. *Agency Committee*, p. 10.

50. *Reporter*, 5 Jan 1831, p. 58.

51. *Ladies Anti-Slavery Associations*, 5 (n.d.) [Goldsmith's Library, Senate House, University of London].

52. Ibid.

53. *Reporter*, 30 Sept 1825, p. 32.

54. Ibid., 31 Aug 1825, p. 24.

55. Ibid., 31 July 1826, p. 212.

56. Ibid., Oct 1829, p. 83; Mar 1839, p. 156.

57. Ibid., 1 Aug 1830, p. 348; 1 Sep 1830, p. 404.

58. *Report of the Sheffield Female Anti-Slavery Society* (n.d.); Mrs Rawson *The Bow in the Cloud* (Sheffield, 1834); *An Address to the Labouring Classes* (n.d.); R. Coupland, *The British Anti-Slavery Movement* (1933) p. 137.

59. Petition from Brook St, Derby, *Journal of the House of Lords*, LXIII (Sept 1830 — Nov 1831) 32.

60. P. Knight, *Knibb 'the Notorious', Slaves Missionary, 1803–1845* (1973) ch. 7.

61. *Journal of the House of Lords*, LXIII, Petitions (1830) 101.

62. Petition from Hull Unitarians, ibid., p. 40.

63. See William Beckford, *A Descriptive Account of the Island of Jamaica* (1790) and *An Appeal to the Candour and Justice of the People of England in behalf of the West Indian Merchants and Planters* (1792), both in M. Craton, J. Walvin and D. Wright, *Slavery, Abolition and Emancipation* (1976) pp. 266–72.

64. Cropper to Macauley, 1822, Add. MS. 41, 267, A, fos 106, 108, 126.

65. *Reporter*, 30 Apr 1827, p. 360.

3.   'OUR CAUSE BEING ONE AND THE SAME'. ABOLITIONISTS
        AND CHARTISM *Betty Fladeland*

1. Standard histories of the British anti-slavery movement do not consider its relationship to the working classes, although a few studies have explored working-class involvement in the movement: James Walvin, 'English Democratic Societies and Popular Radicalism 1791–1800' (University of York, unpublished Ph.D. thesis, 1969: microfilm, Friends, House Library, London); James Walvin, 'How Popular Was Abolition? Popular Dissent and the Negro Question, 1787–1833' (unpublished MS); E. M. Hunt, 'The North of England Agitation for the Abolition of the Slave Trade, 1780–1800' (University of Manchester, unpublished MA thesis, n.d.). Douglas Riach emphasises the exertions made by Dublin abolitionists to reach the working classes in his 'Ireland and the Campaign against American Slavery, 1830–1860' (University of Edinburgh, unpublished Ph.D. thesis, 1975); and Gloria Clare Taylor points out the role of the Scottish churches in disseminating the anti-slavery message to all classes in 'Some American Reformers and Their Influence on Reform Movements in Great Britain from 1830–1860' (University of Edinburgh, unpublished Ph.D. thesis, 1960). Richard Blackett emphasises the degree to which black abolitionists attracted working-class audiences in his study (in progress) of black American abolitionists' missions to Britain.

2. Recent works such as Howard Temperley, *British Antislavery, 1833–1870* (Columbia, SC: University of South Carolina Press, 1972) and Christine Bolt, *The Anti-Slavery Movement and Reconstruction, A Study of Anglo-American Co-operation, 1833–1877* (Oxford University Press, 1969) mention that some abolitionists, most specifically Joseph Sturge, were not insensitive to working-class oppression, but the relation-

ship has not been studied in detail. G. D. H. Cole includes Sturge in his *Chartist Portraits* (New York: Macmillan, 1965). David B. Davis in *The Problem of Slavery in the Age of Revolution* (Ithaca and London: Cornell University Press, 1975) seems to conclude that the anti-slavery movement did more to bolster than to challenge the existing social order. He concedes that probably the abolition movement 'bred a new sensitivity to social oppression', but suspects that 'Walvin exaggerates the continuing appeal of antislavery to working-class leaders'. See chs 8 and 9, esp. pp. 368, 377, 384, 451, 455 and 467. My quotations are from note 30 on p. 368, and p. 467. The most recent work which upholds the traditional thesis of worker antipathy to the anti-slavery movement is Patricia Hollis, 'Anti-Slavery and British Working-Class Radicalism in the Years of Reform', in Christine Bolt and Seymour Drescher (eds), *Anti-Slavery, Religion and Reform* (Folkestone: Dawson Press, 1980).

3. Sharp to Mr Lloyd (Gray's Inn) for the Archbishop of York (Dr Drummond), 30 July 1772, Granville Sharp Letterbook, York Minster Library.

4. Ibid.; Granville Sharp, *The Legal Means of Political Reformation* . . . , 8th edn (1797); Granville Sharp, *An Appendix to the Second Edition of Mr. Lofft's Observations on a late Publication, entitled "A Dialogue on the Actual State of Parliaments"* . . . (1783).

5. Cartwright to Samuel Whitbread, 30 Aug. 1814, quoted in Frances Dorothy Cartwright (ed.), *The Life and Correspondence of Major Cartwright*, 2 vols (1826) vol. II, pp. 80–3. See also vol. I, pp. 66, 82, 134–5, 144–5, 149–50 and 167. Also, John Cartwright, *Give Us Our Rights* . . . (1782); and Cartwright to Henry Lord Brougham, 16 and 22 July 1812, Brougham Papers, University College, London.

6. Thomas H[ardy], to the Rev. Mr Bryant, 2 Mar 1792, Place Papers, Add. MS. 27811, BL.

7. Walvin, 'How Popular Was Abolition?'

8. Alfred held that in its early stages Chartism reflected social aims. See Alfred [Samuel H. G. Kydd], *The History of the Factory Movement from the Year 1802, to the Enactment of the Ten Hours' Bill in 1847*, 2 vols (1857; Reprints of Economic Classics, New York: Augustus M. Kelley, 1966) vol. II, p. 77. Asa Briggs in his introduction to Cole's *Chartist Portraits* agrees that 'Chartism was born before the name'.

9. Alfred, *Factory Movement*, vol. II, pp. 67–72 and 88–9.

10. *The Operative*, 5 May 1839.

11. *Birmingham Journal*, 13 Jan 1838.

12. Letter to the Editor, *Nonconformist*, 26 May 1841.

13. Alfred, *Factory Movement*, vol. I, pp. 198–9 and 254–5; vol. II, pp. 60–1.

14. Simon Maccoby, *English Radicalism, 1832–1852* (Geo. Allen

and Unwin, 1935) pp. 174–6.

15. Nassau William Senior, *Two Lectures on Population* ... (1829); Senior to Henry Brougham, 9 Mar 1833, Brougham Papers; 'Letter of 14 September 1832, to Lord Chancellor Brougham on Poor Law Reform', in Leon S. Levy, *Nassau W. Senior 1790–1864* (Newton Abbot: David and Charles, 1970) Appendix X, pp. 247–54. Martineau's preachments on the need for the poor to limit their numbers are embodied in her *Illustrations of Political Economy* (1833). See also Francis Place to Martineau, 8 Sep 1832, Place Papers, Add. MS. 35149, fo. 189.

16. *Northern Star and Leeds General Advertiser*, 31 Mar 1838.

17. *Northern Liberator* (Newcastle-upon-Tyne), 27 Apr 1839.

18. *London Dispatch and People's Political and Social Reformer*, 23 Apr 1837.

19. Henry Lord Brougham, *The Life and Times of Henry Lord Brougham, Written by Himself*, 3 vols (New York: Harper and Bros, 1871–2), vol. III, pp. 39–40; Chester New, *The Life of Henry Brougham to 1830* (Oxford: Clarendon Press, 1961) p. 149. Cobbett is quoted in E. P. Thompson, *The Making of the English Working Class* (New York: Vintage Books, 1963) p. 824. Thompson himself used the phrase 'half-hearted or equivocal reformers like Brougham' who played a 'ritual' role. See p. 604.

20. Harriet Martineau, *Biographical Sketches* (Macmillan, 1869) p. 164; Harriet Martineau, *A History of the Thirty Years' Peace*, 4 vols (Geo. Bell and Sons, 1877) vol. III, p. 102; vol. II, p. 385. Some of Brougham's anti-slavery colleagues were distrustful of him too. See H[enry] T[hornton] to Wm Wilberforce, 24 Sept 1804, and [James Stephen?] to Wilberforce [22 Sept 1804], Wilberforce Papers, Perkins Library, Duke University, Durham, NC.

21. *The Chartist*, 19 May 1839; *The Operative*, 23 Dec 1838 and 30 June 1839.

22. *The Scotsman* (Edinburgh), 29 June, 17 and 24 July 1839; W. H. Marwick, *A Short History of Labour in Scotland* (Edinburgh: W. and R. Chambers, 1967) p. 11; Francis Place to Brougham, 4 July 1840, Brougham Papers.

23. Maria Weston Chapman (ed.), *Harriet Martineau's Autobiography and Memorials of Harriet Martineau*, 2 vols (Boston: James R. Osgood, 1877) vol. I, p. 159.

24. Vera Wheatley, *The Life and Work of Harriet Martineau* (Fairtown, NJ: Essential Books, 1957) pp. 103–5; R. K. Webb, *Harriet Martineau, A Radical Victorian* (Wm Heinemann, 1960) pp. 130–2 and 346–9.

25. Martineau, *Thirty Years' Peace*, vol. I, pp. 112–14, vol. II, p. 313. She specifically mentions a woman, Esther Hibner, who 'treated

her apprentices as the most barbarous and depraved of slaveholders treats his slaves'.

26. Ibid., vol. IV, p. 204.

27. Ibid., vol. III, pp. 261 and 263—4; *Autobiography*, vol. II, pp. 1 and 3.

28. H. Martineau to R. M. Bacon [editor of *Norwich Mercury*], 14 Nov [n.d.], Add. MS. 6247 (87), University Library, Cambridge.

29. Martineau, *Thirty Years' Peace*, vol. III, pp. 264, 266, 488—90 and 493.

30. H. Martineau to Charles Buller, MP, 21 Aug 1841, *Autobiography*, Appendix D. pp. 587—94.

31. Edward Baines, MP, *The Life of Edward Baines, Late M.P. for the Borough of Leeds*, 2nd ed. (Brown, Green, Longmans and Roberts, 1859) p. 167. Baines did support most features of the new Poor Law. See Dorothy Thompson, *The Early Chartists* (Columbia, SC: University of South Carolina Press, 1971) p. 69 n.

32. *Sheffield Iris*, 4 Sept and 11 Dec 1838.

33. *Northern Star and Leeds General Advertiser*, 28 Mar 1838; Alfred, *Factory Movement*, vol. I, pp. 105—6. Morpeth, once elected, was accused of failing to carry out his campaign promise to amend the Poor Law.

34. Alfred, *Factory Movement*, vol. I, pp. 221—9; G. D. H. Cole, *Chartist Portraits*, p. 84; *Northern Star and Leeds General Advertiser*, 7 and 21 Apr 1838.

35. Alfred, *Factory Movement*, vol. I, pp. 95—102.

36. Ibid., vol. I, p. 104.

37. Quoted in ibid., vol. I, p. 119.

38. The *Sheffield Iris* for 10 Sept 1839 carried an article, 'Chartism, Its Cause and Cure', by Samuel Roberts. Feargus O'Connor wanted Baines elected to Parliament because he opposed the Eleven Hours' Bill. Baines said it was not right to put English children on a work day equal to that of adult blacks in the West Indies. *Northern Star and Leeds General Advertiser*, 3 Mar 1838.

39. *Poor Man's Guardian*, 6 July 1833.

40. Alfred, *Factory Movement*, vol. II, p. 92.

41. See, for example, the case of the Staffordshire potters as presented in the *London Dispatch and People's Political and Social Reformer*, 18 Dec 1836.

42. Quoted in Robert George Gammage, *History of the Chartist Movement 1837—1854*, 2nd edn (1894; Reprints of Economics Classics, New York: Augustus M. Kelley, 1969) p. 88.

43. *Northern Star and Leeds General Advertiser*, 14 Apr 1838.

44. *Northern Liberator*, 24 Aug 1839.

45. Ibid., 8 Nov 1839.

46. *The Reformer* (Birmingham), 6 Aug 1835. The Protest was signed on 1 Aug 1833.

47. Douglas Riach, 'Ireland and the Campaign against American Slavery', pp. 146–7.

48. Minute Book of the Anti-Slavery Society, 1837, p. 41, Anti-Slavery Papers, E/25, Rhodes House Library, Oxford. There are various letters on this issue in Anti-Slavery Papers, C2/80; also, *British Emancipator*, 3 Jan 1838; *The Reformer*, 18 June 1835; Minute Book of the Glasgow Emancipation Society, entries for 9 June and 28 Dec 1835, photostat copy, Mitchell Library, Glasgow.

49. Ralph E. Turner, *James Silk Buckingham, 1786–1855, A Social Biography* (Williams and Norgate, 1934) pp. 60 and 275; T. Perronet Thompson, 'The Suffering Rich', *Westminster Review*, XI (Apr 1834) 265–74; William Howitt, *A Serious Address to the Members of the Anti-Slavery Society, on Its Present Position and Prospects* (Wm Henry Cox, 1843) p. 6; Archibald Prentice, *History of the Anti-Corn Law League*, 2 vols (F. and G. Cash, 1853) vol. I, pp. 4–6; Stephen H. Hobhouse, *Joseph Sturge, His Life and Work* (J. M. Dent and Sons, 1919) pp. 35–6.

50. *British Emancipator*, 3 Jan 1838.

51. *London Dispatch and People's Political and Social Reformer*, 12 Feb 1837. Buxton succeeded Wilberforce as the parliamentary leader for emancipation.

52. *Northern Liberator*, 17 Apr 1838. See issues throughout April, May and June.

53. *Northern Star and Leeds General Advertiser*, 10 Mar and 14 Apr 1838 and 8 Nov 1839.

54. Ibid., 26 May 1838.

55. *Northern Liberator*, 8 Nov 1839; *Poor Man's Guardian*, 17 Nov 1832. Papers surveyed were *The Chartist, The Chartist Circular, The Charter, The Champion, The Northern Liberator, The Operative, Northern Star* and *Poor Man's Guardian*.

56. *Northern Star*, 5 May 1838.

57. Ibid. Joseph Pease, a Quaker abolitionist, was a Darlington manufacturer.

58. A letter signed 'Homo', also Joseph Corbett to Joseph Sturge, *Birmingham Journal*, 30 Mar and 15 Sept 1839.

59. Quoted in Henry Richard, *Memoirs of Joseph Sturge* (S.W. Partridge, 1864) p. 296.

60. Lovett was involved in the anti-slavery movement as early as the mid-1820s. See *The Life and Struggles of William Lovett . . .* (Trubner, 1876) pp. 36, 321. John Collins was a Birmingham shoemaker and is

not to be confused with the radical American abolitionist, John A. Collins.

61. Lovett, *Life and Struggles*, p. 107.

62. Ibid., pp. 129—34 and 150—8. Quotations are on pp. 132 and 152.

63. William Lovett and John Collins, *Chartism; A New Organization of the People, Embracing a Plan for the Education and Improvement of the People Politically and Socially; Addressed to the Working-Classes of the United Kingdom, and More Especially to the Advocates of the Rights and Liberties of the Whole People as Set Forth in the "People's Charter"*, 2nd edn (1841); Dorothy Thompson, *Early Chartists*, p. 171.

64. Among the papers in the William Lovett Collection, Birmingham Reference Library, see O'Connell to John Cleave [n.d.]; 'Report of the Deputation Appointed by the Working Men's Association to wait upon Daniel O'Connell, to ascertain his views and intentions with respect to Trades Unions', 12 Feb 1838; and 'The Reply of the Precursor Society on behalf of the People of Ireland to the Address of the Persons Styling Themselves the Radical Reformers of England, Scotland and Wales', 29 Nov 1838.

65. *Northern Liberator*, 28 Oct 1837.

66. James Silk Buckingham, *Plan of an Improved Income Tax and Real Free Trade*... (James Ridgway, 1845) pp. 62—5; J. S. Buckingham, *Evils and Remedies of the Present System of Popular Elections* . . . (Simpkin, Marshall, 1841) pp. 43—4, 63—5 and 121.

67. L. G. Johnson, *General T. Perronet Thompson, 1783—1869* (Geo. Allen and Unwin, 1957) pp. 213 *passim*, 221 and 224; T. P. Thompson to John Bowring, 26 May 1841, Thompson Papers, University of Hull.

68. Lovett, *Life and Struggles*, p. 172; *London Dispatch and People's Political and Social Reformer*, 3 June 1838.

69. Turner's reputation as a radical went back to 1816 when he had lent the use of his field for a protest against the late war with the United States. Fiona Ann Montgomery, 'Glasgow Radicalism, 1830—1848', (University of Edinburgh, 1974, unpublished Ph.D. thesis) pp. 49—50; *Scots Times*, 15 and 19 Nov 1831.

70. Alex Wilson, 'Chartism in Glasgow', in Asa Briggs (ed.) *Chartist Studies* (Macmillan, 1959) pp. 251—3.

71. William Darling, *Henry Vincent, A Biographical Sketch with a Preface by Mrs. Vincent* (James Clark, 1879) pp. 66—9.

72. *Sheffield Iris*, 8 Jan 1839. Elliott later broke with the Chartists, believing repeal of the Corn Laws should have priority.

73. A. R. Schoyen, *The Chartist Challenge: A Portrait of George Julian Harney* (Heinemann, 1958) pp. 3 and 8.

74. Patrick Brewster, *Chartist and Socialist Sermons* (Glasgow: Forward, [n.d.]) p. iii; Alexander Wilson, *The Chartist Movement in Scotland* (Manchester: Manchester Univ. Press, 1970) pp. 62–3.

75. Brewster, *Chartist and Socialist Sermons*. The ideas are repeated in all of the sermons but see especially Sermon I, pp. 4, 5 and 8–10; Sermon II, pp. 17, 20–1 and 25; Sermon III, pp. 32–3; Sermon IV, pp. 48, 54 and 58.

76. Brewster's suspension was not carried out because of the disruption in the following General Assembly of the Church of Scotland. Wilson, *Chartist Movement in Scotland*, pp. 202–3; Brewster, *Chartist and Socialist Sermons*, introduction.

77. Wilson, *Chartist Movement in Scotland*, p. 68. Bronterre O'Brien blamed Brewster for the split, and Feargus O'Connor called him a 'political priest' whose actions played into the hands of O'Connell and the 'vile Whigs'. See *The Operative*, 16 Dec 1838; *Northern Star*, 12 Jan 1839; *Glasgow Argus*, 14 Jan 1839.

78. *Birmingham Journal*, 6 and 13 July 1839; *Northern Star*, 13 July 1839; *London Dispatch*, 21 July 1839. The *Dispatch* accused the London police of provoking the violence.

79. *Birmingham Journal*, 17 Aug and 14 Sept 1839; Richard, *Memoirs of Sturge*, pp. 258–67.

80. Wm Cardo to Home Office, 6 Nov 1839, HO 40/37 contains the first report on Sturge as a potential leader of agitation. The last I found was in the spring of 1842. See Letterbook, 1839–42, labelled 'Police, Birmingham', in HO 65/10, PRO. C. R. Moorsom, also named in the report of 19 Nov 1839, was active in the Birmingham Anti-Slavery Society and sensitive to the problems of the British working class.

81. Harold U. Faulkner, *Chartism and the Churches* (New York; Columbia Univ. Press, 1916) pp. 35 and 40–1; *The Chartist*, 2 Feb 1839; *The Scotsman*, 11 Jan 1840. It should be pointed out that members of other groups, including the Anti-Corn Law League, retaliated by disrupting Chartist meetings.

82. *The Northern Liberator* launched the attack by describing the Anti-Slavery Convention as a 'grand meeting of humbug' representing the cant and insincerity of the 'slave squad'. See issues for 13 June and 3 Oct 1840.

83. Ibid., 15 Aug 1840.

84. Ibid., 28 Nov 1840; *Northern Star*, 26 Nov 1840.

85. Glasgow Emancipation Society Minute Book II, 10 Aug 1840; *Scots Times*, 12 Aug 1840; *Glasgow Argus*, 13 Aug 1840; Robert L. Bingham, 'The Glasgow Emancipation Society, 1833–76' (University of Glasgow, unpublished M. Litt. thesis, 1973) pp. 139–40.

86. GES Minute Book II, 14 Sept 1840; *Glasgow Argus*, 14 Sept 1840; Wilson, *Chartist Movement in Scotland*, p. 121.

87. GES Minute Book III throughout spring 1841, especially entry for 27 Apr 1841; John A. Collins to Richard D. Webb [of Dublin], 28 [?] Apr 1841, Garrison Papers, Boston Public Library; *Glasgow Argus*, 19 and 29 Apr 1841; C. Duncan Rice, 'The Scots Abolitionists, 1833–1861' (unpublished MS.) p. 151.

88. *Northern Star*, 26 Nov 1840; Anna Gurney to J. J. Gurney, 31 Jan and 20 Feb 1840, Gurney MS, Friends House Library.

89. H. Martineau to Charles Buller, MP, 21 Aug 1841, in her *Autobiography*, Appendix D, pp. 587–94.

90. John Pease, *A Few Hints on Happiness Addressed to the Working Classes of Great Britain by a Tradesman* (Leeds, 1831). The manuscript is in the Pease Papers, D/HO/X1 Durham County Record Office. John Pease, 'To the Labouring Classes', D/HO/X1. An attached note says 'Address intended for publication during the Chartist and other Excitements, . . . only prevented printing by pressure of other engagements'.

91. Elizabeth Pease to Anne Warren Weston, 24 June 1841, Weston Papers, Boston Public Library; Elizabeth Pease to Wendell and Ann Phillips, 16 Aug and 29 Sept 1842, Garrison Papers; Anna M. Stoddart, *Elizabeth Pease Nichol* (New York; J. M. Dent, 1899) pp. 136–41.

92. *Household Suffrage and Equal Electoral Districts Shown to be Unfavourable to Good Government and Purity of Election* . . . (1841); C. Duncan Rice, 'The Scottish Factor in the Fight against American Slavery, 1830–1870' (University of Edinburgh, unpublished Ph.D. thesis, 1969) p. 494.

93. Robert G. Gammage, *History of the Chartist Movement*, p. 209; Mark Hovell, *The Chartist Movement*, 1st edn (Manchester Univ. Press, 1918; Reprints of Economic Classics, New York: Augustus M. Kelley, 1967) p. 255. Macauley lost his seat in Parliament in 1847 at least partly because of Chartist opposition. See Maccoby, *English Radicalism, 1832–1852*, p. 276 and note. Yet Macaulay was not altogether antagonistic to labour. He voted for the Ten Hours' Bill. See Cole, *Chartist Portraits*, p. 104.

94. Samuel Wilberforce to Henry Lord Brougham, 9 Aug 1859, Brougham Papers.

95. W. E. Forster to Barclay Fox, 22 Mar 1842, in T. Wemyss Reid, *Life of the Right Honorable W. E. Forster*, 2 vols, 3rd edn (Chapman and Hall, 1888; reprinted, Bath: Adams and Dart, 1970) pp. 148–52, 153–5, 158 and 278–82.

96. T. Perronet Thompson, 'The Suffering Rich', *Westminster Review*, XI (April 1834) 265–74; Thompson to John Bowring, 2 Aug 1834, Thompson Papers.

97. Thompson to Bowring, 12 Apr 1833, 11 Jan, 3 and 20 Feb 1840 (the last two contain the direct quotations) Thompson Papers.

98. The London *Times* attacked Thompson for his socialism. See

letters from Thompson to Richard Cobden throughout 1842, Thompson Papers.

99. *Birmingham Journal*, 1 Feb 1840.

100. Joseph Sturge, *A Visit to the United States in 1841* (1842; Reprints of Economics Classics, New York: Augustus M. Kelley, 1969) pp. 102–3 and 147; Sturge to the Electors of Nottingham, 1 May 1842, *Nonconformist*, 25 May 1842.

101. The articles appeared in the *Nonconformist*, 13 Oct–1 Dec 1841. The pamphlet, *Reconciliation between the Middle and Labouring Classes* (Birmingham, 1842), is to be found in the Place Papers, BL, Add. MS. 27810, fo. 70. Miall's quotation is on p. 17 of the pamphlet.

102. George Thompson notebook (compiled by his daughter Amelia Ann Everard Chesson), 20 Sep 1839, George Thompson Papers, Rylands Library, Manchester. The excerpts in this notebook seem to have been copied mostly from Thompson letters.

103. Ibid., 27 Oct 1841.

104. *The Scotsman*, 7 May 1842. Thompson's lectures are covered in the *Nonconformist* throughout the summer and autumn of 1842.

105. Thompson Notebook, 27 Oct 1841.

106. Place to Henry Ashworth, 5 Apr 1842, Place Papers, Add. MS. 27810, fo. 185; Richard, *Memoirs of Sturge*, p. 301; *The Scotsman*, 20 July 1842. The *Northern Star* facetiously objected to Sturge's assertion that all who were not burdens on the state should have the vote. This, said the editor, would exclude all of the clergy, the upper class, and most of the middle class. *Northern Star*, 19 Mar 1842.

107. *Nonconformist* (designated as the organ of the Complete Suffrage Union) from Nov 1841 to Apr 1842; *Birmingham Journal* for the same period; Richard, *Memoirs of Sturge*, pp. 301–3; Hobhouse, *Sturge*, pp. 72–3; Place to Sturge, 23 Mar 1842, Place Papers, Add. MS. 27810, fo. 124.

108. J. H. Hinton had co-operated with Sturge in organising the British and Foreign Anti-Slavery Society. He served as editor of the *British Emancipator* and substitute editor of the *British and Foreign Anti-Slavery Reporter*. See Minute Book I, Antislavery Papers E 2/6.

109. J. P. Mursell was pastor of the Bond Street Independent Chapel in Leicester, active in Reform Bill politics and in the Anti-Corn Law League. See A. Temple Patterson, *Radical Leicester, A History of Leicester 1780–1850* (Leicester: for University College, Leicester, 1954).

110. The Rev. Dr J. W. Massie believed that working people needed more than religion and lectured to them on such topics as 'The Importance to the Entire Body Politic in this Country, of the Social Advancement of the Working Classes'. He was an Anti-Corn Law activist, helped to organise the Anti-Slavery League, and during the American Civil War

lectured for the Union cause. See *Nonconformist*, 18 and 25 Aug 1841: 12 Aug 1846; 14 Nov 1849; Betty Fladeland, *Men and Brothers; Anglo-American Antislavery Cooperation* (Urbana: University of Illinois Press, 1972) p. 403.

111. The Rev. Dr John Ritchie of the Secessionist church in Edinburgh had participated in the Scottish abolition movement since the organisation of the Glasgow and Edinburgh societies in 1833. See GES, Minute Book I, 6 Dec 1833. Like Brewster, he was involved in the Chartist—Abolitionist arguments and supported the Complete Suffrage Union, serving on its National Council. Wright, *Scottish Chartism*, p. 139; Faulkner, *Chartism and the Churches*, pp. 18—19.

112. The Rev. Thomas Swan was a Baptist. An active member of the Birmingham Anti-Slavery Society, he was a delegate to the World Anti-Slavery Convention of 1843. He was on the Provisional Council of the Complete Suffrage Union. Later he worked with American abolitionist Elihu Burritt in the League of Universal Brotherhood. See Birmingham Anti-slavery Society, Minute Book, Birmingham Reference Library; *Nonconformist*, 16 Apr 1842 and 23 Dec 1846.

113. Wilson, 'Chartism in Glasgow', in Briggs (ed.), *Chartist Studies*, pp. 273—7; Faulkner, *Chartism and the Churches*, p. 44.

114. Spencer's anti-slavery activities can be traced in Antislavery Papers, Rhodes House, Oxford. His numerous writings include: *The Pillars of the Church of England; or, Are Intemperance and Ignorance, Bigotry and Infallibility, Church Rates and Corn Laws, Essential to the Existence of the Establishment?* (London, 1843); *Religion and Politics; or, Ought Religious Men to be Political?* (London, 1843); and *The New Poor Law; Its Evils and Their Remedies* (London, 1843). Spencer's obituary is in the *Nonconformist*, 2 Feb 1853. *Northern Star and Leeds General Advertiser*, 8 Jan 1842; Spencer to the editor, *The People*, 10 Oct 1848.

115. Henry Solly, *These Eighty Years, Or, The Story of An Unfinished Life*, 2 vols (Simpkin, Marshall, 1893) pp. 328—9, 343—4, 369—72, 375—82, 394 and 397—409. Solly moved to London where he lived amidst the poor with whom he worked. Among his writings are *Working Men; a Glance at Some of Their Wants; with Reasons and Suggestions for Helping Them to Help Themselves*, 4th edn (London: Jerrold and Sons, 1865); *Destitute Poor and Criminal Classes. A Few Thoughts on How to Deal with the Unemployed Poor of London, and with Its "Roughs" and Criminal Classes* (Social Science Ass'n, 1868); and a novel, *James Woodford, Carpenter and Chartist*, 2 vols (Sampson Law, Marston, Searle, and Rivington, 1881) which carries a Chartist message.

116. *Nonconformist*, 16 Apr 1842 carries a list of the delegates to the April conference. See also *The Scotsman* which carried reports of

the meetings throughout the period; and C. Duncan Rice, 'The Scottish Factor', pp. 228–9.

117. T. Perronet Thompson to Richard Cobden, 28 Oct 1842 and Thompson to John Bowring, 9 Oct 1843, Thompson Papers; Johnson, *Thompson*, pp. 26–8 and 43. Thompson subsequently attended several meetings with Sturge in an attempt to form a Complete Suffrage–Anti–Corn Law League coalition.

118. *Nonconformist*, 9 Mar, 28 Sept and 8 Oct 1842.

119. Ibid., 18 May 1842.

120. Printed circular, 'National Complete Suffrage Union', Place Papers, Add. MS. 27810, fo. 201; *Birmingham Journal*, 9 Apr 1842; *Nonconformist*, 6, 13, 27 Apr and 25 May 1842; Richard, *Memoirs of Sturge*, p. 300; Sturge to Lovett, 27 Apr 1842 and Memorial to Queen Victoria, Lovett Collection, Birmingham Reference Library.

121. Richard, *Memoirs of Sturge*, pp. 305–15; Hobhouse, *Sturge*, pp. 76–7; *Nonconformist*, 18 and 25 May, 8 June, 10 Aug 1842. Sturge's opponent was John Walter, Proprietor of *The Times*, who got 1885 votes to Sturge's 1801.

122. *Birmingham Journal*, 31 Dec 1842. Bronterre O'Brien put the primary blame on Thomas Spencer, J. Ritchie, Patrick Brewster and Lawrence Heyworth for obduracy against the Charter. *British Statesman*, 31 Dec 1842.

123. *The Pilot* (Birmingham), 14 Dec 1844.

124. In 1870 Taylor introduced a bill that revived the Chartist plank to pay MPs but it failed. During the American Civil War he was an organiser of the London Emancipation Society and active in support of the Union. Maccoby, *English Radicalism, 1853–1886* (Geo. Allen and Unwin, 1938) p. 162; Fladeland, *Men and Brothers*, p. 393.

125. Fox was interested in the extension of educational opportunities, women's rights and Chartism, but disliked Feargus O'Connor's physical force group. After the Chartist failure of 1848 he wrote *Counsels to the Working Classes* on the need for co-operation with the middle classes. Richard Garnett and Edward Garnett, *The Life of W. J. Fox, Public Teacher & Social Reformer 1786–1864* (John Lane, 1910) pp. 61–2, 111–12, 256 and 257.

126. Villiers, Bowring, Taylor and John Fielden supported Sharman Crawford's motion for complete suffrage. The *Nonconformist*, 10 May 1843 suggests that there was some vote-trading with the Corn Law repealers.

127. Ashurst was a radical London solicitor who championed the poor, the Charter, and equal rights for women. Prior to 1832 he had vowed not to pay taxes until the Reform Bill passed. G. H. Holyoake, *The History of Co-operation* (New York: E. P. Dutton, 1906) vol. I, p. 191; Walter Merrill and Louis Ruchames (eds), *The Letters of William*

Lloyd Garrison (Cambridge, Mass.: Belknap Press of Harvard University, 1971) vol. II, pp. 202n. and 666n.

128. The Howitts took over *The People's Journal* and continued editing it as *People's and Howitt's Journal*. Besides numerous articles dealing with anti-slavery and labour it ran a series by William called 'Letters on Labour to the Working Men of England'. See issues from 11 Apr 1846 to 20 June 1846. The Howitts were active in the Co-operative League and on behalf of Mechanics Institutes. Margaret Howitt (ed.), *Mary Howitt, An Autobiography*, 2 vols (Wm Isbister, 1889).

129. W. J. Linton, a wood engraver, issued a Chartist sheet *The National* from 1848 to 1852. He antedated Henry George by calling for a single tax on land. W. J. Linton, *The People's Land, and an Easy Way to Recover It* (J. Watson, 1850); Mark Hovell, *Chartist Movement*, p. 299.

130. F. R. Lees, who joined the Chartists, published *The Truthseeker* in which he frequently reprinted anti-slavery as well as Chartist materials. J. F. C. Harrison, 'Chartism in Leeds', in Briggs (ed.), *Chartist Studies*, p. 91; Louis Billington, 'Some Connections between British and American Reform Movements 1830–1860. With Special Reference to the Anti-Slavery Movement' (University of Bristol, unpublished MA thesis, 1966).

131. Samuel Roberts of Llanbrynmair supported numerous reforms including anti-slavery, universal suffrage for men over twenty-one, education, abolition of capital punishment and disestablishment of the church. In 1843 he founded a monthly magazine, *Y Cronicl*. See Glanmor Williams, *Samuel Roberts Llanbrynmair* (Cardiff: University of Wales Press, 1950).

132. James Haughton was one of the pillars of the Irish anti-slavery movement. His only stipulations for suffrage qualification were that men – and women – be literate and not on parish relief. See Samuel Haughton, *Memoir of James Haughton . . .* (Dublin: E. Ponsonby, 1877); Douglas Riach, 'Ireland and the Campaign against American Slavery', esp. pp. 190–1, 335, 337, 338 and 351. Haughton and James Silk Buckingham advocated a plan whereby each person could select his own rank on a social scale and then pay taxes accordingly.

133. Duncan McLaren was the brother-in-law of John Bright and active in the free trade as well as anti-slavery, education, peace and suffrage movements. See J. B. Mackie, *The Life and Work of Duncan McLaren*, 2 vols (Thomas Nelson and Sons, 1888).

134. John Dunlop and Alexander Duncanson were both active in Scottish abolitionist activities. Duncanson was pastor of a Congregational church in Falkirk. He wanted a fusion of all reform movements including Chartism, anti-slavery, temperance and anti-capital punishment. See Wilson, *Chartist Movement in Scotland*, p. 245.

135. J. F. C. Harrison, 'Chartism in Leeds', in Briggs (ed.), *Chartist Studies*, p. 96; Billington, 'Some Connections', p. 223; Joseph Barker, *The Life of Joseph Barker. Written by Himself, Edited by His Nephew, John Thomas Barker* (Hodden and Stoughton, 1880) pp. 245 and 289–97; *The Christian*, 14 Feb 1848; Joseph Barker, *The Reformer's Almanac* . . . (Wortley, 1848).

136. Frederick B. Tolles (ed.), *Slavery and "The Woman Question". Lucretia Mott's Diary of Her Visit to Great Britain to Attend the World's Anti-Slavery Convention of 1840*, Supplement No. 23 to *Journal of the Friends' Historical Society* (Haverford, Pa.: Friends' Historical Society, 1952). The quotation is on p. 70.

137. Richard Blackett, 'Black Americans in the Anti-Slavery Connection' (unpublished MS.) pp. 6–7.

138. J. A. Collins to 'My Dear Friend' [Elizabeth Pease], 16 Aug 1841, Garrison Papers.

139. Garrison to Samuel J. May, 6 Sept 1840; Merrill and Ruchames (eds), *Garrison Letters*, vol. II, p. 696–9.

140. Ibid., vol. II, p. 554.

141. The Garrisonians were not invited to the 1843 convention so the American delegates represented the American and Foreign Anti-Slavery Society and those favourable to political action, which Garrison opposed.

142. *Nonconformist*, 21 and 28 June 1843; John F. Johnson, *Proceedings of the General Anti-Slavery Convention, Called by the Committee of the British and Foreign Anti-Slavery Society* . . . (1844). The names of John Bowring, T. P. Thompson, Henry Solly, Dr John Ritchie, Henry Vincent and Sharman Crawford are noticeable in these accounts, indicating the prominent role of the pro-Chartist group in the 1843 convention.

143. William Wells Brown, *Three Years in Europe; Or, Places I Have Seen and People I Have Met. With a Memoir of the Author, by William Farmer, Esq.* (Charles Gilpin, 1852) pp. 12, 91–2, 139–41, 206 and 223; Samuel R. Ward, *Autobiography of a Fugitive Negro: His Anti-Slavery Labours in the United States, Canada and England* (John Snow, 1855).

144. Earl Ofari, *"Let Your Motto Be Resistance," The Life and Thought of Henry Highland Garnet* (Boston: Beacon Press, 1972) p. 58; Joel Schor, *Henry Highland Garnet* (Westport, Conn.: Greenwood Press, 1977) p. 167; *Banner of Ulster*, 7 Feb 1851 (with thanks to R. Blackett for citation).

145. Philip S. Foner, *Frederick Douglass* (New York: Citadel Press, 1964 p. 101; *Nonconformist*, 27 May 1846.

146. H. C. Wright, 'Journal and Commonplace Book', XXIX–XXXVIII, Boston Public Library; *The Inquirer*, 17 and 20 Jan, 11 Apr,

22 Aug and 28 Nov 1846; *Nonconformist*, 27 May and 8 July 1846; George Thompson to H. C. Wright, 23 May 1846, Garrison to R. D. Webb, 19 Aug 1846, and Garrison to Helen Garrison, 3 Sept 1846, Garrison Papers; J. N. Buffum to Caroline Weston, 25 June 1846, Weston Papers.

147. *The Inquirer*, 5 Sept 1846.

148. Lovett, *Life and Struggles*, p. 321; *Nonconformist*, 12 and 19 Aug 1846; *The Inquirer*, 19 Sept 1846; Garrison to John B. Estlin, 19 Aug 1846, Garrison Papers; Mary Howitt to M. W. Chapman, 2 Mar [1847], Weston Papers.

149. Wilson, *Chartist Movement in Scotland*, pp. 259—60; Billington, 'Some Connections', p. 261; Clare Taylor (ed.), *British and American Abolitionists. An Episode in Transatlantic Understanding* (Edinburgh: University of Edinburgh Press, 1974) pp. 357—8. *The Spirit of the Age* (owned by W. H. Ashurst and edited by G. J. Holyoake) 25 Nov 1848 has an interesting article on the Free Soil Party in America as standing for the small farmer and worker. The Free Soil Party was the successor to the Liberty Party and its emphasis was on preventing the extension of slavery into the territories and new western states; but 'free soil' had a double meaning as the party also advocated free land for frontier settlers.

150. Cole, *Chartist Portraits*, p. 22. Eventually Marx and Engels turned against Jones because he was willing to ally with the middle classes. John Saville, *Ernest Jones: Chartist* (Lawrence and Wishart, 1952) pp. 21, 42 and appendix I.

151. A. R. Schoyen, *The Chartist Challenge, A Portrait of George Julian Harney* (Heinemann, 1958) p. 266; Saville, *Ernest Jones*, pp. 66—9 and 76—7.

152. Saville, *Ernest Jones*, pp. 76—7.

153. *Anti-Slavery Watchman; A Magazine of English and American Abolitionism*, 2 (Dec 1853). This may be found in the George Thompson Papers, Rylands Library.

4. SLAVE CULTURE, RESISTANCE AND THE ACHIEVEMENT OF EMANCIPATION IN THE BRITISH WEST INDIES, 1783—1838
Michael Craton

* This essay emerges out of three earlier published papers: 'Christianity and Slavery in the British West Indies, 1750—1865', *Historical Reflections/Reflexions Historiques* (Sept 1978); 'Proto-Peasant Revolts? The Late Slave Rebellions in the British West Indies, 1816—1832', *Past & Present*, 85 (Nov 1979); 'The Passion to Exist; Slave Rebellions in the British West Indies, 1629—1832', *Journal of Caribbean History* (Spring 1980). It is the forerunner of a chapter in a forthcoming book:

Testing the Chains; Slave Rebellions in the British West Indies, 1629–1832 (Ithaca: Cornell University Press, 1981).

1. Mrs A. C. Carmichael, *Domestic Manners and Social Condition of the White, Coloured and Negro Population of the West Indies*, 2 vols (1834) vol. I, pp. 246–7.

2. The debate over abolition and emancipation alone accounts for 170 pages of the monumental bibliography by Lowell J. Ragatz, *A Guide for the Study of British Caribbean History, 1763–1834* (Washington: Government Printing Office, 1932; Annual Report of the American Historical Association, 1930) pp. 405–573. The key works were probably Granville Sharp, *A Representation of the Injustice and Dangerous Tendency of Tolerating Salvery* . . . . (1769); Anthony Benezet, *Some Historical Account of Guinea* . . . . (Philadelphia, 1771; reissued 1787); Rev. John Wesley, *Thoughts on Slavery* (1774; reissued, 1784); John Ady *et al. The Case of Our Fellow Creatures, the Oppressed Africans* . . . . (1783); Rev. James Ramsay, *An Essay on the Treatment and Conversion of African Slaves in the British Sugar Colonies* (1784); Rev. John Newton, *Thoughts Upon the African Slave Trade* (1788); Thomas Clarkson, *An Essay on the Slavery and Commerce of the Human Species, Particularly the African* (1788); William Wilberforce, *The Speech on Wednesday, May 13, 1789, on the Question of the Abolition of the Slave Trade* . . . . (1789); Henry, Lord Brougham, *A Concise Statement of the Question Regarding the Abolition of the Slave Trade* (1804); Zachary Macaulay, *Negro Slavery* (London, 1823); Rev. Thomas Cooper, *Facts Illustrative of the Condition of the Negro Slaves in Jamaica* (1824); James Stephen, *The Slavery of the British West India Colonies Delineated*, 2 vols (1824, 1830); James Cropper, *The Support of Slavery Investigated* (1824).

3. Ragatz, *British Caribbean Guide, 1763–1834*, pts 15 and 16, pp. 391–404.

4. Matthew Gregory Lewis, *The Journal of a West Indian Planter* (1834) p. 228.

5. Thomas Coke, *A History of the West Indies*, 3 vols (Liverpool, 1808–11) as quoted in Madeline Grant, 'Enemies to Caesar? Sectarian Missionaries in British West Indian Slave Society, 1754–1834' (University of Waterloo, unpublished MA thesis, 1976) p. 79.

6. Rev. Hope Masterton Waddell, *Twenty-Nine Years in the West Indies and Central Africa* (Nelson, 1863) p. 37.

7. J. E. Hutton, *A History of the Moravian Missions* (Moravian Publications Office, 1872).

8. Coke, *History of the West Indies, passim*.

9. Michael Craton, *A History of the Bahamas* (Collins, 1962) pp. 183

and 222; Rev. Edwin Angel Wallbridge, *The Demerara Martyr; Memoirs of the Rev. John Smith* . . . . (1848).

10. F. A. Cox, *History of the Baptist Missionary Society from 1792 to 1842* (1842); R. Lovett, *History of the London Missionary Society*, 2 vols (1899).

11. Hutton, *Moravian Missions*, p. 177.

12. Quoted in *Edinburgh Review*, Mar 1824, 244.

13. Rev. Elliott to LMS Directors, 7 Dec 1808, quoted by Bernard Marshall, 'Missionaries and Slaves in the British Windward Islands' (Association of Caribbean Historians, unpublished conference paper, Trinidad, 1980) p. 21.

14. Letter from Rev. Whitehouse to Wesleyan Missionary Society, 1 July 1829, in *British Sessional Papers, Commons, 1830–1*, XVI, p. 91, as quoted in Grant, 'Enemies to Caesar?' p. 79; 'Copy of a Journal Containing Various Occurrences at Le Resouvenir, Demerara, Commenced in March 1817 by John Smith, Missionary', PRO, CO 111/46.

15. Grant, 'Enemies to Caesar?' pp. 37–64.

16. *British Sessional Papers, Commons, 1831–2*, XLVII.

17. Quoted by Peter Duncan, *A Narrative of the Wesleyan Mission to Jamaica* (1849) p. 312.

18. Grant, 'Enemies to Caesar?' Appendix II, pp. 169–70.

19. Rev. John Lindsay, 'A Few Conjectural Considerations upon the Creation of the Humane Race, Occasioned by the Present British Quixottical Rage of Setting the Slaves from Africa at Liberty', BL, Add. MSS. 12439, fo. 258.

20. Rev. George W. Bridges, *A Voice from Jamaica* (1823).

21. One thinks, in contrast, of the initial failure of the missionaries to make converts in Africa. For example, Livingstone, though usually regarded as the greatest of African missionaries, apparently made only one convert during his career, who later backslid. Tim Jeal, *Livingstone* (1973).

22. See, for example, the witty interrogation of the missionaries by the village elders in Chinua Achebe, *Things Fall Apart* (New York: Fawcett Premier ed., 1958) pp. 134–7 and 164–7.

23. Quoted by Bernard Marshall, 'Missionaries and Slaves', p. 15.

24. Peter J. Wilson, *Crab Antics: The Social Anthropology of English-Speaking Negro Societies of the Caribbean* (New Haven: Yale University Press, 1973).

25. For example, see the way in which the Bahamian Baptist churches founded by the blacks Prince Williams and Sharper Morris divided on the coming of white missionaries in 1833–4. Michael Symonette and Antonia Canzonari, *Baptists in the Bahamas; An Historical Review* (Nassau, 1977) pp. 1–27.

26. Eugene D. Genovese, *Roll, Jordan, Roll; The World the Slaves Made* (New York: Pantheon, 1972) p. 7.

27. Robert Moore, 'Slave Rebellions in Guyana', in *Papers Presented at the Third Conference of Caribbean Historians Held at the University of Guyana, April 15—17, 1971*, pp. 62—74.

28. Genovese, *Roll, Jordan, Roll*, p. 207.

29. C. F. Pascoe, *Two Hundred Years of the SPG, 1701—1900* (1901).

30. Rev. John Clarke, *Memorials of Baptist Missions to Jamaica* (1869) pp. 9—31.

31. Ibid., p. 30.

32. Norman Cohn, *The Pursuit of the Millenium; Revolutionary Millenarianism and Mystical Anarchists of the Middle Ages* (1957) pp. 13—16.

33. Sidney Mintz and Douglas Hall, 'The Origins of the Jamaican Internal Marketing System', *Yale University Publications in Anthropology*, LVII (1960) pp. 1—26.

34. Memorial of Merchants and Planters interested in Dominica dated 5 Apr 1791, PRO, CO 71/19; Craton, *Testing the Chains*, ch. 17.

35. Ibid., pt 6, ch. 1.

36. Governor Murray to Lord Bathurst, 24 Aug 1823, PRO, CO 111/39; Joshua Bryant, *Account of an Insurrection of the Negro Slaves in the Colony of Demerara* (Georgetown, 1824) p. 6; Craton, *Testing the Chains*, ch. 19.

37. Bryant, *Account*, p. 9.

38. Trial proceedings for 5 Nov 1823, PRO, CO 111/43, p. 295.

39. PRO, CO 28/86; Craton, *Testing the Chains*, ch. 18.

40. *Proceedings of a General Court Martial held at the Colony House in George Town, on Monday the 13th day of October 1823* (Hatchard, 1824); *Edinburgh Review*, XL (Mar—July 1824) 226—70; 'The Late Insurrection in Demerara and Riot in Barbados', PRO, CO 111/43; Craton *Testing the Chains*, ch. 19.

41. Cecil Northcott, *Slavery's Martyr; John Smith of Demerara and the Emancipation Movement, 1817—1824* (Epworth Press, 1976) pp. 110—12; Edwin Angel Wallbridge, *The Demerara Martyr; Memoirs of the Rev. John Smith, Missionary to Demerara* (1848 and Georgetown, 1943) Appendix V, pp. 257—309.

42. Northcott, *Slavery's Martyr*, p. 111.

43. Craton, *Testing the Chains*, ch. 21; Philip Wright, *Knibb 'The Notorious,' Slaves' Missionary, 1803—1845* (Sidgwick and Jackson, 1973) pp. 56—133.

44. Committee appointed 30 May 1832; evidence taken, 6 June — 11 Aug 1832; Report ordered to be printed, 11 Aug 1832. *British*

Sessional Papers, Commons, Accounts and Papers, 1831–2, XLVII *(482).*

45. Michael Craton, *Sinews of Empire; A short History of British Slavery* (New York: Doubleday; Temple Smith, 1974) pp. 276–80.

46. Henry Bleby, *The Death Struggles of Slavery* (1853) p. 129.

5. BRITISH OPINION AND THE EMERGENCE OF HAITI, 1791–1805 *David Geggus*

1. W. Sypher, *Guinea's captive kings: British anti-slavery literature in the eighteenth century* (Chapel Hill, 1942) pp. 19–23; T. Clarkson, *History of the . . . abolition of the African slave trade* (1808) vol. II, 210–12; R.I. and S. Wilberforce, *Life of William Wilberforce* (1838) vol. I, p. 296.

2. See *The Times,* 24–31 Oct and *English Chronicle* 25 Oct–3Nov 1791.

3. West India Committee Library, Minute Book, vol. III, pp. 157–66; BL, Add. MSS. 38351, fos. 101–3, and 58906, fos. 111–14. The West India garrisons were already very strong but the planters wanted their slaves to see that the government supported them against the abolitionists. For the government's reaction, see D. Geggus, 'The British Government and the Saint Domingue slave revolt, 1791–93', *EHR* (Apr 1981), and for the reaction in Jamaica, D. Geggus, 'Jamaica and the Saint Domingue slave revolt, 1791–93', *The Americas* (Oct. 1981).

4. *The Times,* 10 Nov 1791 and *English Chronicle* 10–12 Nov 1791.

5. Wilberforce, *Life,* vol. I, pp. 340–1.

6. *The Times,* 28, 29, 31 Oct and 5 Nov 1791.

7. *English Chronicle,* 10–12 Nov and *The Star,* 18 and 22 Nov 1791.

8. See *Journals of the Assembly of Jamaica,* vol. IX, p. 6, Address to the Crown, 4 Nov 1791; *The Star,* 30 Nov 1791. The Jamaican planter Bryan Edwards deplored the cruelty of both sides. In his eye-witness reports from Cap Français, printed in the British press, he pitied the 'poor devils' made prisoner by the planters, while in Jamaica's address to the Crown he expatiated on the rebels' 'blackest crimes, as if receiving a deeper dye from the hands of the cruel and merciless enemy'.

9. *The Star,* 21 and 24 Nov, 17 and 22 Dec 1791; *The Times,* 19 and 27 Dec 1791; *English Chronicle* 1–3 Nov, 29–31 Dec 1791.

10. Clarkson, *History,* vol. II, pp. 348–50; Wilberforce, *Life,* vol. I, pp. 338–9.

11. R. I. and S. Wilberforce, *The correspondence of William Wilberforce* (1840) vol. I, pp. 89–90; above, note 5.

12. *A particular account of the commencement and progress of the insurrection of the negroes in St. Domingo* (1792).

13. T. Clarkson, *The true state of the case respecting the insurrection at St. Domingo* (Ipswich, 1792); [W. Roscoe], *An inquiry into the causes of the insurrection of the negroes in the island of St. Domingo* (1792).

14. See *The debate on the motion for the abolition of the slave trade in the House of Commons on Monday 2nd April 1792* (n.p., n.d.); Clarkson, *History*, vol. II, pp. 355—449; and on the importance of Long's evidence, T. Gisborne, *Remarks on the late decision . . . respecting the abolition of the slave trade* (1792) pp. 17—20. *PD*, XXIX, Cols 1055—158 provides fewer details.

15. See Geggus, 'British government'.

16. *Debate on the motion*, pp. 7—9, 44, 92 and 118; *The Star*, 18 and 21 Nov 1791.

17. Clarkson, *True state*, pp. 7—8; Roscoe, *Inquiry*.

18. See the Bodleian Library copy, annotated by Burke, of [Y. Cormier] *Mémoir sur la situation de Saint Dominigue à l'époque de janvier 1792* (n.p., n.d.) pp. 22 and 24. He also thought cannibalism, however, 'frequent in France also'.

19. *A letter from Percival Stockdale to Granville Sharp Esq., etc.* (Durham, n.d.) pp. 20—6.

20. W. Fox, *A defence of the decree of the National Convention . . . for emancipating the slaves, etc.* (1794).

21. See below, note 27. In the *Annual Register, 1793*, the poetry section included an *Ode on seeing a negro funeral* (taken from Bryan Edwards's history of the British West Indies, published that year) which described revolted slaves 'transformed to tigers, fierce and fell' glutting their 'rage for blood'.

22. *The Times*, 15 Aug, 5 Oct and 7 Nov 1794.

23. *Annual Register, 1797*, p. 128. The tombstone of one officer, buried in Salford, Lancashire, still bears witness to 'Domingo's' 'horrid wars', 'fierce barbarian wiles' and 'the yellow pest that stalks, gigantic, through the Western Isles'.

24. See D. Geggus, *Slavery, War and Revolution: the British occupation of Saint Domingue, 1793—98* (Oxford, 1981) ch. 9, pt 1; *Annual Register, 1796*, p. 66, and *1797*, pp. 121—6.

25. *PD*, XXXIII, cols 575—94.

26. B. Edwards, *An historical survey of the island of St. Domingo* (1797) preface and ch. 12.

27. *Gentleman's Magazine*, LXII (1794) 167, expresses the same idea.

28. However, in the 1801 edition he predicted that the former free coloureds would overthrow the blacks.

29. See Geggus, *Occupation*, ch. 5, pt 1, and ch. 9, pt 1. Edwards was also later accused of distorting his evidence concerning the slave revolt: *Christian Observer*, II (1803) 624.

30. *Gentleman's Magazine*, LXII (1794) 319–322 and 406–10.

31. See *The spirit of the public journals for 1797* (1802) pp. 240–1.

32. See Geggus, *Occupation*, ch. 10, pt 6.

33. *Annual Register, 1798*, pp. 234 and 247–9.

34. The passage is cited with suitably acidic commentary in C. L. R. James, *The black Jacobins* (New York, 1963) pp. 226–7.

35. PRO, HO 30/2, pp. 162–7 and WO 1/170, p. 345.

36. M. Rainsford, *St. Domingo or an historical, political and military sketch of the Black Republic* (1802) p. 5.

37. J. Stephen, *The crisis of the sugar colonies* (1802) pp. 14–15. Cf. *The Christian Observer*, I (1802) 134.

38. Rainsford, *Sketch*, p. 5. A second edition of Edwards's *Survey* was now brought out.

39. Stephen, *Crisis*, p. 7.

40. Capt. Rainsford, *A memoir of the transactions that took place in St. Domingo in the spring of 1799, etc.* (1802). Internal evidence shows the date in the title, doubtless added by the publisher, is incorrect. It was completely changed for the second edition.

41. Rainsford, *Memoir*, pp. 1–2, 17–18 and 20–3.

42. In mid-March it was learned that the French troops had landed in St Domingue and were meeting stiff resistance.

43. Rainsford, *Sketch*, pp. 17–18 and 59–63, and *Memoir*, p. 18. In the second work Rainsford's praise of the British planters is noticeably less fulsome.

44. Stephen, *Crisis*, pp. 27 and 72–5.

45. Ibid., pp. 79–80 and 113–15.

46. Government policy was, after allowing the expedition to sail, to remain neutral and hope for a speedy victory, as did the British planters. Even the Colonial Secretary Lord Hobart, who was an abolitionist, considered 'Toussaint's Black Empire' an 'evil': see H. Hughes, 'British policy towards Haiti, 1801–1805', *Canadian Historical Review*, XXV 4 (1944) 398. Yet only two years before a French attempt to raise a slave rebellion in Jamaica had been betrayed by Toussaint to the British: see PRO, CO 245/1, p. 34.

47. Stephen, *Crisis*, pp. 5, 113–15 and 150–1.

48. Ibid., pp. 113–16.

49. Ibid., p. 117. As soon as the signing of the peace preliminaries was known in Jamaica, Governor Nugent immediately declared void the new convention he had just negotiated and asked the Dominguan envoys to leave the island. The British resident was withdrawn from Port au Prince and all trade with St Domingue forbidden: *The Times*, 15 Mar 1802.

However, this was meant to ensure strict neutrality. Governor Johnson of Dominica, a planter, did without permission assist the French, but the Commander in Chief in the east Caribbean, General Trigge, agreed with Stephen's arguments and praised them highly to Prime Minister Addington: Devon Record Office, Addington Papers, 1802/OC2/3. Addington, too, read *The Crisis*.

50. Stephen, *Crisis*, pp. 15—16 and 29.

51. *The Christian Observer*, I (1802) 134—5, 200—2, 305—9, 333 and 403.

52. See Rainsford, *Sketch*, preface; [J. Stephen], *The opportunity, or reasons for an immediate alliance with St. Domingo* (1804) pp. 1—5 and 50, However, the recent French debacle in Egypt and Syria, now obscured by hindsight, was also fresh in contemporaries' minds.

53. W. Cobbett, *Letters to . . . Lord Hawkesbury and . . . Henry Addington, etc.*, 2nd edn (1802) p. 64; *Cobbett's Political Register*, vol. I, pp. 43, 188, 283—6 and 731—6. Cobbett claimed that the government only pretended the blacks were dangerous so as to justify its weakness in having allowed the French expedition to sail.

54. Fox was at this time in Paris paying court to Bonaparte.

55. *The Times*, 1 Jan, 5 Apr, 16 and 17 June 1802.

56. *The Times*, 18, 19, 20 Mar, 25 and 26 May.

57. See the *Annual Register, 1801*, p. 284 ff. and *1802*, preface; below, note 71.

58. *The Times*, 16 and 17 June 1802; *The Christian Observer*, I (1802) 401—3.

59. Cobbett, *Letters*, pp. 64—6 and 163—5; *Cobbett's Political Register*, vol. I, pp. 731—6. Cf. *Annual Register, 1802*, p. 209.

60. European commanders were infuriated by the blacks' refusal to stand still, like their own troops, and be shot.

61. Colonel Chalmers, *Brief remarks on the late war in St, Domingo* (1802) pp. 1, 36, 42—8, 55—66 and 81. On Chalmers, see Geggus, 'British government', note 51.

62. *Edinburgh Review*, I (1802) 216—37.

63. See *The True Briton*, 29 Jan 1803; H. Brougham, *An inquiry into the colonial policy of the European powers* (Edinburgh, 1803) vol. II, pp. 60—140 and 310—14.

64. Hughes, 'Policy', pp. 401—3.

65. *Morning Post*, 1 Feb 1803.

66. The convention did not promise assistance and had been abrogated. The freedom offered to the Dominguan recruits had been conditional upon five years service, which none had completed.

67. Wilberforce, *Correspondence*, vol. I, pp. 258—61 and 265; *The Christian Observer*, II (1803) 186.

68. *The Times*, 16 Mar 1803.

69. None the less, Charles Fox could still chide the British in 1803

for being more concerned with the Swiss, while regarding French inhumanity in St. Domingue as being beneficial to Britain's commercial and military interests: see D. V. Erdman (ed.), *The collected works of Samuel Taylor Coleridge* (Princeton, 1978) vol. III, pt i, p. 434 n.15.

70. *The Times* 22 July 1802; *The Christian Observer*, I (1802) 676–7 and 751; *Annual Register, 1802*, pp. 209–20; *Morning Post*, 9 Nov 1802. The blacks, *The Times* observed, had been 'cruelly deluded into all their crimes, all their sufferings' by the hypocritical French and their Rights of Man.

71. [J. Stephen], *Buonoparte in the West Indies, or the history of Toussaint Louverture, the African hero* (1803) pt 1, p. 2. Cf. the preface to the revised version, *The history of Toussaint Louverture* (1814). In its first year or so, the work went through four editions, including one Irish one.

72. For example, *Cobbett's Political Register*, vol. IV, pp. 933–7.

73. See Stephen, *Opportunity*, p. 10; *Morning Post*, 27 Jan 1804; Hughes, 'Policy', p. 405.

74. *The Times*, 28 Jan 1804.

75. Ibid., 27 and 28 Jan and 31 May 1804.

76. *The Christian Observer*, I (1802) 202.

77. See *the Edinburgh Review*, I (1802) 216–37; *The Christian Observer*, II (1803) 618–24.

78. C. Southey (ed.), *The life and correspondence of Robert Southey* (1850) vol. II, pp. 203–4.

79. H. Brougham, *A concise statement of the question regarding the abolition of the slave trade* (1804); *Edinburgh Review*, IV (1804) 476–86.

80. Wilberforce, *Life*, vol. III, pp. 180–1.

81. *The Christian Observer*, III (1804) 306–10. For the relative absence of colour prejudice in Britain at this time, see *Cobbett's Political Register*, vol. IV, 933–7.

82. *Edinburgh Review*, V (1804) 238; Stephen, *Opportunity*, pp. 12–14.

83. *The Times*, 18 Apr 1803, 28 Jan and 28 May 1804.

84. *Annual Register, 1802*, pp. 211–12, and *1803*, p. 333.

85. *The Times* 18 June 1804; *Cobbett's Political Register*, vol. V, pp. 125–6.

86. Hughes, 'Policy', pp. 405–8. By Sep 1804, it had been decided that a full treaty was neither desirable nor necessary, as Haiti's politics were deemed too unsettled and no longer threatening.

87. *The Christian Observer*, III (1804) 381; Wilberforce, *Correspondence*, vol. I, p. 350.

88. Erdman, *Collected works*, vol. III, pt ii, pp. 195 and 207. On Egypt, cf. Brougham, *Inquiry*, vol. II, pp. 354–99.

89. Southey, *Life*, vol. II, pp. 247 and 263–4.

90. S. Whitchurch, *Hispaniola, a poem* . . . (Bath, 1804) printed on cheap badly-cut paper. Whitchurch, then in his mid-forties, had long been interested in anti-slavery and had been a supporter of the self-proclaimed prophet Richard Brothers.

91. Ibid., pp. 66–7.

92. *Annual Register, 1802*, p. 220, and 1803, p. 335.

93. *The Times*, 28 May and 18 June 1804.

94. Brougham, *Inquiry*, vol. II, pp. 120–1, 141–84 and 409–44.

95. Cf. Geggus, *Occupation*, ch. 4, pt. 2.

96. Stephen, *Opportunity*, pp. 18–21; *The Christian Observer*, II (1803) 618–24 and 688–94; [Stephen], *Buonoparte*, pt 1, p. 15.

97. Stephen, *Opportunity*, pp. 33–44. We find the same illogicality as in *The Crisis*. If, as he said, the British colonies were not threatened internally and the Haitian threat could be deflected, then there was no material reason to ameliorate slavery or consider it doomed.

98. M. Rainsford, *An historical account of the black empire of Hayti* (1805) pp. x–xi, 103 and 360–4.

6. THE MISSIONARY CONTEXT OF THE BRITISH ANTI-SLAVERY MOVEMENT   *C. Duncan Rice*

1. Morgan Godwyn, *The Negro's and Indian's Advocate, Suing for their admission into the Church* (1680).

2. M. Warren, *The Missionary Movement from Britain in Modern History* (1965) p. 24.

3. *A Letter to William Wilberforce, M.P., on the Subject of Impressment* (1816); D. McLeod, *Gloomy Memories in the Highlands of Scotland . . . or a Faithful Picture of the Extirpation of the Celtic Race from the Highlands of Scotland* (Toronto, 1857) pp. 82–8.

4. G. Battiscombe, *Shaftesbury. The Great Reformer, 1801–1885* (Boston, 1975) pp. 70–85.

5. *Liberator*, 2 Oct.1840, 1 Jan, 14 May and 30 July 1841.

6. *Edinburgh Review*, VIII 16 (July 1806) 434.

7. *Edinburgh Review*, XII 23 (Apr 1808) 371.

8. 'Exeter Hall Pets', *Punch*, VI (1844) 210.

9. 'The Niger Expedition', (1848) in F. G. Kitton (ed.), *To Be read at Dusk and Other Stories, Sketches and Essays by Charles Dickens* (1898) p. 71; H. House, *The Dickens World* (1941) pp. 86–91.

10. Z. Macaulay to R. Paul, 4 Sep 1817, Paul Papers, Scottish National Library.

11. S. Jakobsson, *Am I not a Man and Brother? British Missions and the Abolition of the Slave Trade and Slavery in West Africa and the West Indies, 1786–1838* (Lund, 1972).

12. *Edinburgh Almanac or Universal Scots and Imperial Register for 1835* (Edinburgh, 1835) p. 453 and *passim*.

13. O. Ransford, *David Livingstone. The Dark Interior* (1978) p. 11.

14. G. Lambert, 'Dark Providence no Just Reason of Discouragement in Missionary Exertions', *Four Sermons* (1796) p. 34, quoted in J. A. De Jong, *As the Waters Cover the Sea. Millenial Expectations in the Rise of Anglo-American Missions, 1640—1810* (Kampen, 1970) p. 188.

15. Warren, *Missionary Movement*, pp. 46—7.

16. H. R. Temperley, *British Anti-Slavery, 1833—1870* (1972) pp. 72—3; C. Duncan Rice, *The Scots Abolitionists, 1833—1861* (Baton Rouge, 1981, forthcoming) appendices.

17. P. Hollis, 'Anti-Slavery and British Working-Class Radicalism', in C. Bolt and S. Drescher (eds), *Anti-Slavery, Religion and Reform: Essays in Memory of Roger Anstey* (Folkstone, Kent, 1980) pp. 303—4; S. Meacham, *Henry Thornton of Clapham* (Cambridge, Mass., 1964) pp. 136—46; J. Pollock, *Wilberforce* (New York, 1978) pp. 255—63.

18. D. B. Davis, *The Problem of Slavery in the Age of Revolution, 1770—1823* (Ithaca, 1975) pp. 453—68 and *passim*.

19. B. W. Noel, *Christian Missions to Heathen Nations* (1842) p. 348.

20. W. G. Enright, 'Urbanization and the Evangelical Pulpit in Nineteenth Century Scotland', *Church History*, XLVII (1978) 400—7.

21. D. Rothman, *The Discovery of the Asylum. Social Order and Disorder in the New Republic* (Boston, 1971).

22. C. Allen (ed.), *Plain Tales from the Raj. Images of British India in the Twentieth Century* (1975) p. 25. On the social background of early missionary recruitment see M. Warren, *Social History and Christian Mission* (1967) pp. 36—57.

23. *Edinburgh Review*, XIV 28 (Apr 1809) 40.

24. P. Hinchcliff, 'The Selection and Training of Missionaries in the Early Nineteenth Century', in G. J. Cuming (ed.), *The Mission of the Church and the Propagation of the Faith* (Cambridge, 1970) pp. 131—5.

25. D. M. Scott, 'Abolition as a Sacred Vocation', in L. Perry and M. Fellman (eds), *Anti-Slavery Reconsidered. New Perspectives on the Abolitionists* (Baton Rouge, 1979) pp. 51—74. See also Scott, *From Office to Profession. The New England Evangelical Ministry, 1750—1850* (Philadelphia, 1978); B. Heaney, *A Different Kind of Gentleman. Parish Clergy as 'Professional' Men in Early and Mid-Victorian England* (Hamden, Conn., 1976).

26. W. H. McKelvie, *Annals and Statistics of the United Presbyterian Church* (Edinburgh, 1873) pp. 678 ff.

27. G. Thompson, *Letters and Addresses . . . During his Mission in the United States* (Boston, 1837) p. 2.

28. M. Horne, *Letters on Missions, Addressed to the Protestant Ministers of the British Churches* (Andover, Mass., 1815) p. 19.

29. *Christian Missions to Heathen Nations*, pp. 347—8.

30. R. Anstey, 'The Protestant Ethic and Slavery', paper delivered at Waterloo Slave Studies Conference, 15 Mar 1979, p. 1.

31. See for instance C. Buchanan, *The Star in the East; a Sermon, preached . . . in . . . 1809* (Boston, 1811).

32. Unidentified quotation in Anstey, 'Protestant Ethic', p. 2.

33. Thompson, *Letters and Addresses*, p. 70.

34. T. Clarkson, *The History of the Rise, Progress, and Accomplishment of the Abolition of the African Slave Trade by the British Parliament*, 2 vols (1808) vol. II, p. 586.

35. J. Sturge and T. Harvey, *The West Indies in 1837* (1838) p. 380.

36. R. Wardlaw, *The Jubilee: A Sermon Preached . . . on . . . the Memorable Day of Negro Emancipation in the British Colonies* (Glasgow, 1834) p. 34.

37. C. K. Whipple, *Relation of the American Board of Commissioners for Foreign Missions to Slavery* (New York, 1861) p. 43.

38. Noel, *Christian Missions to Heathen Nations*, pp. 25—6.

39. S. Tomkins, 'The Psychology of Commitment: The Constructive Role of Violence and Suffering for the Individual and his Society', in M. Duberman (ed.), *The Anti-Slavery Vanguard: New Essays on the Abolitionists* (Princeton, 1965) pp. 270—98.

40. J. E. Gordon to T. Chalmers, 10 June 1818, MS. 4.8.7, Chalmers Papers, New College, Edinburgh.

41. B. Wyatt-Brown, 'Conscience and Career: Young Abolitionists and Missionaries', in Bolt and Drescher (eds) *Anti-Slavery, Religion, and Reform*, p. 196.

42. *Conference on Missions Held in 1860 at Liverpool* (1860) pp. 257—8.

43. H. Martineau, *The Martyr Age of the United States of America* (Newcastle, 1840) p. xviii.

44. E. Wigham, *The Anti-Slavery Cause in America and its Martyrs* (1863) pp. 61—3.

45. B. Edwards, *The History . . . of the British Colonies in the West Indies*, 3 vols (1801) vol. I, 431 ff; J. H. Bennet, Jr, *Bondsmen and Bishops; Slavery and Apprenticeship on the Codrington Plantations of Barbados, 1710—1838* (Berkeley, 1958).

46. Henry Brougham, *Speeches of Henry Lord Brougham*, 4 vols (Edinburgh, 1838) vol. II pp. 51—128.

47. H. Whiteley, *Three Months in Jamaica in 1832: Comprising a Residence of Seven Weeks on a Sugar Plantation* (1833); W. L. Burn, *Emancipation and Apprenticeship in the British West Indies* (1937) pp. 94—7.

48. Quoted in J. H. Hinton, *Memoirs of William Knibb, Missionary in Jamaica* (1847) p. 45.

49. W. Knibb and P. Borthwick, *Colonial Slavery. Defense of the Baptist Missionaries* (1833). See also P. Wright, *Knibb 'The Notorious,' Slaves' Missionary, 1803–1845* (1973) pp. 112 ff.

50. Whipple, *Relation of the American Board . . . to Slavery, passim*; R. J. Berkhofer, *Salvation in the Savage. An Analysis of Protestant Missions to the American Indian and the American Indian Response, 1787–1852* (Lexington, Kentucky, 1965) pp. 141–2.

51. For example, *Anti-Slavery Reporter*, 15 Oct 1845, 1 June 1850, 1 Apr 1853, 1 Dec 1854; *Anti-Slavery Advocate*, Oct and Nov 1854.

52. L. Tappan to W. Lillie, 16 Mar 1855, *Letterbooks*, IX, Tappan Papers, Library of Congress.

53. J. Dunlop, *American Slavery: Organic Sins, or the Iniquity of Licensed Injustice* (Edinburgh, 1846) p. 12.

54. Pollock, *Wilberforce*, p. 64.

7.   SLAVERY AND THE DEVELOPMENT OF DEMOGRAPHIC
THEORY IN THE AGE OF THE INDUSTRIAL REVOLUTION
B. W. Higman

* The author wishes to thank Stanley Engerman for his comments on a draft of this paper.

1. Michael Drake (ed.) *Population in Industrialization* (Methuen, 1969) p. 1.

2. See: ibid.; Thomas McKeown and R. G. Brown, 'Medical Evidence Related to English Population Changes in the Eighteenth Century', in D. V. Glass and D. E. C. Eversley (eds), *Population in History* (Edward Arnold, 1965) ch. 12; Thomas McKeown, *The Modern Rise of Population* (Edward Arnold, 1976); M. W. Flinn, *Origins of the Industrial Revolution* (Longman, 1966); J. D. Chambers, *Population, Economy, and Society in Pre-Industrial England* (Oxford University Press, 1972); M. W. Flinn, 'The Stabilisation of Mortality in Pre-industrial Western Europe', *Journal of European Economic History*, III 1 (Fall 1974) 285–318; Michael Flinn (ed.), *Scottish Population History* (Cambridge University Press, 1977); D. Levine, 'Some Competing Models of Population Growth during the First Industrial Revolution', *Journal of European Economic History*, VII 2 and 3 (Fall and Winter 1978) 499–516; David Levine, *Family Formation in an Age of Nascent Capitalism* (New York: Academic Press, 1977); Ronald Lee, 'Models of Preindustrial Dynamics with Applications to England', in Charles Tilly (ed.), *Historical Studies of Changing Fertility* (Princeton University Press, 1978) ch. 4; K. H.

Connell, *The Population of Ireland 1750—1845* (Oxford: Clarendon Press, 1950).

3. B. W. Higman, 'The Slave Populations of the British Caribbean: Some Nineteenth-Century Variations', in Samuel Proctor (ed.), *Eighteenth-Century Florida and the Caribbean* (Gainesville: University of Florida Press, 1976) pp. 60—70; Michael Craton, 'Hobbesian or Panglossian? The Two Extremes of Slave Conditions in the British Caribbean, 1783 to 1834', *William and Mary Quarterly*, XXXV (Apr 1978) 324—56.

4. Philip D. Curtin, *The Atlantic Slave Trade: A Census* (Madison: University of Wisconsin Press, 1969) pp. 29—30.

5. Richard Sheridan, *An era of West Indian Prosperity 1750—1775* (Barbados: Caribbean Universities Press, 1970) p. 108.

6. Lowell Joseph Ragatz, *The Fall of the Planter Class in the British Caribbean, 1763—1833* (New York: Octagon Books, 1963). Cf. R. Keith Aufhauser, 'Profitability of Slavery in the British Caribbean', *Journal of Interdisciplinary History*, V (1974) 45—67; Seymour Drescher, *Econocide: British Slavery in the Era of Abolition* (University of Pittsburgh Press, 1977).

7. E. J. Hobsbawm, 'The British Standard of Living 1790—1845' and 'History and "The Dark Satanic Mills" ', in *Labouring Men* (New York: Anchor Books, 1967) chs 5 and 6; R. M. Hartwell, 'The Rising Standard of Living in England, 1800—1850', *EcHR* XIII (1961) 397; J. E. Williams, 'The British Standard of Living, 1750—1850', *EcHR*, XIX 3 (Dec 1966) 581—9; M. W. Flinn, 'Trends in Real Wages, 1750—1850', *EcHR*, XXVII 3 (Aug 1974) 395—413; G. N. Von Tunzelman, 'Trends in Real Wages, 1750—1850, Revisited', *EcHR*, XXXII 1 (Feb 1979) 33—49.

8. D. V. Glass, *Numbering the People: The Eighteenth-Century Population Controversy and the Development of Census and Vital Statistics in Britain* (Farnborough: Saxon House, 1973) p. 11; Kenneth Smith, *The Malthusian Controversy* (Routledge and Kegan Paul, 1951) pp. 25—7.

9. William Godwin, *Of Population* (Longman, Hurst, Rees, Orme and Brown, 1820) p. 91.

10. Glass, *Numbering the People*, p. 12.

11. Robert V. Wells, *The Population of the British Colonies in America before 1776: A Survey of Census Data* (Princeton University Press, 1975) pp. 14 and 195.

12. See B. W. Higman, *Slave Population and Economy in Jamaica, 1807—1834* (Cambridge University Press, 1976). The registration returns are at T. 71, PRO.

13. See especially the reports of James Robertson, Registrar of Slaves for British Guiana, in Minutes of Court of Policy for Essequebo

and Demerara, 1824, vol. I, p. 329, and 1828, vol. II, pp. 153–73; *PP* 1833 (700) XXVI, 427–49.

14. Babington to Howick, 9 July 1832, T.71/678–1.

15. *Grenada Free Press* (St Georges), 2 July 1828, quoting the *Glasgow Courier*.

16. *A Review of the Colonial Slave Registration Acts, in a Report of a Committee of the Board of Directors of the African Institution* (African Institution, 1820) p. 68.

17. William H. Burnley, *Opinions on Slavery and Emancipation in 1823* (James Ridgway, 1823) p. xi.

18. Joseph J. Spengler, *France Faces Depopulation* (New York: Greenwood Press, 1968); Tilly, *Historical Studies*.

19. Thomas Robert Malthus, *An Essay on the Principle of Population*, ed. Philip Appleman (New York: W. W. Norton and Co., 1976) p. 3.

20. Joseph J. Spengler, *French Predecessors of Malthus* (Duke University Press, 1942) pp. 163, 215, 255 and 260.

21. D. E. C. Eversley, *Social Theories of Fertility and the Malthusian Debate* (Oxford: Clarendon Press, 1959) pp. 54–8. For modern discussions of this question see W. L. Westermann, *The Slave Systems of Greek and Roman Antiquity* (Philadelphia: American Philosophical Society, 1955) p. 32; Cedric A. Yeo, 'The Economics of Roman and American Slavery', *Finanzarchiv*, XIII (1952) 459; A. H. M. Jones, 'Slavery in the Ancient World', *EcHR*, IX (1956) 193: M. I. Finley, *The Ancient Economy* (Chatto and Windus, 1973) p. 86.

22. Malthus, *Essay* (Appleman edn) p. 31.

23. T. R. Malthus, *An Essay on Population* (J. M. Dent and Sons, 1960) vol. I, pp. 150–1.

24. See also Sir James Steuart, *An Inquiry into the Principles of Political Economy* (Edinburgh: Oliver and Boyd, 1966) vol. I, pp. 47–51 and 147–9; Eversley, *Social Theories*, pp. 54–8.

25. For a review of the reasons for this contrast, see Stanley L. Engerman, 'Some Economic and Demographic Comparisons of Slavery in the United States and the British West Indies', *EcHR*, XXIX 2 (May 1976) 258–75.

26. James H. Cassedy, *Demography in Early America* (Cambridge, Mass.: Harvard University Press, 1969) p. 178; J. Potter, 'The Growth of Population in America, 1700–1860', in Glass and Eversley (eds), *Population in History*, ch. 27; C. Vann Woodward, 'Southern Slaves in the World of Thomas Malthus', in *American Counterpoint* (Boston: Little, Brown and Co., 1971) p. 90.

27. Malthus, *Essay* (Dent edn) vol. I, pp. 7–8.

28. Ira Berlin, 'Time, Space, and the Evolution of Afro-American

Society on British Mainland North America', *American Historical Review*, LXXXV (1980) 46; Arthur Zilversmit, *The First Emancipation: The Abolition of Slavery in the North* (University of Chicago Press, 1967) p. 222.

29. Godwin, *Of Population*, p. 439; Michael Thomas Sadler, *Ireland; Its Evils and Their Remedies* (John Murray, 1829) p. xxv.

30. Malthus, *Essay* (Dent edn) vol. I, p. 91.

31. Malthus, *Essay* (Appleman edn) pp. 46–7. See also *PP* 1826–7 (550), V, 'Third Report from the Select Committee on Emigration from the United Kingdom', pp. 311–27.

32. J. J. Spengler, 'Malthusianism and the Debate on Slavery', *South Atlantic Quarterly*, XXXIV 2 (Apr 1935) 170–89; Joseph J. Spengler, 'Population Theory in the Ante-Bellum South', *Journal of Southern History*, II 3 (Aug 1936) 360–89; Woodward, 'Southern Slaves'.

33. David Brion Davis, *The Problem of Slavery in the Age of Revolution, 1770–1823* (Ithaca: Cornell University Press, 1975) p. 359; Harold A. Boner, *Hungry Generations: The Nineteenth-Century Case Against Malthusianism* (New York: Columbia University Press, 1955) p. 56.

34. Patricia James, *Population Malthus: His Life and Times* (Routledge & Kegan Paul, 1979) pp. 124–5, Smith; *Malthusian Controversy*, p. 250.

35. *PD*, 1st series, II, 13 June 1804, cols 658–9.

36. Malthus was also referred to freely in the United States debates on abolition. See Duncan J. MacLeod, *Slavery, Race and the American Revolution* (Cambridge University Press, 1974) pp. 58 and 203, n. 150.

37. *PD*, 1st series, VIII, 5 Feb 1807, col. 667.

38. Ibid., 23 Feb 1807, col. 987.

39. Ibid., col. 993, and 1st Series, IX, 16 Mar 1807, col. 118. On 27 February 1807 Malthus wrote to his close friend the Rev. Edward Clarke: 'I went to Town on Monday with the intention of being present at the debate on the abolition, but was too late; I was just in time however to see Mr. Wilberforce before he went into the house, and to furnish him with data to rescue my character from the imputation of being a friend to the slave trade. I should have been much distressed if the accusation had been made without being contradicted'. Quoted in James, *Population Malthus*, p. 125.

40. James, *Population Malthus*, pp. 39, 125–6 and 340–1.

41. George Ensor, *An Inquiry Concerning the Population of Nations* (Effingham Wilson, 1818) p. 79.

42. Ibid., p. 251.

43. Ibid., p. 254.

44. *PD*, 1st series, VIII, 23 Feb 1807, col. 949.

45. Ibid., 1st series, XXVIII, 20 July 1814, col. 803.

46. James Stephen, *Essays in Ecclesiastical Biography* (Longman, Green and Co., 1891) p. 547.

47. *PP* (Lords) 1832, II, p. 828.

48. Ibid., p. 828.

49. *Instructions for the Management of a Plantation in Barbados, and for the Treatment of Negroes* (1786) p. 2.

50. A West Indian, *Notes in Defence of the Colonies: On the Increase and Decrease of the Slave Population of the British West Indies* (Jamaica, 1826) p. 19.

51. *Further Proceedings of the Honourable House of Assembly of Jamaica* (1816) p. 30.

52. Burnley, *Opinions on Slavery*, pp. vi—vii.

53. *PP* (Lords) 1832, II, p. 828.

54. Ibid., pp. 828—9.

55. Ibid., pp. 830 and 883.

56. James Stephen, *The Slavery of the British West India Colonies Delineated*, vol. II (Saunders and Benning, 1830) p. 76.

57. Ibid., pp. 76—7.

58. See John D. Post, *The Last Great Subsistence Crisis in the Western World* (Baltimore: Johns Hopkins University Press, 1977); John D. Post, 'Famine, Mortality, and Epidemic Disease in the Process of Modernization', *EcHR*, XXIX 1 (Feb 1976) 14—37; Paul Slack, 'Mortality Crises and Epidemic Disease in England, 1485—1610', in Charles Webster (ed.), *Health, Medicine and Mortality in the Sixteenth Century* (Cambridge University Press, 1979) ch. 1; T. S. Ashton, *Economic Fluctuations in England, 1700—1800* (Oxford: Clarendon Press, 1959); Andrew B. Appleby, *Famine in Tudor and Stuart England* (Stanford University Press, 1978); M. L. Parry, *Climatic Change, Agriculture and Settlement* (Folkestone: Dawson, 1978).

59. Richard B. Sheridan, 'The Crisis of Slave Subsistence in the British West Indies during and after the American Revolution', *William and Mary Quarterly*, XXXIII (Oct 1976) 615—41.

60. Maxwell to Bathurst, 11 Mar 1823, CO 239/9; Nicolay to Goderich, 2 May 1832, 239/29; *Grenada Free Press*, 19 Sept and 10 Oct 1832; T.71/261—3.

61. Michael Craton, 'Death, Disease and Medicine on Jamaican Slave Plantations; the Example of Worthy Park, 1767—1838', *Histoire Sociale — Social History*, IX (Nov 1976) 237—55.

62. See, for example, *PD*, 1st series, IX, 16 Mar 1807, col. 121 (Hibbert).

63. Stephen, *Slavery*, p. 79.

64. *PD*, 1st series, II, 30 May 1804, col. 450.

65. Ibid., 1st series, II, 30 May 1804, col. 453; 1st series, III, 28 Feb 1805, col. 670.

66. Ibid., 1st series, III, 28 Feb 1805, col. 672.

67. Minute Book of the Society for the Improvement of West India Plantership, 1811–12, and of the Agricultural Society, 1812–16, pp. 115–16 (MSS. University of Keele Library; microfilm at University of the West Indies Library).

68. Ibid., pp. 116, 118 and 133.

69. Woodford to Bathurst, 12 June 1825, CO 295/66, fo. 53 (evidence of Burton Williams, 18 Jan 1825).

70. Skeete to Murray, 2 Dec 1828, CO 28/102, p. 145.

71. *Barbados Mercury*, 19 Mar 1833, quoted in *St. Georges Chronicle and Grenada Gazette*, 30 Mar 1833. For a further illustration of the ambiguity of the Bardadian planters on the issue, see Bruce M. Taylor, 'Our Man in London: John Pollard Mayers, Agent for Barbados, and the British Abolition Act, 1832–1834', *Caribbean Studies*, XVI 3 and 4 (Oct 1976, Jan 1977) 77–9.

72. G. W. Roberts, 'Emigration from the Island of Barbados', *Social and Economic Studies*, IV 3 (Sep 1955) 252.

73. Colebrooke to Russell, 25 Jan 1840, CO 239/58; David Lowenthal and Colin G. Clarke, 'Slave-Breeding in Barbuda: The Past of a Negro Myth', *Annals of the New York Academy of Sciences*, CCXCII (June 1977) 510–35.

74. Davis, *Problem*, p. 359.

75. Eversley, *Social Theories*, pp. 23–88.

76. See Engerman, 'Some Economic and Demographic Comparisons'; Herbert S. Klein and Stanley L. Engerman, 'Fertility Differentials between Slaves in the United States and the British West Indies: A Note on Lactation Practices and Their Possible Implications', *William and Mary Quarterly*, XXXV (Apr 1978) 357–74; Craton, 'Hobbesian or Panglossian?'; Higman, *Slave Population and Economy*; Higman, 'Slave Populations'.

77. Davis, *Problem*, p. 356.

78. For example, *PD*, 1st series, II, 13 June 1804, col. 660 (William Young); 2nd series, XIII, 31 May 1825, col. 1010 (Richard Gordon); 2nd series, XIX, 1 May 1828, col. 241 (Earl of Darnley).

79. Francis D. Klingender, *Art and the Industrial Revolution* (Frogmore: Paladin, 1972) p. 100.

80. Malthus, *Essay* (Everyman edn) vol. II, p. 278, quoted in Richard B. Simons, 'T. R. Malthus on British Society', *Journal of the History of Ideas*, XVI 1 (Jan 1955) 75.

81. James P. Huzel, 'Malthus, the Poor Law, and Population in Early Nineteenth-Century England', *EcHR*, XXII 3 (Dec 1969) 430–52; Raymond Cowherd, *Political Economists and the English Poor Laws* (Athens: Ohio University Press, 1978); S. G. and E. O. A. Checkland

(eds), *The Poor Law Report of 1834* (Harmondsworth: Penguin Books, 1974).

82. Davis, *Problem*, p. 358; David Brion Davis, *The Problem of Slavery in Western Culture* (Harmondsworth: Penguin Books, 1970) p. 366.

8. ABOLITIONIST PERCEPTIONS OF SOCIETY AFTER SLAVERY   *David Eltis*

1. See David Brion Davis, *The Problem of Slavery in the Age of Revolution* (Ithaca, 1975); Roger T. Anstey, *The Atlantic Slave Trade and British Abolition, 1760–1810* (1975); Seymour Drescher, *Econocide* (Pittsburgh, 1977); Howard Temperley, 'Capitalism, Slavery and Ideology', *Past & Present*, 75 (1977) 94–118. For a partial synthesis of these and a development of the argument in this paragraph see Stanley L. Engerman and David Eltis, 'Economic Aspects of the Abolition Debate', in Seymour Drescher and Christine Bolt (eds) *Anti-Slavery, Religion and Reform* (Folkestone, 1980).

2. William Wilberforce, *An Appeal To The Religion, Justice and Humanity of The Inhabitants of The British Empire On Behalf of the Negro Slaves in the West Indies* (1823). See also James Cropper, *A Letter Addressed to the Liverpool Society for Promoting the Abolition of Slavery* . . . (1823) p. 5, and Thomas Clarkson, *Thoughts on the Necessity of Improving the Condition of the Slaves in the British Colonies* . . . (1823) p. 51. For a sensitive discussion of James Stephen's position see Davis, *The Problem of Slavery*, pp. 366–8.

3. Seymour Drescher, 'Capitalism and Abolition', in Roger T. Anstey and P. E. H. Hair (eds), *Liverpool, the African Slave Trade and Abolition* (Liverpool, 1976) pp. 167–95. James Walvin, 'The Public Campaign in England against Slavery, 1787–1834', in David Eltis and James Walvin (eds), *The Abolition of the Atlantic Slave Trade* (Madison, Wisconsin, 1981), pp. 63–79.

4. *PD*, 3rd series, XV, 18 Mar 1833, cols 729–30.

5. David Brion Davis, 'The Emergence of Immediatism in British and American Anti-Slavery Thought', *Mississippi Valley Historical Review*, XLIX (1962–3) 209–30, in particular pp. 219–22.

6. See for example Wilberforce in William Cobbett (ed.), *The Parliamentary History of England*, XXIX (2 Apr 1792) 1072.

7. Thomas More Madden (ed.), *The Memoirs (chiefly autobiographical) from 1798 to 1886 of Richard Robert Madden* (1891) pp. 95–7.

8. The issue addressed by David Brion Davis, *The Problem of Slavery in Western Culture* (Ithaca, 1966).

9. Drescher, *Econocide*, pp. 142–86; W. A. Green, 'The Planter

Class and British West Indian Sugar Production before and after Emancipation', *EcHR*, XXVI (1973) 448–63. In the continuing debate on the US slave economy, the latest chapter of which was triggered by Robert W. Fogel and Stanley L. Engerman, *Time on the Cross* (Boston, 1974), the high efficiency of the southern plantation relative to the northern farm appears to have been accepted by all participants. Differences remain on the origin of the efficiency but no one is arguing that the planter would have been better off with free labour. See Paul David *et al.*, *Reckoning with Slavery* (New York, 1976) pp. 202–23; Fogel and Engerman, 'Explaining the Relative Efficiency of Slave Agriculture in the Antebellum South', *American Economic Review*, LXVII (1977) 275–96 and replies by Donald F. Schaeffer and Mark D. Schmitz, Paul A. David and Peter Temin, and Gavin Wright, ibid., LXIX (1979) 208–26. An additional element of the northern critique of the southern economy not present in the British case was the South's failure to industrialise. See Eugene D. Genovese and Elizabeth Fox Genovese, 'The Slave Economies in Political Perspective', *Journal of American History*, vol. 66, no. 1 (June 1979) 7–23. Abolitionist explanations of planter behaviour were usually given in terms of the 'passions of man being excited' by the exercise of supreme power to the point where the planter could not discern where his best interests lay.

10. Stephen conceded the difficulty of attracting free labour to the West Indies but not its inferior productivity relative to slave labour. See *Crisis of the Sugar Colonies* (1802) p. 191 and *The Slavery of the British West India Colonies Delineated* (1824–30) vol. I, pp. xxxiii, and vol. II, pp. 381–3.

11. Reginald Coupland, *Wilberforce, a Narrative* (Oxford, 1923) pp. 405–46.

12. Davis, *The Problem of Slavery*.

13. A. W. Coats, 'Changing Attitudes to Labour in the mid Eighteenth Century', *EcHR*, II (1958–9) 35–51; Stanley L. Engerman, 'Coerced and Free Labor: Property Rights and the development of the Labor Force' (forthcoming).

14. See the evidence of Thomas Fowell Buxton, Rev. John Thorpe, William Knibb and others in the *Report of the Select Committee on the Laws and Usages of the West Indian Colonies in relation to the Slave Population*, *PP* (Lords), CCCVII (1831–2) pp. 805, 855 and 1055. Also the *Report from the Select Committee on the Extinction of Slavery Throughout the British Dominions* (*PP* 1831–2, XX) p. 182.

15. Rev. P. Duncan in *Report from the Select Committee on the Laws and Usages . . . (PP* Lords), 1831–2, p. 669.

16. *Anti-Slavery Reporter*, I (1826) 242. William Wilberforce to King of Hayti, 8 Oct 1818, in R.I. and S. Wilberforce, *The Correspondence of William Wilberforce* (1840) vol. II, pp. 385–6.

17. *The West Indies in 1837* (1838) p. 374; cf. *The Report of the Committee of the African Institution . . . 15th July, 1807* (1811) p. 24, 'indolence is a disease which it is the business of civilization to cure'; *Edinburgh Review,* XXIV (1808) p. 375; Henry Meredith, *An Account of the Gold Coast of Africa* (1812) p. 213.

18. Undated memorandum in PRO CO 320/1 cited in W. L. Burn, *Emancipation and Apprenticeship in the British West Indies* (1937) p. 105.

19. Sturge and Harvey, p. 51. See also William Knibb's evidence in *Report of the Select Committee on West Indian Colonies* (*PP* 1842, XIII) p. 422, and Philip Wright's discussion in *Knibb the Notorious* (1973) pp. 229–30. Mary Turner, however, following Hinton's lead in his *Memoir of William Knibb* (1847) p. 207, suggests that the Baptists envisaged a newly structured economy built on small proprietors in *Slaves and Missionaries* (forthcoming). But note that prosperity was still linked indissolubly with market participation even though Knibb acknowledged the possibility of a decline in sugar exports (Knibb to Sturge, 5 Jan 1839; Hinton, p. 310).

20. See for example Adam Hodgson, *A Letter to J. B. Say on the Comparative Expense of Free and Slave Labour* (1823) p. 28.

21. D. L. Murray, *The West Indies and the Development of Colonial Government 1801–1834* (Oxford, 1965) pp. 104–5, 141–2 and 153–4; J. Stephen, *The Slavery of the British*.

22. *Anti-Slavery Reporter,* I (1826) 88.

23. *The West India Question* (1832) p. 15.

24. Clarkson, *Thoughts on the Necessity of Improving,* p. 27.

25. *Anti-Slavery Reporter,* I (1826) 360.

26. Henry Brougham, *An Enquiry into the Colonial Policy of the European Powers* (Edinburgh, 1803) vol. II, pp. 507–18. This was an extension of the stages model widely current at the time – see the discussion in Philip D. Curtin, *Image of Africa, British Ideas and Action 1780–1850* (Madison, Wisconsin, 1964) pp. 63–5.

27. William Taylor, *Report from the Select Committee on the Extinction . . .* (*PP* 1831–2) p. 29. For evidence of this view see Sturge and Harvey, p. 72; James Cropper, *The Interests of the Country and the Prosperity of the West Indian Planters mutually secured by the immediate abolition of slavery . . .* (1833) p. 25; Woodville K. Marshall (ed.) *The Colthurst Journal* (New York, 1977) p. 166; *Report from the Select Committee on the Laws and Usages . . .* (*PP* (Lords), 1831–2) p. 617. For a later exposition see W. Neilson Hancock, *The Abolition of Slavery Considered with reference to the state of the West Indies since Emancipation* (Dublin, 1852) pp. 5–7.

28. *Report from the Select Committee on the Laws and Usages . . .* (*PP* (Lords), 1831–2) p. 905. See his complete evidence, pp. 836–940;

see also Stuart, pp. 30–1; Clarkson, pp. 19–29; and Josiah Condor, *Wages or the Whip* (1833) pp. 81–90. The limitations of the abolitionist's conception of freedom came out much more clearly in the French case than in the English. See Seymour Drescher's discussion of de Toqueville's abolitionism in *Dilemmas of Democracy* (Pittsburgh, 1968) pp. 151–95.

29. R. I. and S. Wilberforce (eds), *The Correspondence of William Wilberforce* (1840) vol. I, pp. 385–6; Marshall, p. 161. Almost all the witnesses examined by the 1832 select committees, planter and abolitionist alike, urged that occupation of the provision grounds be made conditional on the occupant working on the estate.

30. Clarkson, p. 38; see also *Report from the Select Committee on the Extinction* . . . (*PP* 1831–2) pp. 69, 120, 176 and 310.

31. Condor, p. 44; Sturge and Harvey, p. 31. The argument was incorporated into the *Report of the Select Committee on the Commercial State of the West Indies* (*PP* 1831–2, XX) p. 21.

32. *Report from the Select Committee on Laws and Usages* . . . (*PP* (Lords), 1831–2) p. 1048.

33. Marshall, pp. 197–8.

34. *Report from the Select Committee on the Extinction* . . . (*PP* 1831–2, XX) pp. 151–2, 161 and 170. See Buxton's speech in *PD*, 3rd series, XXVIII (19 June 1835) Col. 924 and Governor Sir Charles Metcalfe's summary of the issue cited in Douglas G. Hall, *Free Jamaica, 1838–65: An Economic History* (New Haven, 1959) pp. 158–9.

35. The best summaries of British emancipation plans are in Lowell J. Ragatz, *The Fall of the Planter Class in the British West Indies, 1763–1833* (New York, 1928) pp. 449–52 and Burn, pp. 107–14.

36. See in particular John Davy, *The West Indies, Before and Since Slave Emancipation* (1854) and William G. Sewell, *The Ordeal of Free Labor in the British West Indies* (New York, 1862).

37. The best general survey is William A. Green, *British Slave Emancipation: The Sugar Colonies and the Great Experiment, 1830–65* (Oxford, 1976), but for outstanding surveys of individual colonies see Hall, for Jamaica, and Alan H. Adamson, *Sugar without Slaves* (New Haven, 1972) for British Guiana.

38. N. Deerr, *The History of Sugar* (1949–50) pp. 193–203. For a summary of Deerr's figures and more recent work see Stanley L. Engerman, 'Notes on the Patterns of Economic Growth in the British North American Colonies in the Seventeenth, Eighteenth and Nineteenth Centuries', to appear in Paul Bairoch and Maurice Levy Leboyer, *Disparities in Economic Development since the Industrial Revolution*.

39. Macpherson makes the distinction between a market economy where the self-employed sell their produce on the open market, and a market society where labour itself is a marketable factor of production:

C. B. Macpherson, *The Political Theory of Possessive Individualism* (Oxford, 1962) p. 48. Most abolitionists would probably have been happy with the former if it had been consistent with the maintenance of exports. For the development of internal markets see Sidney Mintz, 'Slavery and the Rise of Peasantries', *Historical Reflections*, VI (1979) 213—42 and his *Caribbean Transformations* (Chicago, 1974) pp. 180—224; Gisela Eisner, *Jamaica, 1830—1930: A Study in Economic Growth* (Manchester, 1961). For production of a minor export staple see J. S. Handler, 'The History of Arrowroot and the Origin of Peasantries in the British West Indies', *Journal of Caribbean History*, II (1971) 59—83.

40. Philip D. Curtin, *Two Jamaicas* (Cambridge, Mass., 1955) pp. 122—57; Douglas G. Hall, 'The Flight from the Estates Reconsidered: the British West Indies, 1838—42', *Journal of Caribbean History*, X (1978) 8—34; Brian W. Blouet, 'Land Policies in Trinidad, 1838—50', ibid., VII (1976) 43—59; Woodville K. Marshall, 'The Ex-Slaves as Wage Labourers on the Sugar Estates in the British Windward Islands, 1838—1846', paper presented to the 1979 ACH meetings, Curacao; Adamson, pp. 34—56; the most convenient survey is in *Report of the Select Committee on the West Indian Colonies* (*PP* 1842, XIII) in particular pp. 1, 3, 46, 93, 116—17, 121 and 299—303.

41. Howard Temperley, *British Anti-slavery, 1833—1870* (Columbia, SC, 1972) pp. 121—36; Christine Bolt, *The Anti-Slavery Movement and Reconstruction* (Oxford, 1969) pp. 1—25.

42. The Colonial Office commitment to maximising sugar output lasted till the 1880s. See William A. Green, 'James Stephen and British West India Policy, 1834—1847', *Caribbean Studies*, XIII (1972) 33—56 for a discussion of the harder official line of the 1840s.

43. *Report of the Select Committee on the West Indian Colonies* (*PP* 1842, XIII) pp. 291—314, 440—3 and 548.

44. Burn, p. 373; Marshall (ed.), *The Colthurst Journal*, 165.

45. E. M. Davis to Elizabeth Pease, 15 Feb 1842, in Clare Taylor, *British and American Abolitionists* (Edinburgh, 1974) p. 167; Temperley, p. 157. The emergence of this group which may be traced back to James Cropper and before him William Roscoe and his Jacobinical friends (see Kenneth Charlton, 'James Cropper and Liverpool's Contribution to the Anti-Slavery Movement', *Transactions of the Historic Society of Lancashire and Cheshire*, CXXIII (1972) 57—80) is one of the most striking developments in British abolitionism between the 1780s and the 1840s. It is not that Tory dominance of the movement concurrently disappeared but that the movement could always lay claim to the sympathies of the economically progressive, whether they were Tory, Whig or radical. In the 1780s the nexus of this group was Tory, by the 1840s it was located predominantly amongst the latter two.

46. James Cropper to William Lloyd Garrison, 17 May 1834, in Taylor, p. 29. Howard Temperley has dealt with the free labour theme in the emancipation campaign but tends to treat it as a tactical device rather than a vital part of the anti-slavery core. See *Past & Present*, p. 94—118.

47. Unknown (but from the rest of the letter obviously a British Garrisonian) to Maria Weston Chapman, 24 May 1844; J. B. Estlin to Webb(?), 5 Nov 1845, both in Taylor, pp. 219 and 241.

48. *PD*, 3rd series, XCIX (26 June 1848) col. 1222.

49. 'Humanity sold for Sugar; the British Abolitionists' Attitude to Free Trade in Slave Grown Sugar', *HJ*, XIII (1970) 411—12.

50. Henry George Grey, *The Colonial Policy of Lord John Russell's Administration* (1853) vol. II, p. 303. Grey was probably the most doctrinaire 'moderniser' to hold cabinet rank at this time. He was a convinced abolitionist, of course, but when Undersecretary for the Colonies in 1832 (as Lord Howick) he advocated the harshest of the emancipation plans considered by the Colonial Office. Ten years later he attempted to get the 1842 Select Committee to include resolutions incorporating similar measures in its report. His record as Colonial Secretary, 1846—52, is described in Adamson, pp. 50—5.

51. Estlin papers, Williams Library, London.

52. J. B. Estlin to R. D. Webb, 13 Nov 1845 (Taylor, p. 242).

53. Gilbert Osofsky, 'Abolitionists, Irish Immigrants and Romantic Nationalism', *American Historical Review*, LXXX (1975) 889—912; Carl Siracusa, *A Mechanical People; Perceptions of the Industrial Order in Massachusetts, 1815—1880* (Middletown, Conn., 1979) pp. 144—8; Peter F. Walker, *Moral Choices: Memory, Desire and Imagination in Nineteenth-Century American Abolition* (Baton Rouge, 1978) pp. 15—20.

54. James Haughton, *Should the holders of slave property receive compensation on the abolition of slavery* (Dublin, 1853) pp. 1—13.

55. *Proceedings of the American Anti-Slavery Society at its Second Decade* (New York, 1854) p. 112.

56. Temperley, *British Antislavery*, pp. 111—36.

57. Haughton, pp. 1—8; W. Neilson Hancock, pp. 10—14; John Candler and G. W. Alexander, *The British West Indies in 1850* (1851); [W. E. Forster], 'British Philanthropy and Jamaica Distress', *Westminster Review*, LIX (1853) 171—89; Charles Buxton, *Slavery and Freedom in the British West Indies* (1860).

58. Douglas Lorimer, *Colour, Class and the Victorians* (New York, 1978) pp. 127—8. For earlier and more private abolitionist criticism of the Jamaican labourer see Lewis Tappan to John Scoble, 31 July 1844, in Annie Abel and F. J. Klingberg, 'The Correspondence of Lewis Tappan and others with the British and Foreign Anti-Slavery Society',

Journal of Negro History, XII (1929) 317.

59. See Lushington's eloquent exposition in *PD*, 3rd series, LVIII (7 May 1841) cols 82–4; cf. *Report of the Select Committee of the House of Lords on the Slave Trade with Minutes of Evidence* (*PP* 1849, XIX) pp. 93–4.

60. W. Emanual Riviere, 'Labour Shortage in the British West Indies after Emancipation', *Journal of Caribbean History*, IV (1974) 10; Stanely L. Engerman, 'Economic Aspects of the Adjustments to Emancipation in the United States and the British West Indies' (forthcoming).

61. Herman Merivale, *Lectures on Colonization and the Colonies* (1861) p. 303.

62. As one of the special magistrates put it, 'It is quite overlooked that compulsion may exist without coercion but of a rationale that is of the highest and strongest kind, a moral compulsion arising from the presence of felt wants whether natural or artificial and from the force of attachment to place and neighbourhood of which the negro is keenly susceptible': Sligo to Genelg (enc.) 28 July 1836, CO 137/212, cited in Burn, p. 373. A gauge of the change may be obtained by comparing abolitionist evidence before the 1832 committee with the equivalent given to the 1842 committee. One of the first indications of it was in Richard R. Madden's evidence in *Report of Select Committee on the Working of the Apprenticeship System in the Colonies . . .* (*PP* 1836, XV) pp. 75–85.

63. Sir Charles Metcalfe stated the dilemma when he claimed estate labour is necessary to the 'civilization and future welfare of the negroes' but found it objectionable 'to adopt any measures with a view to coercion in that respect': *Report of the Select Committee on the West Indian Colonies* (*PP* 1842, XIII) p. 517. An unresolved issue here is the extent to which the flight from the estates was a rational response to poor pay or a function of an overwhelming desire to be independent. To put it another way, was the ex-slave exhibiting a 'pre-industrial' utility in opting out of wage labour or were wages simply too low? See Stanley L. Engerman, 'Economic Aspects of the Adjustments to Emancipation'.

64. The first imperial expenditures in Jamaica for developmental purposes of any kind did not come until 1869 (Burn, p. 379). This, of course, is not to ignore the large-scale educational activities organised by the missionaries and the anti-slavery leaders.

65. *Report of the Select Committee on the West Indian Colonies* (*PP* 1842, XIII) p. iv. For the benefits of abolition as perceived by American abolitionists see James M. McPherson, 'Was West Indian Emancipation a Success? The Abolitionist Argument During the American Civil War', *Caribbean Quarterly*, IV (1964) 28–34.

66. See for example Hancock, pp. 5–7, and William Knibb. For the

latter's views see his evidence to the 1842 committee, in particular the following exchange:

'McGrantley Berkeley: "What with the fourpost bedsteads, the side-boards, the mahogany chairs, the riding horses, the brood mares, the provision grounds . . . (do) you consider the labourers in Jamaica at present better off than the labourer in this country?"

Knibb: "Decidely: I should be very sorry to see them as badly off as the labourers in this country; half of them of starving . . . . Owner occupied or securely held smallholdings will increase the demand for consumer goods by the ex-slaves." '

(*Report of the Select Committee on the West Indian Colonies, PP* 1842, XIII).

67. Ronald Robinson and John Gallagher, *Africa and the Victorians* (1961) p. 3.

68. Lorimer, pp. 123–30. Gordon K. Lewis comments that Victorian society at large regarded the events of the 1830s as a 'happy ending to a sad story soon to be forgotten' in *Slavery, Imperialism and Freedom* (1978) p. 78.

69. *The Anti-Slavery Appeal: American Abolitionism after 1830* (Baltimore, 1976) p. 17.

70. Walters, pp. 147–8.

Notes on Contributors

DAVID GEGGUS is a Hartley Research Fellow in the History Department, University of Southampton. He has been a British Academy 'Thank-Offering to Britain' fellow and in 1980 was awarded the Roger Brew Memorial Prize for Latin American History. He is the author of *Slavery, War and Revolution: The British Occupation of Saint Domingue* (OUP, 1981) and several articles on slavery.

DAVID ELTIS teaches history and economics at Algonquin College, Ottawa. He is the author of several articles on the slave trade and abolition and has co-edited a volume of essays entitled *The Abolition of the Atlantic Slave Trade*. He is currently writing a book on the nineteenth-century slave trade.

BETTY FLADELAND is a Professor of History in Southern Illinois University at Carbondale. She is the author of *Men and Brothers: Anglo-American Antislavery Co-operation* (Urbana and London: University of Illinois Press, 1972) and is currently working on a more complete study of the connection between anti-slavery and working-class movements from the late eighteenth to mid-nineteenth century.

SEYMOUR DRESCHER is Professor and Chairman of History at the University of Pittsburgh. He has written books on Alexis de Tocqueville as well as on anti-slavery in Britain and France. He has written several studies on anti-slavery, including *Econocide: British Slavery in the Era of Abolition* (Pittsburgh, 1977). He is also co-editing *Political Symbolism in Modern Europe* (1981).

B. W. HIGMAN is Senior Lecturer in History at the University of the West Indies, Mona, Jamaica, but will hold the position of Senior Research Fellow at the Australian National University during 1981—3. His book *Slave Population and Economy in Jamaica 1807—1834* won the Bancroft Prize in American History for 1977.

JAMES WALVIN has taught at the University of York since 1967. In addition to various books on modern British social History, his books on slavery and black history include *Black and White. The Negro and English Society 1555—1945* (1973); *Black Personalities in the Era of Slavery* (with P. Edwards) (1982); and *A Short History of Slavery and the Slave Trade* (1982), the latter two both published by Macmillan.

MICHAEL CRATON is Professor of History at the University of Waterloo, Ontario. He is the author of *History of the Bahamas* (1962, 1968); *A Jamaican Plantation. The History of Worthy Park, 1670—1970* (1970, with James Walvin); *Sinews of Empire: A Short History of British Slavery* (1974); *Searching for the Invisible Man: Slaves and Plantation Life in Jamaica* (1978); *Testing the Chains: Resistance to Slavery in the British West Indies* (forthcoming 1982).

C. DUNCAN RICE is Dean of the College and Professor of History at Hamilton College, New York. His publications include *The Rise and Fall of Black Slavery* (1975); *The Scots Abolitionists 1831—61* (1981); and articles on related subjects in journals and collections. He is now working on Anglo-American middle-class reform, 1770—1860, and on the response of the Scottish Enlightenment to slavery and savagery.

Index